M. F. K. Fisher,
Julia Child,
and Alice Waters

Also by Joan Reardon

Poetry by American Women, 1900–1975: A Bibliography (with
Kristine A. Thorsen)
Poetry by American Women, 1975–1989: A Bibliography
Oysters: A Culinary Celebration (with Ruth Ebbling)

M. F. K. Fisher,

CELEBRATING

Julia Child,

THE PLEASURES

and Alice Waters

OF THE TABLE

Joan Reardon

HARMONY BOOKS • NEW YORK

Grateful acknowledgment is given for permission to reprint the
following: Photograph by John Engstead. Provided to the author
courtesy of M. F. K. Fisher; Photograph copyright by James D. Wilson;
Photograph by Paul Child. Provided to the author courtesy of Julia
Child; Photograph copyright by Brian Leatart; Photograph copyright by
Robert Messick; Photograph copyright by Michele Clement.

Published by Harmony Books, a division of Crown Publishers, Inc., 201
East 50th Street, New York, New York 10022. Member of the Crown
Publishing Group.

Random House, Inc. New York, Toronto, London, Sydney, Auckland

HARMONY and colophon are trademarks of Crown Publishers, Inc.

Manufactured in the United States of America

Design by Debbie Glasserman

Library of Congress Cataloging-in-Publication Data
Reardon, Joan.
M. F. K. Fisher, Julia Child, and Alice Waters : celebrating the
pleasures of the table / Joan Reardon.
p. cm.
Includes bibliographical references and index.
1. Cooks—United States—Biography.   2. Food writers—United
States—Biography.   3. Fisher, M. F. K. (Mary Frances Kennedy).
4. Child, Julia.   5. Waters, Alice.   I. Title.
TX649.A1R43   1994
641.5'092'273—dc20
[B]   94-8650
CIP

ISBN 0-517-57748-8

10 9 8 7 6 5 4 3 2 1

First Edition

*For the three women who first
introduced me to the pleasures of the table—
my mother, godmother, and grandmother*

CONTENTS

A C K N O W L E D G M E N T S

Although this book reflects my personal and professional commitment to the pleasures of the table, its pages also acknowledge my gratitude to all those who have contributed to that commitment.

M. F. K. Fisher, Julia Child, and Alice Waters gave me the foundation for this book, invited me into their kitchens, and entrusted me with their memories, letters, notes, and papers. I thank them for that and also for sharing with me the inspiration, incandescence, and incentive that distinguish their careers.

I am grateful to B. Gargan, who urged me to purchase a copy of the Penguin edition of *Mastering the Art of French Cooking* at W. H. Smith on the rue de Rivoli in 1965, and to my former colleague Lauri Lee, who introduced me to M. F. K. Fisher's fine prose in 1978. My gratitude extends also to Richard Black, whose enthusiasm for reruns of Julia Child's TV shows was infectious.

Since the early 1970s The Culinary Collection at The Arthur and Elizabeth Schlesinger Library has been a magnet; the library's manuscript holdings are a rich resource, and the staff are a source of support for projects great and small. I am, especially, in the debt of Barbara Haber, who believed in this book from the beginning, encouraged me to seek the necessary permissions, and never failed to assist in every way possible. I would also like to thank the Radcliffe Research Support Program for supporting in part the research of this book. And I would like to acknowledge in a special way the late Patricia King, the Director of The Arthur and Elizabeth Schlesinger Library, and her assistant, Sylvia McDowell, who concurred with M. F. K. Fisher and her executor Robert Lescher and with Julia Child, Judith Jones, and Eleanor Friede (executor for Donald Friede) in granting permission to publish material from The Julia McWilliams Child Papers 1953–1980, Unprocessed Collection—1964–1983 in The Schlesinger Library Manuscript Collection and from The Mary Frances Kennedy Fisher Papers 1929–1985, Unprocessed Collection 71-58—87-M68, also in The Schlesinger Library Manuscript Collection.

Added to the wealth of manuscript material in The Schlesinger Library, private papers in the homes of M. F. K. Fisher, Julia Child, and Alice Waters were made available to me, and these gracious women answered any and all questions with generosity. I also wish to thank Joyce McGillis, Jean-Pierre and Denise Lurton Moulle, Lindsey Shere, Martine Labro, Nathalie Waag, Joyce Goldstein, Marsha Moran, Michele Anna Jordan, Patricia Wells, and countless others for sharing their ideas and memories with me. Patricia Kelly's photographs of the interior of La Pitchoune gave me a view of rooms I had not been able to see when I visited Bramafam in the summer of 1989. And M. F. K. Fisher's kind offer to take any photographs I might need from a box in her bedroom also gave me a wonderful insight into scenes from her Whittier and Hemet days.

The surge in popular culinary literature during the past twenty years provided a rich source of books and magazine and newspaper articles for this book, as did many studies of popular culture. I wish to thank their authors in a more personal way than the select bibliography permits.

A thank-you must also be extended to the people who believed in this book so early and so continuously. Without the encouragement and critical eye of my husband, John J. Reardon, I would never have ventured into a genre he has mastered so well. Without my agent Doe Coover's publishing expertise, the manuscript would not have evolved. And without the enthusiasm of Harriet Bell, Kathy Belden, John Michel, Janet McDonald, and, especially, Valerie Kuscenko, at Harmony Books, the book simply would not have become a reality. I thank them all.

As Laura Shapiro's influential *Perfection Salad: Women and Cooking at the Turn of the Century* documented, dedicated and determined women caused a revolution in America's culinary history and substantially made a difference in our country's cooking and eating habits a century ago. Move forward in time from the end of the nineteenth through the twentieth century and again innovative women have distinguished themselves as prime movers in what has come to be called America's second "cooking revolution."

For Mary Lincoln, who referred to eating as something more than animal indulgence and advocated "cooking with a nobler purpose than the gratification of appetite" at the World's Congress of Women in 1893, substitute M. F. K. Fisher's art of eating. For Fannie Farmer's "scientific cookery" turn to Julia Child's mastery of the art of French cooking. And for Sarah Tyson Rorer's resourceful use of Indian corn in demonstrating recipes in the Model Kitchen at the Columbian Exposition (1893) put in its place Alice Waters' use of local and seasonal foodstuffs in the open kitchen of Chez Panisse. A fanciful comparison, perhaps, because the microwave and convection ovens of our day are light-years away from the Jewell Range, as is L'Ecole des Trois Gourmandes from The Boston Cooking School and *The Chez Panisse Menu Cookbook* from *Mrs. Rorer's Cook Book*. There is, however, a similarity in the circumstances of change that cannot be ignored. In the last years of the nineteenth century the interest Americans took in food provoked scores of cookbooks, food magazines, cooking schools, and the concept of the kitchen as "a home laboratory for food production." The food industry in tandem with teachers bent on reforming the American diet looked to the twentieth century with the hope that technology and nutritional knowledge would replace tradition-bound culinary tastes.

The three last decades of the twentieth century have brought about a very different revolution in American foodways. Overseas transport necessitated by war and the recent spur of travel for pleasure have opened doors to foreign foods, menus, and culinary apprenticeships. From the Kennedy White House to starred restaurants in every large American city, a French chef in the kitchen indicated the cosmopolitanism of both host and guest. In 1959 *The James Beard Cookbook* provided its users with recipes for roasting a turkey, frying oysters, and making chili con carne from scratch—in short, with recipes redolent of Beard's childhood in Oregon. Two years later, Craig Claiborne, a restaurant reviewer who took his role seriously, edited *The New York Times Cookbook*, in which he included at least seven recipes for pâté; one was developed by Paula Peck, who had toured the restaurants and bistros of Paris in search of the perfect pâté. And the same year Knopf published *Mastering the Art of French Cooking*, a French cookbook for Americans that described all the techniques necessary to cook the dishes of the repertoire at home. Within two years Julia Child was known across America as Public Television's "French Chef," cooking became a national pastime, restaurant-going emerged as high drama, and searching for the tastes of prefrozen and packaged foods was a cause.

Now, as at the turn of the last century, there is a convergence of both social forces and talent that focuses attention on individual contributions and influences and on the importance of interrelationships. Narratives about women's lives also have come into sharper focus, thereby expanding autobiographical and biographical writings into countless forms. The 1990s have also witnessed a diminishing of the reluctance formerly held by professional and academic commentors on our culture to explore a subject as ordinary as food or a feeling as compelling as pleasure. And as more and more men and women with academic degrees enter the culi-

nary profession, the rigid separation between culinary professionals and culinary historians, archeologists, and social scientists has
substantially narrowed. Culinary history alone, however, has not
dictated the shape of this book. Because of the unique roles played
by M. F. K. Fisher, Julia Child, and Alice Waters, it becomes a
series of portraits of the individuals, linked by their common interests and inspirations.

In the beginning of the twentieth-century culinary revolution
there was M. F. K. Fisher continuing the tradition of Brillat-Savarin
by documenting tales of feasts ancient and modern. From her early
forays into medieval cookery books in the 1930s through more
than fifty years of distinguished publishing, often on the subject of
food and wine, she seized culinary writing from the domestic scientists, the packagers and promoters, even the "gourmets," and with
cunning and daring, she placed it at the center of those "ageless
celebrations of life." M. F. K. Fisher dignified our hungers in a
prose style that was as enthusiastically praised by the poet W. H.
Auden as it was by the cookbook writer and teacher James Beard.
By vesting words like *appetite, nourishment, ripeness, decay,* and *pleasure* with metaphoric meanings, she made her kitchens, whether in
Provence or California, and her table symbols for the world; wine,
cheese, and bread became its poetry.

M. F. K. Fisher created a rhetoric of food and subtly challenged
all those who followed her "at the hot literary cookstove of gastronomical comment" to weigh every word they wrote with care,
and she bequeathed the habit of recalling past pleasures of feasts
great and small, especially in those times of inner drought and
stress. In addition to the gastronome Brillat-Savarin, whose *Physiology of Taste* she translated in the late 1940s, M. F. K. Fisher introduced into the mainstream of American letters not only *An
Alphabet for Gourmets* but also a memorable portrait of *The Gastronomical Me* with whom we could in some measure identify.

While M. F. K. Fisher's audience was often small and select, Julia
Child's conquest of the American public occurred in living rooms
and kitchens across the country. Julia Child chopping, folding, and
sautéeing in her studio kitchen captured live on the TV screen and
Julia tossing an omelette in her kitchen at home were synonymous.
The medium, whether monkfish, chicken livers, eggs, butter, or

chocolate, was her message. Never pedantic, always enthusiastic, Julia Child demystified French cooking and spoke to us in an idiom we could understand. Her intention was "to take a lot of the la-dee-dah out of French cooking because I think a lot of it was a sort of one-up-manship and 'We Happy Few.' " Thousands of TV viewers, devotees of her cookbooks, and potential students who she inspired to don toques knew that she also gave Americans the techniques of French cooking, dramatized the scenario of our entertaining, and offered expertise and confidence. Neither a chef in the traditional sense nor a Frenchwoman by birth, Julia Child was almost solely responsible for America's rush to try its hand at the art of French cooking.

The interest in French food that Julia popularized and the politicized climate of revolt against the status quo that swept Berkeley, California in the 1960s enabled Alice Waters to feed our hunger in a more immediate way with apple cider sherbet and Tarte Tatin in fall, quail eggs, wild asparagus, and salmon roe in spring. As a proprietor-chef, she was in a unique position "to insist that [her patrons] eat in a certain way, try new things, and take time with food." The impact of her culinary philosophy reverberated throughout the culinary community. The catch phrase "California cuisine" soon described everything from zucchini blossoms to pizza to mesquite-grilled salmon. By the mid-70s, Alice Waters' restaurant Chez Panisse became one of the most talked-about restaurants in the Bay Area and was acknowledged as a force of culinary change in America.

From 1982 to the present, the books that have become known as the "Chez Panisse cookbooks" have publicized Alice Waters' untiring efforts to secure fresh, unadulterated, seasonal food. Her open kitchen at Chez Panisse is a direct statement of a mission to remove the barriers between those who prepare food and those who savor it. Successful as a restaurateur, Alice Waters has broken gender barriers and provided an apprenticeship for a new generation of chefs while continually searching for ways to revolutionize the taste of America.

Exploring the seminal roles that M. F. K. Fisher, Julia Child, and Alice Waters have played in changing our attitudes about food and cooking, dining and pleasure, and the composition of a meal means looking at the conceptual frameworks available to them. La Belle France, with its food and wine, its gastronomers and architectonic culinary heritage, and its potagers and enviable outdoor markets, is a common source of inspiration in their lives and careers, as is California, where each has lived and worked, and part of their story is how they each learned to live in another landscape.

Respect, admiration, and friendship is another and a lesser known facet of their lives. M. F. K. Fisher and Julia Child met for the first time in 1966 when they were both working on Time-Life's *Cooking of Provincial France*. M. F. K. Fisher and Alice Waters met at Chez Panisse when Alice Waters assembled a group of Mary Frances's friends and admirers (including James Beard) to celebrate her seventieth birthday in 1978. Julia Child read the manuscript of Alice Waters' first book, dined at Chez Panisse, and cohosted a segment with Alice Waters for the television series *Cooking with Master Chefs*. In the highly charged and competitive food world, these talented women coexist easily and well. Their friendship, their mutual love of France, and their shared passion for food and wine add a wonderful dimension to the developing story of American gastronomy. Their contribution to what has been called a modern food revolution has not been isolated; they have shared the work and the rewards with culinary masters as impressive as James Beard and Craig Claiborne, chefs as creative as Henri Soulé and Albert Stöckli, and many of the translators of foreign cuisines, such as Virginia Lee, Marcella Hazan, Madeleine Kamman, and Jacques Pépin.

When three women command our attention to the degree that M. F. K. Fisher, Julia Child, and Alice Waters do, however, a book devoted to the evolution of their professional careers commands our attention in a special way. Their careers, individually and collectively, changed America's culinary landscape by redefining food and cooking. Each one built upon the work of her predecessor and the spectrum of their achievements stands for something larger.

Their books, moreover, force us to reexamine the canon, to look at culinary writing as a genre with its own potential for excellence. Their recipes tempt us to seek the woman behind the conscious construct of ingredients and methods and prompt us to ask questions about her life: What kind of house does she live in? What is her writing schedule like? What does she eat for breakfast? How does she dress for dinner? Why does she write about food and cooking and not love, war, and peace? Why did Mary Frances Fisher use the ambiguous M. F. K. Fisher for the byline of her first article and all of her subsequent books? What made Knopf see the possibilities in an overwritten, much-too-long book on French cooking by Julia Child, Louisette Bertholle, and Simone Beck that other publishers had turned down? And what made Berkeley graduate Alice Waters a successful entrepreneur? Why did their culinary odysseys begin in France? Flourish in California?

M. F. K. Fisher, Julia Child, and Alice Waters: Celebrating the Pleasures of the Table offers a hint of an explanation.

Joan Reardon
Seaward II
Lake Forest, Illinois

The pleasures of the table—that lovely old-fashioned phrase—depict food as an art form, as a delightful part of civilized life. In spite of food fads, fitness programs, and health concerns, we must never lose sight of a beautifully conceived meal.

JULIA CHILD

La Belle France

And France is La Belle France, friendly foreign home.

JULIA CHILD

Even for Parisians the authentic France is still to be found in the
countryside. There the days are calmer, the pleasures simpler, the food
straightforward, colorful and full of the flavors of the garden.

M. F. K. FISHER

And I believed that in order to experience food as good as I had had in
France, I had to cook and serve it myself.

ALICE WATERS

The culinary seduction of M. F. K. Fisher, Julia Child, and Alice Waters began in France, where the abiding pleasures of food and wine, gastronomy, and a well-documented history of cuisine are fatal attractions. It, of course, had happened to many other Americans before and after them, and they were not alone in the enduring love affair that ensued. From the early days of America, when Thomas Jefferson appointed Chef Julien as the White House's first French chef, to Patricia Wells's presentation of Joël Robuchon's three-star cuisine, France has tempted gourmands, chefs, writers, and journalists to taste, to savor, and to learn. Few have resisted.

The lure of traveling through the provinces, and offering their readers a bouquet of France, has sustained both well-known and unknown writers. For every American who aspired to the title *chevalier du tastevin*, the vineyards of France, whether they produce a vaunted Grand Cru or a humble *vin de pays*, have been the subject of viticultural study and connoisseurship. And from the end of World War II to the present in ever-increasing numbers, many of the movers and shakers of America's culinary establishment have secured a firm grounding in France's culinary principles and techniques either by apprenticing in French restaurants or by working with French chefs in the United States. During the postwar era, particularly, military assignments, business transfers, and travel opportunities have introduced France in its undisputed role as the maker, the shaper, and the ruler of Western cuisine to the average American citizen with more insistence than ever before.

Why French cuisine has achieved such an elevated status is a story that never diminishes in the telling, and it has something for everyone from the professional who develops his basic techniques within the cuisine's inherent structure to the cook whose inspiration comes from the array of ingredients available at an outdoor market. And although French cuisine shared a common origin with that of most of the countries once under Roman rule, the accidents of climate and geography have generously favored the emergence of French cuisine into an art form.

Since the reign of Louis XIV, moreover, history has chronicled the important contributions of certain chefs, not with the same insistence that artists, writers, and musicians have been honored but with recognition accorded to the most illustrious culinary practitioners. François Pierre de la Varenne has often been called the first noteworthy chef of modern times and the author of "the first great French cookbook." Together with Henri Vatel, the romantic model of perfectionism who is reputed to have committed suicide rather than disgrace his patron with an inadequate meal, he was a culinary hero of the ancien régime.

With the revolution at the end of the eighteenth century, however, came the idea, and to some extent the reality, that everyone should eat well. Yet the anarchic violence of the revolution was never directed against sumptuous feasts or those responsible for them. Rather the revolution democratized the role of the chef from service in the houses of the nobility to bourgeois restaurateur.

Through the influence of professional chefs who either established restaurants in Paris and other French cities or fled their native country in the aftermath of the revolution, the principles of classic French cuisine, including most of the basic methods of cooking and the fundamental sauces, were codified and exported. And a succession of brilliant chefs believed that the foundations of that cuisine were eternal, although they also acknowledged that with changing times French cuisine would continue to adapt to the ever-increasing refinement of the palate.

Consequently, while the basics of French cuisine were in place, emphasis and style changed as cuisine developed according to the spirit of the times and the dictates of certain chefs. During the nineteenth and early twentieth centuries, two names dwarf all others. Marie-Antoine Carême (1784–1833), a Parisian born into a large and impoverished family, virtually dominated the early nineteenth century. Beginning as an apprentice in a pâtisserie, he went on to study cookbooks and architecture, eventually linking the two in his culinary endeavors. As either sweet or savory fantasies, his *pièces montées* were reflections of his daring and inventiveness as well as reminders of his patron Talleyrand's conviction that cuisine should be spectacular and expensive. But, Carême also concerned himself with the conditions in which chefs worked, protesting the harmful effects of preparing banquets in kitchens equipped with enormous charcoal-burning stoves. Even though these conditions made the chef's career precarious, the cause of French cuisine warranted the risk. In truth, he believed that cuisine should be spectacular, worth more than battles, congresses, and assemblies. In France gastronomy had become a creative endeavor and a subject for endless discussion.

A distinctively French phenomenon also was the cultivation of the gourmet-writer as opposed to the producer of cookbooks. Since the mid-eighteenth century Great Britain and the United States have had a tradition of prescriptive and often authoritarian writers of cookbooks in the tradition of Hannah Glasse, Mrs. Beeton, and Amelia Simmons. France, in contrast, encouraged the written words of descriptive and cosmopolitan gastronomical raconteurs, of whom the greatest was Anthelme Brillat-Savarin (1755–1826). When his *Physiologie du Goût* ("Physiology of Taste") was published in 1826, it set the literary parameters for civilized man's concern with sustenance and provided a model for gastronomical prose.

Carême and other culinary writers had all included advice and recipes for a wide class of people, but as time went on a gradual trend developed addressing books specifically to professional chefs. And the not too subtle distinction between *haute cuisine* and *cuisine bourgeoise* took form. Prestigious cuisine came to be regarded as one that requiring a battery of assistants and equipment to which even the most prosperous housewife could never aspire. The social status of chefs, high after the revolution, also underwent a series of advantageous changes, only to dwindle again when chefs became more confined to kitchens, which were brutally hot and dangerous during the latter half of the nineteenth century.

Georges-Auguste Escoffier (1846–1935) restored prominence to the role of chef and dominated the first quarter of the twentieth century by distilling the culinary efforts of the past and adding to them his own extraordinary flair. Born in a small Riviera village, he began his culinary career in an uncle's restaurant in Nice and moved on to acquire culinary expertise in three Parisian restaurants until he began his legendary collaboration with César Ritz in 1883. Not content to reform the atmosphere of the kitchen, he also organized the method of work, and his hierarchy from *chef-patron* to *sous-chef* to designated *commis* all contributed to the making of a dish. But it was not only in initiating a chain of command that Escoffier was an innovator. He substituted lighter and fragrant *fumets* for *espagnole* and *allemande* sauces, thereby concentrating the natural juices of meat, fish, and vegetables in water, broth, butter, or olive oil. And in *Le Guide Culinaire* (1903), he published 5,000 shorthand recipes as a guide to proper identification of the dishes of the *répertoire*.

Largely because of the efforts of Carême and Escoffier and those who worked with them, professional chefs acquired the know-how to perpetuate the tradition of French grand cuisine. If an apprentice from Paul Bocuse's contemporary three-star kitchen in the suburbs of Lyon were miraculously transported into Carême's nineteenth-century kitchen, he would feel reasonably at home. Conversely, if one of Carême's *commis* found himself in the kitchen at Collonges-au-Mont-d'Or, he would see little that would bewilder him except the lighting, air-conditioning, and the microwave oven—none of which affects the *art* of cooking. Similarly, because of the efforts of Escoffier (expanded by Louis Saulnier in 1914), chefs in kitchens around the world make *beurre escargots* with shallots, garlic, parsley, salt, pepper, brandy, and butter; they prepare *crème pâtissière* with egg yolks, sugar, flour, milk, and vanilla. These are but two of the recipes found in *Le Guide Culinaire*, the standard text utilized by professional chefs.

While Escoffier spread the gospel of French cuisine, he also unwittingly committed classical cooking to a holy canon whereby the cognoscenti could display their sophistication by pronouncing on the authenticity of a dish. Chefs also tended to rely on the formulated ideas of Escoffier rather than use their own imaginations. As a consequence, cooking stagnated until the years between the two world wars, when in both his restaurant and his cookbooks Edouard Nignon (1865–1935) put into practice his inner conviction that "routine in cuisine is a crime." By focusing attention on the quality of the produce he used and advocating honesty in presentation, he paved the way for other restaurateurs to move away from the rigid codification that Escoffier had unintentionally imposed upon French cuisine.

Nignon's emphasis on originality was emulated by three younger chefs, and their contributions literally chart the movement away from restaurants managed by a maître d'hôtel who employed chefs to the elevation of the role of chef to *chef-patron*. André Pic, Alexandre Dumaine, and Fernand Point, while giving justifiable credit to Escoffier, also sought to inspire the creativity of French cuisine as it is understood today. André Pic inherited a family *auberge* in Valence and during the 1930s developed it into a famous stopping place for travelers on the way to the south of France. Alexandre Dumaine and his wife transformed the Hôtel de la Côte d'Or at Saulieu into a gastronomic retreat. And Fernand Point and his wife put their restaurant La Pyramide in the vanguard of Michelin's three-starred establishments. After apprenticing in Point's *auberge de campagne*, Paul Bocuse, Alain Chapel, Jean and Pierre Troisgros, Louis Outhier, and François Bise went on to popularize the simpler and lighter style of cooking that Escoffier called for in his motto, "Faites Simple," and that Point and Dumaine initiated in their restaurants.

The second half of the twentieth century, therefore, can be gastronomically charted in a succession of decades in which almost every ten years produced a chef who could be called the heir to a tradition of greatness. In the late 1940s, it was Fernand Point who maintained a successful restaurant in Vienne during the war and became teacher and mentor to a host of promising chefs. In the 1950s, Paul Bocuse assumed a unique position of leadership among French chefs and popularized Lyonnaise cuisine and Burgundian wines in the restaurant that bears his name. In the 1960s Michel

Guérard advanced the free and imaginative interpretation of French cooking already in progress by creating *cuisine minceur* as one of the features of his famous spa in Eugénie-les-Bains. In the 1970s Swiss-born chef Fredy Girardet refined the techniques he learned while working with the Troisgros brothers in Roanne and introduced his *cuisine spontanée* into the menu of the restaurant named for him in Crissier, Switzerland. And in the 1980s Joël Robuchon acquired three Michelin stars for his Parisian restaurant Jamin just twenty-eight months after its opening, but more to the point, according to David Bouley, he "crossed the gulf between classic cuisine and the modern approach without sacrificing the refinements of the last three hundred years of French cooking."

In Brillat-Savarin's wake as a literary chronicler of France's gastronomy, Curnonsky (1872–1956) had identified four categories of French cuisine. Because they are somewhat outdated, haute cuisine, French family cooking, regional cooking (a marriage of gastronomy and tourism), and impromptu cooking (managed with whatever came to hand) have given way to a new vocabulary implicitly linked to the *chefs-patron*. But Curnonsky's injunction, "Cuisine—it's when things taste of themselves," has been prophetic. During the 1970s the new style of cooking was collectively labeled *nouvelle cuisine*, and was frequently confused during the same decade with Michel Guérard's *cuisine minceur*. Largely because of the abuses associated with the popularization of both, *cuisine actuelle*, a style of cooking committed to the rediscovery of the savors, flavors, and tastes of an ingredient, emerged in the 1980s, and it emphasized the culinary style of a *chef-patron*.

Since innovation had not been a cardinal rule of pre-nouvelle cooking, the standard preparations of crustaceans, chicken, duck, quenelles, truffles, and foie gras began to change dramatically in the late 1960s. But the identification of those ingredients with haute cuisine continued even though *foie gras en brioche* became foie gras with smooth lentil cream sauce; chicken served *demi-deuil* or *en vessie* became *poulet grillé au citron*, and duck served as *caneton Tour d'Argent* became *filet de canard au Cassis* at Boyer's restaurant in Reims. Challenged also were the favorite preparations of the past: *en brioche*, *en croûte*, or *en vessie*, together with farces, *émincés*, croustades, vol-au-vent, sauces, gratins, and *flambages*.

Although they were influenced by the tradition of French regional dishes, Asian cooking styles, medieval recipes, readily available exotic fruits and vegetables, time-saving kitchen equipment,
and dietary concerns, inspiration became the key word in the world
of the *chefs-patron*. Since the 1970s, chefs have become more engaged in research and the study of potential sources of authentic
dishes and, by so doing, have radically altered their own status.
While the grand cuisine of the past was concerned with replication
and recollection, the new aimed for evocation and nostalgia; where
the old took comfort in the sureties of venerable tradition, the new
built imaginative constructions on the foundations of the old,
which in Curnonsky's classifications included provincial and regional foods as well as that simplification of classic cuisine known
as *cuisine bourgeoise*. In the past the role of chef had ranged from
household servant or kitchen practitioner to high priest. In the era
of the *chefs-patron*, the chef became a creative artist who had trained
for his position for years.

But neither haute cuisine nor nouvelle cuisine was regarded as
the province of the nonprofessional. And while the new emphasis
on seasonality and simplicity as well as the integration of vegetables, fruits, saltwater fish, pastas, and exotic spices into three-
starred menus were celebrated, the innovative dishes of the
chefs-patron were not regularly prepared and served in French
homes. Unlike professional cooking and until well into the twentieth century, *cuisine de femmes* existed, for the most part, in recipes
passed from woman to woman, from country households to other
country households—all virtually not published and not accessible
outside a given community, but well known to Frenchmen who
savored them.

Literally, a collection of basic recipes analogous to those that *The
Fannie Farmer Cook Book* and *The Settlement Cookbook* had given to
the women of eastern and middlewestern America in the early
years of the twentieth century was only offered to French home-
makers in 1925 when a compilation of 1,300 recipes incorporating
"la pratique et les principes rationnels de notre vraie bonne cuisine" was
published by Madame Saint-Ange. Although her book, *La Bonne
Cuisine*, featured traditional recipes for sauces and the preparation
of seafood, poultry, meats, vegetables, and entremets long as-

sociated with hearth and home, it was also different from its American counterparts. Social, economic, and, above all, aesthetic differences between the way a Frenchman cooked and dined at home and the way an American approached a meal were considerable. Methods of preparation, regional specialities, local wines, and a tradition of courses dictated not only the content but the service of a French meal, and when experienced by Americans for the first time, these differences begged emulation.

Against a professional and domestic backdrop so rich in culinary scenarios, Americans were free to range widely. The many changes brought about by the economy, transportation, and governance were evident everywhere, but the well-known Gallic fascination with food and France's reputation as the epicenter for both the style and the art of living remained in place. The particular *savoir vivre* that linked the art of conversation with a *café crème* could still be found in any sidewalk café. The markets, whether on the rue de Buci or in the small hill towns of Provence, still offered an array of garden vegetables and fruits picked in their prime. And many a bistro served a plat du jour cooked by a *patronne* with the same care she lavished on a *poulet à l'ail* or a *gratin de pommes de terre* that she prepared for her family.

Like so many Americans who had traveled to France before and after them, M. F. K. Fisher, Julia Child, and Alice Waters were not quite prepared for the culinary experiences that awaited them when they visited that country for the first time. And certainly they could not have foreseen the highly individual way that those experiences would influence both their lives and their careers. First impressions, however, became lasting ones. A potato soufflé served as a separate course at the old post hotel in Avallon, *sole meunière* enjoyed with a fine Chablis at La Couronne in Rouen, and a simple pairing of homegrown melon with country ham in Brittany were culinary initiations that inspired M. F. K. Fisher, Julia Child, and Alice Waters to translate their indebtedness to France into an American idiom. In the beginning there were "never to be forgotten" meals.

"Do come, you'll love it" echoed through M. F. K. Fisher's letters after her first few months of residence in Dijon in 1929. It was an invitation to a country she wanted to share with family and friends, and her initial response to the wonderful food and wine, magnificent buildings, boulevards, and monuments became a continual refrain. Like that of so many other young people who traveled "student third" on ocean liners departing from New York, her destination had been a hexagon-shaped land bordered by northern beaches and southern sands, by the Atlantic on the west and mountains and rivers to the east, a country so diverse in its provinces that only the accidents of history, the pride of a common language, and a determined sense of exclusivity bonded its people together. Her first stop was Paris, and for those who had literary aspirations, like her husband, Alfred Fisher, the hotel of choice was on the Left Bank, one of the cafés along the boulevard Saint Germain was the perfect place for a breakfast of café au lait and croissants, and Sylvia Beach's bookshop Shakespeare & Company was the first stop along the way.

After the excitement of dining in the quaint little restaurants in the fifth arrondissement, there was the pleasant surprise of a lunch that Mary Frances and Al Fisher enjoyed at an *auberge de route* on the way from Paris to Dijon, where potatoes were served as a separate course rather than the other half of a "meat and potatoes meal." And then there was the sense of awe associated with standing in the center of the place d'Armes, "which was in the center of Dijon, and therefore in the center of France itself." Seemingly only a few days after the Fishers arrived in Dijon, Mary Frances Kennedy Fisher knew that living in France would be more than a onetime experience.

The map of the inner city of Dijon, whose ancient streets she memorized as she walked to and from the pension on the rue du Petit-Potet where she and her husband rented two tiny rooms, and the landscape of roads and villages that crisscrossed the Côte d'Or that they visited on Sundays with dedicated members of the Club Alpin became a palimpsest. What was written there would never be erased but simply written over.

Climbing up the rickety stairs to their third-floor rooms, taking their midday meal in the communal dining room, and meeting the cast of characters who composed the Ollangnier family, with whom the Fishers boarded, became a source of never-ending curiosity. The best restaurants, the finest vintages, and the latest news published in the newspaper *L'Action Française* were common topics of conversation at the Ollangnier dinner table, as were the famous cathedrals of Burgundy, the latest films, and the complaints of Madame Ollangnier about her desultory music pupils. Food was, moreover, spoken about in a way that had usually been frowned upon in Mary Frances's home in Whittier, California. Perhaps conversing about it was as pleasurable as it was because Madame Ollangnier, despite her many faults, had an enviable reputation for serving tempting meals, or because Monsieur Ollangnier had been born in Belley, the city of gastronomes. Whatever the reason, her host introduced Mary Frances to an array of new dishes as well as to his hometown's famous gastronome Brillat-Savarin and to a literary genre theretofore unfamiliar to her.

Studying drawing and sculpture at the Beaux Arts, and attending lectures and classes in French language and literature at the university were simply ancillary activities compared with the more subtle education Mary Frances sought and found in Dijon. Without her even realizing it, dining in Madame Ollangnier's small, messy, but lively dining room taught Mary Frances that penuriousness and astute bargaining with storekeepers could produce delicious meals. Every day the *pensionnaires* were served enormous fresh salads, either before or after the meat course, and the meal always included cheese. In season, they ate crispy deep-fried Jerusalem artichokes and all kinds of little apples, and drank wine, which was often diluted. Whether the fruit had been undersized, the cheese a reject, or the potatoes sprouting, the meals were always well cooked and "seasoned with a kind of avaricious genius that could have made boiled shoe taste like milk-fed lamb *à la mode printanière.*"

Within a year, when a family named Rigoulot purchased the Ollangniers' house on the rue du Petit-Potet, the Fishers went from improvised culinary rags to riches. Not only was the food served to the *pensionnaires* delicious but it was also marked by the extravagance that Madame Rigoulot desperately tried to maintain in the face of impending financial embarrassment. Hot, creamy soups, fine legs of lamb, the most expensive vegetables, and casks of wine were the order of the day. And when Madame Rigoulot's father, a retired famous Alsatian *confiseur*, visited on Sunday, they concluded their dinner with an apple tart as large as a cartwheel. Madame Rigoulot supervised the kitchen and often did most of the cooking, offering to teach Mary Frances the art of the soufflé and the preparation of her famous holiday entrée, truffled goose. For a complex set of reasons, Mary Frances declined the offer, but simply observing as well as tasting the exquisite quenelles, *les escargots d'or*, and *diplomate au kirsch* helped her develop an educated palate and strong convictions about the kind of menu that would eventually distinguish Mary Frances's own table.

Because of the subtle suggestions offered by the Fishers' favorite waiter at Racouchot's, a special restaurant for their occasional celebrations, and because of the opportunity to taste notable Burgundian wines at the annual Foire Gastronomique, Mary Frances also developed a discriminating taste for good wine. Above all, she learned to speak of wine, cheese, oysters, and pastries the way an art instructor would speak of a still life painting or a sculpture, elevating food to prominence as an element in a refined existence and dignifying the serving of it to a manifestation of style.

Always and everywhere the strange, ancient city of Dijon provided new and interesting experiences. The pungent smell of gingerbread emanated from the *boulangeries*. In the fall, the strong whiff of cassis filled the air. The sounds of café phonographs and the tolling of the great clock on the facade of Notre-Dame often interrupted her while she read Colette's novels and Brillat-Savarin's sage observations. And then there was the sensual excitement of a 1919 Gevrey-Chambertin accompanied by a feast or the cool pleasure of a *vin blanc d'Alsace* served with a dozen *Portugaises Vertes Extra*. While the newness of the language and surroundings afforded little time for synthesis, daily meals—whether served in the dining room of their pension on the rue du Petit-Potet or savored at the Crespin, the simple little seafood restaurant they frequently patronized—were memorized, never to be forgotten, but to be revisited years later and found to be "as good as it had ever been some decades or centuries ago on my private calendar."

And then there were the loud, happy Burgundians. Because they were in straitened circumstances, the Ollangniers and Rigoulots housed and fed the newly married Fishers and a few other students, thereby establishing personal relationships with their boarders that they would never have thought of forming in more affluent times. Living in the midst of family celebrations and crises gave Mary Frances an intimate knowledge of the closed circle of French family life, and it supplied her with a cast of characters she would intro-duce into her books over the years. It was in Dijon also that she developed her special fondness for waiters, shopkeepers, and coachmen (in later years, taxi drivers).

Although Mary Frances and Al Fisher spent time in Cassis, Strasbourg, and on the Côte d'Azur during the three years they were in France, Dijon was their home from 1929 until Christmas 1931. In retrospect, Mary Frances liked to say, "It was there that I started to grow up, to study, to make love, to eat and drink, to be me and not what I was expected to be." And the "gastronomical me" that evolved from those early experiences was a collage of images drawn from the soil of *la France profonde* and from life at the university. Her enjoyment in reading about Colette as both gour-mande and novelist, her attraction to the early films of Marcel Pagnol with their scenes of Provence and *cuisine rustique* that she and her husband saw at the D'Arcy theater in Dijon, and her continuing love affair with Brillat-Savarin contributed in no small measure. And although the fine wines of Burgundy, the lofty souf-flés, and the sealed casseroles of *tripes à la mode de Caen* remained the benchmarks against which all the other styles and multiple facets of French cuisine were compared, it was the transformation of dining into a high cultural event that Mary Frances learned in those early days in France and would never forget.

World War II and more than sixteen years separated M. F. K. Fisher's residence in France from Julia and Paul Child's years of service in that country. Julia's account of her first meal at La Couronne in Rouen, upon their arrival in France in November 1948, varies from time to time. Whether they savored oysters on the half shell, *sole meunière*, or *sole à la normande*, however, makes little difference. The meal, accompanied by a fine Chablis and a blissful feeling that it was totally wonderful, contributed to Julia's appreciation of a country that she would soon call La Belle France.

Leaving behind the war-damaged docks of Cherbourg and the city of Rouen, she and Paul drove south to the City of Light. Julia also left behind a fondness for childhood's codfish balls with egg sauce, pan-fried trout served at a campsite in the Sierras, and broiled salmon on the Fourth of July as she embarked on her *éducation piscivore.* Discovering the possibilities of poaching in wine and tasting the various sauces, mousses, and quenelles, however, were only the beginning; the bistros and small restaurants of Paris dazzled Julia with their offerings of *poulet sauté à l'estragon, rognons de veau flambé,* and lobster à l'américaine.

A bride of little more than a year but a woman of no little experience who had traveled and worked with the OSS in Ceylon during the war, Julia was simply astonished that food could be taken so seriously, that groups could be formed for the sole purpose of dining on good food, and that devotion to the arts of the kitchen and table could consume so much time and energy. As she gained facility in the French language at Berlitz, she spent her time between lessons visiting the markets within walking distance of the Childs' apartment on the rue de l'Université, and, on special occasions, she and Paul watched the farmers unpack their produce at Les Halles in the early hours of the morning. Displays of copper cookware at Dehillerin, and the shop's vast assortment of molds, knives, and pans, also fascinated her. A lifetime of collecting cookware would ensue to ensure the smooth functioning of Julia's many kitchens. But during those first months in Paris, enjoying the food of France was one thing; culinary expertise still eluded her.

When she discovered that several GI's were enrolled in a professional cooking course at the Cordon Bleu, Julia decided to join their ranks. And when a few of the more than competent chefs, who had taken up teaching because of the constraints of the war, discovered that this tall, thin, exuberant American woman was not only able but also willing to arrive early in the morning to do everything from filleting fish to forcing pike through a *tamis* in the painstaking preparation of quenelles, they decided she was a serious student. As Julia whisked, boned, peeled, and sautéed her way through the six-month program, something clicked. She realized that the cuisine of France was a comprehensible system of fundamental techniques with specific methods repeated over and over again with different ingredients. Whether preparing a navarin of lamb, a coq au vin, or a beef bourguignon, several steps, including browning, simmering, straining, skimming, and flavoring, were required; if they were combined, omitted, or substituted, the end result suffered. Techniques could be taught, master recipes learned, balanced menus devised. It was all doable.

Studying at the Cordon Bleu was Julia's initiation into mastering the fundamental techniques of classical French cooking. What began as an exercise in acquiring sufficient skill to prepare the meals that she and Paul could enjoy together, especially when paired with one of Paul's favorite wines, soon became a career for the Smith College graduate who dreamed of being a novelist and who had settled for managing a registry during the war years. But taking classes at the Cordon Bleu was not the only factor in Julia's culinary education. Without her even realizing it, how things were accomplished in France influenced her way of thinking.

The astonishing value that the French placed on skill struck a deep cord in Julia. In Paris, writers acted like writers creating certain standards of genius for the world to emulate, just as good *écaillers*, or oyster openers, looked liked experienced oyster openers, and waiters in a café adopted an attitude that represented the authority of the establishment they served. Not only was it important to be skilled, but in the public role of sommelier, barman, chef, waiter, and maître d'hôtel, the public expected and honored expertise as well. Julia admired this display of Parisian élan, called simply *métier*. With Cordon Bleu behind her, she began her search for a way to make something more than a good dinner out of her newfound skills.

Fortunately, she met Simone Beck. Upper-class, stubborn, and striving to be a culinary professional in a field not recognized as congenial to women, Simca, as she was known, had been working with Louisette Bertholle in developing recipes for a cookbook introducing French food to an American audience, and she was as passionate as Julia was about cooking. From their first conversation at a cocktail party in the home of George Artamonoff in the suburb of Saint-Germain-en-Laye, in which influential Parisian businessmen mingled with personnel attached to the American embassy, the two women "hit it off," as Simca described it. And at Julia's invitation, they met the next day at the Childs' apartment on the rue de l'Université to decide, in Simca's words, "how to tell American cooks all about French techniques and cooking bases, the intricacies of pastry and sauces, the differences in American tastes and produce."

At Simca's urging, also, Julia joined the Cercle des Gourmettes, where the two women, together with Simca's collaborator, reveled in France's postwar immersion in the pleasures of the table. For Julia it meant membership in an exclusive all-French club and an opportunity to observe and, on occasion, assist guest chefs who had well-established reputations. Because of her friendship with Simca, other gastronomic contacts were also established. Julia met the famous Curnonsky (Maurice-Edmond Sailland), who was then editor of the popular cooking magazine *Cuisine et Vins de France*, and he enjoyed telling her his famous stories. But more important, he passed along his insistence that all foods should be cooked to show off their natural flavors. And in a country that boasted hundreds of food and wine organizations, Simca and her husband opened doors for Julia and Paul that might not have been opened by Paul's professional associates at the American embassy.

By 1951 Julia, Simca, and Louisette were giving cooking lessons to visiting American friends and embassy personnel at a school they called L'Ecole des Trois Gourmandes, located in the kitchen of the Childs' apartment. Simca called Julia a natural teacher. Impressively tall, witty, and personable, she communicated her enthusiasm for the task at hand and thoroughly enjoyed the opportunities to work side by side with guest chefs recruited from the Cordon Bleu or the Cercle des Gourmettes. It was not long before there was a scheme to enlarge the first Beck–Bertholle cookbook with Julia as the third collaborator. And the long process of rethinking French recipes in terms of American ingredients and preferences began.

While living in Paris, Julia had learned the basics of French culinary technique at the Cordon Bleu. As she later reflected, however, "Simca gave me the finesse, enlarged my culinary vocabulary, and imbued me with the French attitude about food. Both Simca and Louisette, and the chefs with whom we worked, took their craft with utter seriousness, as a beautiful, marvelous, and creative art form—but an art form with rules. It was that attitude, really, that drew me irresistibly to the profession."

After Paris, Paul was assigned to the U.S. consulate in Marseille, where the Childs lived until May 1954. For Julia, Paris had been a movable feast; Marseille, however, introduced her to the flavors of the south of France. And through her almost weekly letters and exchanges of recipes with Simca, Julia acquired more knowledge of the kinds of cuisine that distinguished many of the other provinces of France. Simca's family roots were Norman, and it was under the tutelage of the family cook that she had learned not only how to make sauce bases, good desserts, and short pastry but also how to use the ingredients that were Normandy's pride. The family also had a home near Cannes in the south of France, where beautifully fresh seafood stews were frequently prepared with chopped tomatoes, onions, leeks, and garlic sautéed in olive oil and flavored with *herbes de Provence* and saffron. After her divorce and her subsequent marriage to Jean Fischbacher, Simca had also added dishes from his native Alsace to her repertoire. As Julia remarked after working with Simca for more than forty years, "Hers is home cooking of the finest sort—*la bonne cuisine bourgeoise*, which is really the basis for all good French food." Testing and continually refining Simca's recipes gave Julia an extraordinary and personalized insight into the cooking of France.

The four years in Paris, however, had been the "honeymoon years." Of subsequent visits she later confided to Simca, "Paris is not the same Paris to me when I do not have my home and my kitchen. We are no longer Parisians, that is." But for those four years that began in 1948 she was "eternally grateful."

During the ten years after the Childs left France for assignments in Bonn and Oslo, traffic between America and France became commonplace. Vacations and pleasure trips probably took second place to business travel, but students enjoying the euphemistically cataloged "semester abroad" seemed to claim more boarding passes than any other group of travelers. And their various reactions to France as the antithesis of American "food fads and convenience products" added another dimension to the perception of France as the gastronomic epicenter of the world.

Drinking a *café crème* in one of the cafés that lined the streets of Montparnasse in 1964, University of California student Alice Waters observed the daily ritual of French men and women with one, two, or several baguettes tucked under their arms rushing home for breakfast. And she saw them repeat the process several hours later when they returned from work. She also noticed how Parisian ladies carried beautifully wrapped boxes of pastries out of pristine, jewel-like shops, and how they selected vegetables and fruits from the outdoor stalls on the rue Mouffetard, the same street that she and her friends often walked up and down reading the menus posted outside the many brasseries and restaurants. As the hours spent over a delicious meal grew longer, and the discriminating activity of choosing the best place for the midday and evening meal became more deliberate, Alice realized that her studies would probably be abandoned in favor of simply eating her way through France.

Both the land and the way its people lived were a revelation, and she said, "I took it in by osmosis. It just became a part of me. I didn't learn it, I just swallowed it, the whole approach from beginning to end." It was a meal, one meal, however, that irrevocably decided her future. It is described as occurring in either a restaurant along the Seine (her father's account) or a little stone house in Brittany with a stream running behind it (her account). Alice remembered a first course of cured ham and fresh melon from the garden, trout caught minutes before in the stream served as the main course, and a tart made from perfectly ripened raspberries for dessert. She also remembered the standing ovation given to the cook by the diners, the applause of people who knew the implications of a pleasurable meal. In retrospect, she knew that "something crystallized that day. It was all so immediate and obvious. . . . That guy I went out with in France—if he only knew how he affected the course of my life." She had planned to travel to other countries on the Continent but spent the entire semester in France, celebrating her twentieth birthday in Paris.

In many ways, Alice's coming of age was typical of Berkeley, a wired mix of actual and vicarious experiences, an academic major in French culture and a studied effort in the remembrance of things past, an eclectic combination of sense and sensibility. But after less than a year abroad, Alice returned to Berkeley with a commitment to learn to live in another landscape dotted with *auberges rustiques*, *potagers*, and *esprit communautaire*.

In the fall of 1964, Alice and her three Berkeley roommates

became involved in the Free Speech Movement, and two years later they campaigned for *Ramparts* editor Robert Scheer, who ran for Congress on an anti-Vietnam platform. They eventually completed their courses at the university. Along the way, Alice and graphic designer David Goines shared an apartment, where Alice began to cook for friends and fellow activists. Seeing her role as bringing politics and food together, she tried to "seduce" others into thinking that although dingy T-shirts, peanut-butter-and-jelly sandwiches, granola, and Campbell's tomato soup were trademarks of the Berkeley Left, even the French communists enjoyed good food. Alice worked her way through Elizabeth David's *French Country Cooking* because the British author, who had brought the color and fragrances of the Mediterranean to a ration-weary England after the war, also captivated her. Inspired by this self-taught cook devoted to the cuisines of the sun, Alice admitted to a kind of "plagiarism" of her recipes and, perhaps more significantly, her ideas. "Her aesthetic is about simplicity and a kind of fragrance. . . . She had a great sense of the seasons and always about life around the table— the setting, the conversation. It was always more than just the food because her recipes were not very specific, to say the least. I remember being frustrated, but it made you think. She was saying something pretty profound about the recipe process—that food changes all the time. It's never, never the same. The climate, the location, all made a difference."

Martine Labro, a French friend whose husband was enrolled in a graduate program at Berkeley, remembered her visit to the Waters-Goines apartment in those early, heady days of cassoulets and *garbures*. Although Alice's cooking was far from perfect, Martine labeled the meal "the food of goodwill," and so obvious was Alice's interest in preparing it that it seemed but a prelude to greater meals.

And, of course, it was. After a year, Alice left Goines and Berkeley to study at the Montessori School in London, and when she returned to Berkeley to teach she soon became emotionally involved with film archivist Tom Luddy and moved into his Berkeley cottage. Passionate about French cinema, he introduced her to the films of Jean Renoir and Marcel Pagnol, and their home became a virtual salon where politics, food, and films held sway. If Brittany had offered Alice the ultimate meal four years earlier, the trilogy of films made by Pagnol in the early 1930s presented an ideal of friendship and community in which Alice could see herself gathering her friends around her table, nourishing them in the spirit of an earlier time. "Pagnol is a big window into where I'm coming from," she has always admitted. "There's this fantastic ambience in the films. All of these characters are such friends. They're trying to get through life together. There's such a joie de vivre."

By 1971 the desire to return to the ambience of that earlier and simpler world and the wish to provide a table and meeting place for their many friends prompted Alice Waters, Victoria Wise, and Lindsey Shere to open a little bistro on Shattuck Avenue, which they called Chez Panisse. Serving a different four-course menu every night, the three women learned the restaurant business hands-on—and were soon in debt. But the effort continued.

During the early years of Chez Panisse, French country cooking based on recipes in both Elizabeth David's and Richard Olney's cookbooks continued to dominate the restaurant's menus, along with playful forays into Escoffier, Michel Guérard, and the Troisgros brothers. But eventually all recipes were adapted to reflect Alice's basic conviction that there are no perfect formulas for good cooking, that pleasure doesn't come through perfection but through tasting the food.

Whenever possible, she traveled to the south of France, staying in her French friend Nathalie Waag's big stucco farmhouse, which was situated in the middle of lavender fields and cherry groves just outside the small hill town of Bonnieux. While in Provence, she also visited Martine and Claude Labro in Vence and joined in the festivities of the vendange by cooking with Lulu and Lucien Peyraud, the proprietors of Domaine Tempier near the seaside town of Bandol. Food was always the preoccupation, the common language that frequently was translated into the "Memorable Menus" of the restaurant—"The Bandol Wine Dinner" to celebrate the arrival of the 1971 vintage, "A Mas des Serres Menu" to feature the lavender honey ice cream served in a small restaurant outside Vence.

"Alice has these romantic fantasies about France," said Luddy, "the food, the men (the Marseille sailmaker Panisse was her dream of a warm fatherly Provençal man with humor and wisdom), and the life." And, indeed, Alice's discovery of Provence in the 1970s perpetuated the dream. There was still an enchantment at that time. And the field-to-table availability of such an Eden-like array of fruits and vegetables was not lost on the aspiring restaurateur. The tastes of Provence, especially, were inspiring, and olive oil, garlic, tomatoes, *mesclun*, the various *herbes de Provence*, and the wines from the small vineyards in and around Bandol infused the dishes served at Chez Panisse.

In the early days of the restaurant, many of Alice's dreams about nourishing, cooking in concert, and becoming fluent in tastes only before imagined were slowly and painstakingly evolving. And gradually the colorful and simple preparation of food that distinguished the dishes of southern France became more possible because of a network of foragers who sought out growers and producers of fresh foodstuffs. It was and continues to be Alice's way of approximating that first meal in Brittany.

France has been a generous benefactor, but today the legacy of that country's gastronomic centrality is as threatened by state-of-the-art *supermarchés*, frozen meals, imported produce, genetically engineered foods, and "le Big Mac" as American cuisine is. "The French just aren't as demanding as they used to be," wrote the *Herald Tribune*'s restaurant critic Patricia Wells. "They used to tell the shopkeeper, 'This is not acceptable, it's not fresh fish, it's not a good loaf of bread.' But fewer people today are brought up with that intense critical eye toward all food." And change does not seem imminent; warnings about adulteration and poor quality fall on deaf ears because, as Elizabeth David often said during her lifetime, "cookery writers are very minor fry."

The culinary world is more than ever in a state of chassé. In the mid-1980s, French-born chef and teacher Madeleine Kamman wrote, "There is, according to some somber prophets, a distinct possibility that French cuisine is on an irreversible downward course." And two years ago, protesting the adoption of the Maastricht treaty, Jean Pierre Quelin, an editor at *Le Monde*, warned, "Beware the Barbarians are at our gates. The remedy is great cuisine—the danger is a united Europe."

But at another time, France as the epicenter of style and the art of living offered Americans a view of a very different culinary world. And three women who were passionate about their experiences in La Belle France uniquely shaped the way America thinks about food. More than fifty years ago, M. F. K. Fisher introduced the French tradition of gourmet writing to an American reading public attuned to nutritional menus and the recipes of home economists. More than thirty years ago, Julia Child successfully translated France's *cuisine bourgeoise* into an American idiom and became its most visible exponent. And more than twenty years ago, Alice Waters began a venture that would eventually culminate in the Best Restaurant of the Year (1992) award for her restaurant, Chez Panisse, and validate her career as one of California's most innovative *chefs-patronne*.

Vive la France!

CHAPTER TWO

Bold at the Stove

*A writing cook and a cooking writer must be bold at the desk
as well as the stove.*

M. F. K. FISHER

If an author's repeated use of favorite words and phrases has an inward as well as an outward story to tell, then the refrain that echoes through the pages of M. F. K. Fisher's books—from a chapter called "Hamburgers à la Mode de Moi-Même" to frequent sentences beginning "I, myself"—may offer more than a few biographical speculations. Famous for creating a prose style that has always been resolutely first-person, without the attendant perils of narcissism or prejudice, she emerges from the pages of her books as a woman of conviction and great independence, answerable to herself and no other. And her compulsion to transform certain kinds of material—childhood, meals shared, refuges, cures, inner maps, hungers satisfied or not—into a curious blend of narrative and essay, recipes and romance may well provide more than a hint of an explanation for her well-deserved literary reputation.

That she was literate, opinionated, and dedicated to her craft is no accident; it was her birthright. As the oldest of the four surviving children of Edith and Rex Kennedy, Mary Frances was born in Albion, Michigan, on July 3, 1908 and grew up in a household of strong personalities. Not only was her mother a dedicated Anglophile but she was also quite literally a "Prairie Princess, a Daisy Miller, whose shy manners were always taken as aloof pride." Edith shared her home with her widowed mother and a parade of relatives, and she sought refuge in the novels she loved to read. In all ways she was a caring mother and a lifelong companion to the complicated Iowan gentleman she loved and could not be dissuaded from marrying. And, in her eldest daughter's eyes, she was one of the most conservative people living.

Rex Kennedy, on the other hand, was adventurous and a risk taker. A fourth-generation newspaperman, he categorically refused to follow the family's journalistic tradition and sold his interest in the *Albion Recorder* in 1910, to go westward with his wife and two small daughters. After two years of various adventures—beachcombing on Puget Sound, cultivating an orange grove in Ventura, and working as city editor of a daily paper in San Diego, he bought *The Whittier News,* "a small daily of ill-repute which no decent Quaker would operate." For forty-two years he met the three o'clock deadline six days a week, attended evening meetings of various organizations, and reported the news with honesty and skill. But the enigmatic editor-publisher always had a special affinity for "lame ducks," those wanderers who passed through Whittier on their way to some unknown adventure that he felt had eluded him. Some of Mary Frances's most persistent memories of her father were flashes of those unfulfilled longings and the "wild gleam" she occasionally noticed in his eye when she heard someone share a story of derring-do with him.

Another adult also influenced the goings-on in the big house on Painter Avenue. Grandmother Holbrook morally and financially sustained her daughter and son-in-law during their first years in Whittier. A Campbellite, lifetime member of the Women's Christian Temperance Union, and frequent patient at Dr. Kellogg's sanatorium in Battle Creek, Michigan, she had definite ideas about behavior, diet, and childbearing and -raising. Living with her, Mary Frances thought, was like "living within sight of the Rock of Gibraltar."

Added to the interplay of these three imposing figures were the shadows of Kennedys, Olivers, and Holbrooks who moved in and out of family discussions. Mary Frances's Great-grandfather Oliver fled Ireland because he had printed scurrilous messages about Queen Victoria. Grandfather Holbrook spent most of his life in his book-filled study, and Grandmother Kennedy filled up the empty columns of her husband's weekly journals with poems patterned on the work of the nineteenth-century British poet Felicia Hemans.

An impressive lineage of undaunted individualists was Mary Frances's inheritance. And the uncles, cousins, and "dear batties" who occasionally visited the house on Painter Avenue and often remained there for months contributed no small share of wonderment with their tales of unusual accomplishments.

Genealogy and her role as the oldest child, therefore, encouraged Mary Frances to distinguish herself early on. Anne, her younger sister by two years, had already captured the lion's share of the family's attention with a delicate stomach. Mary Frances took care of her and played with her during their preschool days. And when Anne joined her as a student at the Whittier elementary school, Mary Frances accompanied her to and from school. Her mother depended upon her to set a good example, which she usually did, although Mary Frances also discovered that there were other ways to win approval. Making a good white sauce for Grandmother Holbrook and scrambling eggs on the cook's night off was one way; giving her mother a notebook filled with her own stories and verses was another, especially when the gift was rewarded with praise.

From the age of four, she confessed, she read books with the addiction of an alcoholic, from morning until night, moving from left to right and top to bottom of the bookcase shelves. Beginning with *The Wizard of Oz*, she went on to a small leather-bound copy of *The Imitation of Christ* that she had been eyeing for some time in her grandmother's sacrosanct apartment; then she began to read the Bible aloud while her grandmother knitted. There was a "children's shelf" that included the Oz books, *Five Little Peppers*, all of Louisa May Alcott, *The Little Colonel*, and various series that "were good at first but not worth a second go." In addition to the library the family had inherited from her grandfather, which included complete editions of Dickens, Thackeray, Jane Austen, the Waverley novels, standard editions of classic myths, and *The Thousand and One Nights*, there were the complete poems of Tennyson, Burns, Poe, and Longfellow and whatever her mother ordered from catalogs, auction notices, and traveling salesmen.

Whenever Mary Frances was asked the meaning of a word she did not know, she was sent to the unabridged Webster's dictionary, which was kept on an iron stand in a corner of the dining room, the scene of most of the family's semantical discussions. The sound of her own voice reading the definition to the hushed diners was "a heady and welcome taste of the limelight." And on Sunday afternoons, Mary Frances and Anne often accompanied their father to the office of *The Whittier News*, walking through the back room of idle presses, amusing themselves in the paper room by writing letters, making paper boats and pigeons, and poring over a copy of *Nostrums and Quackeries* that Mary Frances deftly removed from her father's revolving bookcase when they passed through his office. It was printed on slick paper and had a number of bad photographs of cough syrup labels, trusses, and healing lotions. For some odd reason she loved it, and it stirred her imagination with the same intensity that *Ivanhoe* did. Remembering those years, she was convinced that with the discovery of the printed word she came into focus: "From the minute I could read, I was not separated but whole, of a piece, and not only with other people but my own self. And it is probable that being able to look at print and recognize it has kept me in one piece since that first far day."

If reading was something she did because "everybody in the house who could follow a printed sentence read aloud," shaping sentences and punctuating them correctly were also a part of life in the Kennedy home. "Writing was as natural as breathing," and Mary Frances was adept at its many forms. From her seventh to fifteenth year, she wrote, edited, and published family newspapers at about six-month intervals. Most of them had only two or three editions, but one, an illustrated weekly, ran almost four months. And during her high school years when the society editor, the gardens and PTA man, and even the sports editor at *The Whittier News* went on vacation, she substituted and had her copy on the spindle by the designated deadline.

Mary Frances's role as the oldest child also expanded during those years. When she was nine, her mother gave birth to Norah, and two years later David was born. Edith and Rex thought of them as their second family; Mary Frances and Anne referred to them as the "children" and never quite abandoned the habit. When the children became more mobile and their house seemed too small, to everyone's delight, Rex purchased a ranch on a continuation of Painter Avenue just outside the city limits. Mary Frances assumed more duties in the kitchen, learning to churn and mold butter, and joined her mother when she made cakes on Saturday morning. After Grandmother Holbrook's death in 1920, their meals became more "heathenish." With pigeons, chickens, turkeys, a pig, and a cow, and with orchards and citrus groves, artichokes, asparagus, and every kind of vegetable that grew in the garden, life was filled with new experiences in the lighter, brighter kitchen, which exuded exciting smells and tastes.

As the eldest, Mary Frances also instigated and drafted petitions to convince her parents to alter real or imagined injustices. One of the earliest involved castor oil. Mary Frances and Anne loved oranges, but they flatly stated that they would soon loathe them if their mother persisted in the dreadful custom of mixing doses of castor oil into the fruit drink of their choice. Soon after, they drafted another petition expressing their horror of "bobbed" hair: "We, the undersigned, do not want Mother and Aunt Gwen to get their hair bobbed, now or ever. We cannot stand the thought, and will not stay here if it happens." A third and much more elaborate manifesto was prepared on a small handpress shortly after the Kennedys moved to the ranch. It contained the girls' most impassioned plea to date and concerned weekly attendance at Sunday school. Attending church on Christmas and Easter and even now and then was acceptable, but, they wrote, "We feel that staying home on Sunday mornings and working hard to help Father and perhaps helping with the laundry will bring us closer to God." With the image of Great-grandfather Oliver fleeing Ireland one mile ahead of a posse etched in their memories, Edith and Rex Kennedy were forcibly reminded of the influence of heredity as well as environment on their eldest child.

Mary Frances wrote for and occasionally edited school newspapers during high school, producing everything from reportage to high-flown columns of literary criticism. She remembered, "I was always the English teacher's pet, wrote like mad for her, and assumed casually that I was a genius." That changed somewhat when an old and venerable teacher at the Bishop's School in Palo Alto shattered a few of her pupil's illusions by introducing her to hard work. Praise for a piece well written may have, in fact, "put a germ somewhere about writing to please more people."

For the most part, however, boarding schools and a semester at

Illinois College in Jacksonville, Illinois, failed to enhance her academic record. She returned to Whittier, attended Whittier College for the second semester of her freshman year, then transferred to the University of California at Los Angeles for a makeup botany class during the summer session. It was there that Mary Frances met Princeton graduate Alfred Young Fisher. He was tall, good-looking, six years her senior, the son of an Episcopalian minister— and he was under contract to teach at the Princeton Preparatory School in Cody, Wyoming, that fall.

Mary Frances and Al corresponded throughout the winter, and he told her about his plan to pursue a doctoral degree in English literature at the University of Dijon the following year. Mary Frances continued to mark time at Occidental College and "dreamed of *action*, of intellectual challenges, even of being a chorus girl . . . anything to break from the staid pattern of small-town respectability and waiting for Mr. Right." When asked, she unhesitatingly agreed to become Mrs. Alfred Fisher on September 5, 1929. Eleven days later, traveling in student third, they crossed the Atlantic on the *Berengaria*.

Married, almost twenty-one, and an émigré from a small California town, Madame Fisher celebrated her one-month wedding anniversary with a *dîner de luxe au prix fixe* in eight courses at Racouchot's restaurant in Dijon; then she and her husband returned to their sparsely furnished rooms in a pension on the rue du Petit-Potet. While Al attended lectures and began his thesis, Mary Frances studied drawing and sculpture at the Beaux Arts academy, learned the language and literature of France, and kept a journal. She also wrote a few stories, corresponded with family and friends, and stored in her memory the "inner maps" of Dijon, Marseille, Cassis, Cagnes-sur-Mer, Strasbourg, and the villages and rural scenes that would forever be associated with her coming of age.

Although most of the journals no longer exist and the stories have been reshaped into tales often twice or thrice told, the letters she wrote in France resound with the voice of the developing writer. Reading between the lines of these accounts of day-to-day occurrences—friends' visits, movies seen, tutoring sessions, purchases made, and budgets revised—a portrait emerges. There is a pervasive sense of assimilation of, preference for, and even conviction about the cosmopolitanism of the French scene.

Within three months after her arrival in Dijon, she told her parents that she felt "one-trackish mentally" when her French host, Monsieur Ollangnier, was able to tell her about the superiority of an oyster pie in the tiniest village in France and then go on to discuss old churches, Roman ruins, latest plays and books, and the political maneuverings in Paris with equal gusto and knowledge.

When her sister Anne wrote to her about a possible trip to France after the Christmas holidays, she responded that there was no "dating," that oxfords and simple, dark woolen clothes were worn by young women, and that the French did not "spend money the way they do at home." But she added, "Darling, you'll love it. It's thrilling, fascinating, marvellous—and it gets better and better. Lamplighters and men who sing little songs to sell the candy they carry in trays on their heads, and hot chestnuts on the street corners, and wonderful doorways and cathedral windows, and funny movies and revues and opera for almost nothing, and famous restaurants and perfectly marvellous wines and liqueurs, and hundreds of cafés where you either sit on the pavement and watch the people or go inside and listen to the music—and watch the people—you'll love it."

But day-to-day living in France was not the only thing Mary Frances wrote about. Reading the works of Colette, Balzac, and Hugo in their native language made her more conscious of writers and their style. When her younger sister Norah sent a poem to her for comment, Mary Frances promised that her reply would not be the criticism of an older sister but "the candid ideas of a young person who once tried to write poems, and now only reads them." And she recalled her own efforts when she was twelve years old like Norah and she "saw beautiful things and tried to make them into words." Reading her poems, she claimed, people had either smiled kindly or ignored them, "and I was either flattered by my teachers and relatives, or tolerantly endured. Finally I stopped showing anything to anyone."

She extended her advice with a sad account of how no one really had told her "one damned thing about poetry, about lines and metres and feet and rhythms and word sounds. Sometimes I think of that, and scream inside with bitter disappointment with myself and with the world." Then she wrote of the thousand beautiful forms—sonnets, lyrics, triolets, couplets, quatrains— that would have provided a structure around which to shape her words if she had only known of them. And she urged Norah to learn every twist of the language, to strive for a deep and delicate feeling for words, and to develop her own style by writing imitations of other poets and authors. She concluded the letter with an interesting revelation and an invitation: "Tonight I've told you sad truth about myself that to some would sound silly, to others just conceited, to you, I hope, nothing but the sad truth—and you can trust me with your poems, if you want to. . . . I'd like to send you some things I've written this year. I'd like your criticism of them—your honest thoughts."

With her husband deeply involved in research for his thesis on Shakespeare's plays, and with Lawrence Powell, their American friend from Occidental College and fellow *pensionnaire* chez Rigoulot, explicating the poetry of Robinson Jeffers, Mary Frances was almost always in the midst of discussions about writing and writers. And she had her own opinions about writing that she venturously expressed, then never repeated in the same company. The three were engaged in one of their usual discussions about literature when Powell announced that he was going to learn to be a writer. Mary Frances disagreed completely and said the most he could hope for was to become an accomplished author. Writers are born, she maintained, and no matter how much study and skill are expended one could never "become" a writer. Although they disagreed, she truly believed in the rightness of her opinion.

During the summer of 1931, Mary Frances returned to California to visit her family and escort Norah back to Dijon, where she planned to enroll in a convent school to learn French. That fall, Mary Frances and Al decided to leave their rooms at the Rigoulots' and spend their remaining months in an apartment of their own, where their friends and Norah could occasionally join them for meals. Once she was situated in a small one-room-plus-kitchen on the rue Monge, in the working or "low" quarter of the city, Mary Frances spent more time marketing, preparing meals, and helping her husband with the final preparation of his thesis than she did on her own writing.

When Norah had a Thursday afternoon free from the convent where she studied and boarded, Mary Frances served her pitchers of fresh milk, honey, sweet butter, and the plain kind of Dijon gingerbread called *pavé de santé*. When Lawrence Powell dined at the Fishers'apartment instead of at the Rigoulots' table, she served either a cauliflower or a potato casserole, salad, bread, wine, and fruit for dessert. Sometimes the main course was a steak she managed to grill on top of the stove or fish and fresh mushrooms baked in heavy cream. The entrée was always accompanied by a salad of fresh watercress or marinated green beans, peppers, or endive, and bread and wine. She purchased ripe cheeses, fruit, and, on special occasions, tarts from one of the best pâtisseries. That she had a right to indulge her own gastronomic preferences at her table became a conviction. Believing that her guests should forget "home" and all it stands for at least during the few hours that they were in her home, she cooked meals that she said she hoped would "shake them from their routines, not only of meat-potatoes-gravy, but of thought, of behavior."

In spite of carrying water for cooking and personal needs from the ground floor and learning to keep butter without ice and salad greens fresh, Mary Frances loved the challenge the limited kitchen posed and treasured the privacy. But when her husband was awarded his degree in November and their life turned into a social whirl of faculty teas and dinners, Mary Frances and Al escaped to Strasbourg, where he wanted to do some additional research.

Unable to duplicate their living quarters on the rue Monge, they stayed in a pension. For the first time in many months, Mary Frances began to spend a considerable amount of time on first drafts of stories and on her journal entries. Then suddenly their days in France were almost over. In late March 1932, joined by Norah, they went to a small fishing village between Nice and Cannes to enjoy a last holiday before returning to California in June.

After living as poor students on a fixed stipend for three years, the Fishers were appalled by the conditions created by the Great Depression. College appointments were difficult to acquire, even menial jobs were scarce, and they could not afford to rent an apartment or house during that summer of 1932. And while years later Mary Frances said that she and her husband would have given anything to have worked with Rex Kennedy on *The Whittier News*, the offer was not forthcoming. Her mother and father, however, did invite them to stay at the ranch and use the beach house in Laguna, where the Fishers welcomed the opportunity to maintain the house and pick up odd jobs until Al could find a teaching position.

While Al continued to work on what Mary Frances described as "the great American novel," his young wife kept house, sculpted, and wrote and illustrated an article about Laguna Beach. Calling the artist colony Olas, she described the almost overnight changes, the straightening of streets and felling of trees, the visitors, vacationers, artists, and developers, and the antipathies that flared up and sub- sided as the population grew. When the article was accepted and published by *Westways*, she was paid twenty-five dollars for the three drawings and ten dollars for the accompanying text. "I have never had as sweet and untroubled time in my whole life with something I earned by myself," she wrote. "I spent the money, all of it, on riotous living. Not a penny of it went for taxes, or agents, or anything like that in those full Depression days." She surprised her husband, parents, sisters, and brother with gifts. And she be- came confident that she could write about a place, any place, and what it meant to her, although in this first published piece she resolutely avoided using the first person that would distinguish her work later on. She signed the article M. F. K. Fisher in imitation of her mother's habit of signing checks E. O. H. Kennedy. At that time, however, she had no idea of establishing a byline or doing any more writing professionally.

After spending two years in Laguna Beach, the Fishers moved inland to Eagle Rock when Occidental College offered Al a position in the English department for the fall semester in 1934. To supple- ment their income, Mary Frances got a job working afternoons in an "art" shop in Los Angeles. To occupy her mornings, she often visited the public library. She spent hours there poring over a treasure trove of musty Roman, medieval, and Elizabethan cookery books, which triggered intellectual *amuse-gueules* that were as stimulating and savory as the dishes she had learned to prepare in Dijon. "Before I knew it I was writing little essays about quaint, peculiar, and fantastic cookery habits," she said. "I do not know why cookery rather than anything else: perhaps I liked the good smell of the ancient unread books that were brought up to me from the stacks. (I also liked good food, both in the eating and making, and still do.)"

Mary Frances showed her "gastronomical gleanings" to her husband and to Gigi and Dillwyn Parrish (friends from their Laguna days) whenever they came for dinner. Dillwyn, in turn, showed them to his sister Anne Parrish. As cousins of the famous artist Maxfield Parrish, and children of the portrait painter Anne Lodge Parrish, Dillwyn and Anne were talented writers and artists in their own right. Anne, especially, had a good publishing record at Harper's, so she sent Mary Frances's gastronomical pieces to her editor, Gene Saxton, who expressed interest in them and wanted to publish them as a "Harper Find" if Mary Frances would agree to add several more essays to the collection.

Meanwhile Gigi and Dillwyn Parrish separated in 1935. Gigi remained in the Los Angeles area, while Dillwyn returned to his family's home in Delaware. For more than seven months Mary Frances wrote to him, sending more of her gastronomical essays for his amusement and criticism. And Dillwyn's worldliness, deep sensitivity, and compassion made his return letters especially meaningful to Mary Frances—so much so that her sister Norah later credited Dillwyn with helping Mary Frances focus her talents as a writer. Fourteen years her senior, he easily assumed the role of mentor.

It did not seem unusual, therefore, that Dillwyn and his mother invited Mary Frances to accompany them on a two-month trip to France and England in February 1936. She happily accepted with her husband's blessing. As prearranged, Mary Frances was to meet Gene Saxton and the British publisher of her book while she was in England.

If the trip was something of an opéra bouffe (by this time Mary Frances was in love with Dillwyn Parrish), the meeting in the offices of Hamilton Ltd. was high comedy. Gene Saxton and Hamish Hamilton were both expecting a bookish Oxford don when the very attractive M. F. K. Fisher walked through the door in newly acquired Parisian clothes. After much confusion, they offered her tea, then hesitantly requested that she use M. F. K. Fisher "as an adequately equivocal name for someone who did not write about the pleasures of the table in correctly female and home economics fashion.''

If meeting with her publishers in London was one of the more memorable occasions during her trip abroad with Dillwyn Parrish and his mother, visiting Le Paquis near Vevey, Switzerland, was another. On an earlier trip to Europe, Dillwyn and Anne Parrish had purchased an old stone house and vineyard that overlooked Lake Geneva, and he enthusiastically showed the property to his mother and Mary Frances during their 1936 visit.

Mrs. Parrish, Dillwyn, and Mary Frances returned to America in May, with Mary Frances more in love with Dillwyn than before. She realized that he would always be romantically in love with Gigi, and she was still loyal to Al. Because there was nothing in her background that made adultery a viable choice, she felt that there was no possible solution to her dilemma. After they parted in New York, Dillwyn returned to Delaware. Mary Frances thought seriously about leaving the California-bound train in Chicago to seek employment and a divorce from Al Fisher but decided to return to Eagle Rock instead.

She found her husband greatly changed, in part because of the death of his father, who had been a stern presence in his son's life, and in part because of his newfound freedom. Tensions between his perception of his wife's increasing independence and developing career and his image of her as a winsome naïf continued to grow, however, and then the unexpected happened. Before the fall semester began at Occidental, Dillwyn Parrish invited the Fishers to join him and Anne in Switzerland to form the literary and artistic community they hoped to create at Le Paquis. Knowing that Al's teaching schedule had made writing difficult, Dillwyn, through either friendship or calculation, or both, offered him a chance to escape. Without considering the consequences, the individuals involved in the scheme thought it would work, and the Fishers left California for Switzerland.

After a few weeks of living in a pension in Vevey, Dillwyn, Al, and Mary Frances rented and furnished an apartment to accommodate them while Le Paquis was being renovated. Dillwyn drew up some of the architectural plans himself, Al became interested in enology and even considered taking on the role of winemaster at Le Paquis, and Mary Frances shopped, prepared meals, and kept a journal about their life together and the renovation.

The events of the past year, especially her trip to Europe and the decision to return to Switzerland, and the tensions of living with two men who loved her, albeit in very different ways, blurred for Mary Frances the publication of *Serve It Forth* in early 1937, and she paid very little attention to the occasion. Her book was reviewed favorably by the *New Statesman & Nation*, the *Chicago Daily Tribune*, and the *New York Times* and somewhat unfavorably by *The Times* (London) *Literary Supplement*, but only the review written by S. I. Hayakawa caught her attention as a "perfect review" of this unusual collection of essays about eating, what to eat, and people who eat. And a short note from Alfred Knopf telling her that he wished he had published her book was important to her as well as a foreshadowing of things to come. Although *Serve It Forth* was dedicated to Rex and Edith Kennedy, they took little notice of it. In the Kennedy family, writing was simply something one did.

In the short introduction to the book, Mary Frances drew some fine distinctions between books about *eating*, which either imitated Brillat-Savarin's *Physiology of Taste* or not, and books about *what to eat*, which either gave nutritional information or suggested menus. Then she described books about *people who eat*, which were frequently either memoirs of the rich and famous or gastronomical bicycle tours. She stressed that she intended "to fall between the three fires, or straddle them all." She knew that the spirit of the ghost of Belley would certainly influence her. The household hints compiled by Mrs. Glasse and Mrs. Kander as well as the recipes codified by Carême and Escoffier would also lend their authority. But her book would not be a collection of recipes, she said, although recipes might be there like "birds in a tree—if there is a comfortable branch."

Serve It Forth is a mélange of fact and fancy, incorporating vignettes of culinary history from ancient Egypt to twentieth-century America. Woven among the historical essays are personal essays of secret indulgences, restaurants revisited and the subtle mysteries of time past and time present, the snobbery of certain kinds of food, the rituals of preparation, and her idea of an ideal kitchen. With almost a sly wink, she included a recipe for *pain d'épice* and *diplo-mate au kirsch*—two birds without a branch.

Food is the linchpin for every piece, and the characters and scenes involved in its preparation and consumption are personalized by the author-heroine. Beginning with an overview, she moves from an initial gastronomical "seven ages of man" essay and progresses through twenty-two more chapters to the concluding portrait of César, the embodiment of "what every man in a small fishing village in the south of France wants to be." There is an obvious chronology in the progression of the eight historical essays, from the oldest cookbook, the *Hon-zo*, written in Egypt in 2800 B.C., to memorable cookbooks written by women in nineteenth-century England and America. And there is also a personal past-to-present series of essays with references to the restaurants of childhood and adult life, pensions in Dijon and Strasbourg, and kitchens both filthy and immaculate, noble and commercial.

The centerpiece of the book, and the last embedded tale that she added to the manuscript, is "The Standing and the Waiting," an account of the author's attempt to bring the experiences of the past, idealized and unchanged, into the present. Using the occasion of dining at Racouchot's restaurant in Dijon with Chexbres (Dillwyn Parrish) in 1936, she confronts changes in life and love wrought by the passing of time. Although they are served by the same waiter whom Mary Frances and her husband had befriended six years earlier and the quality of the food and wines remains the same, the "ugly tiled corridors, faint trail of bad air from the corners of the kitchen, and the fumblings of my perfect waiter (dismissed for drunkenness hours before)" subtly undercut Chexbres's toast, "to our pasts—to yours and mine." And the author sadly realizes that everything changes, everything passes. Only the ancient "plebian" tiles on the Burgundian roofs that she sees through her tears escape their fate for a longer time than the fragility of human love.

In a book about the most insistent of human hungers, and the various ways people have, for the most part, dignified the satisfaction of hunger, M. F. K. Fisher employs a form that is as immediate as conversation, and as informed as the most carefully researched article. Between the parable of Jacob (the first restaurateur) and Esau (the first gastronomer) and the heady stories of Vatel and

Lucullus, the serialized memoirs of the author-heroine emerge in a variety of landscapes and timeframes—all quite unforgettable.

By juxtaposing the contemporary preparation of *escargots d'or* with Roman cookery, and the secret indulgence of toasted tangerine sections with the abstinence of medieval monastic regimes, she introduces American readers to a traditionally French mode of culinary writing that avoids both the constraints of culinary history and the self-absorption of the memoirist, focusing her playful imagination and continuing attention on the whys, whens, and wheres of eating.

During the spring of 1937, Mary Frances weighed the possibility of writing a very different kind of book, and she sought Gene Saxton's advice about applying for a Guggenheim grant. She even considered starting a personal book because, she said, "my present life is a strange, complicated, interesting one. . . . But my deep distrust—or is it timidity, cowardice even? of such self-revelations will, perhaps, prevent me from thus relieving myself." As the months passed, however, except for the entries in her journal, she found it difficult to write. Planting a vegetable and flower garden at Le Paquis occupied much of her time. And word that her parents would travel to France and Switzerland in June created a sense of anticipation as well as a plan to meet them in Paris.

Meanwhile, going from their apartment in Vevey to Le Paquis to check on work and perform various chores grew wearisome for Al, and the triangle in which he found himself posed more problems than he could ever hope to resolve. For her part, Mary Frances felt at long last that her relationship with her husband could never survive his realization that she was not "The Woman He Loved and Married, an ideal he formed when he was very young and Christian." And she was increasingly aware of the growing rift between them. She insisted to herself and to those close to her that she was not leaving him for Dillwyn, but she also knew that they must part because they had irreconcilable differences. Before her parents' visit, she asked Al Fisher to stay while Edith and Rex were in Vevey to save them pain but to leave when they returned to California.

Al Fisher spent the rest of the summer of 1937 in Salzburg and returned to the States and a teaching position at Smith College in the fall. Mary Frances and Dillwyn moved into Le Paquis and began an idyllic life together in the midst of a vigorous cycle of gardening and grape growing. Mary Frances harvested the onions, garlic, and shallots, then braided them into ropes to hang over the rafters in the attic. The Italian-Swiss villagers taught her to cook sweet peppers, eggplants, and onions in their own juices, flavored at the last minute with sweet butter or thick olive oil. Dillwyn fried tomatoes the way the family cook did in Delaware. And they harvested corn that they had grown from seed brought back from the States. When alone they ate corn oysters, freshly fried in butter, accompanied by glasses of beer cooled in the fountain.

They entertained guests in front of the fireplace in winter, inviting them to serve themselves from a large casserole simmering on the kitchen stove and the chilled salad bowl on the sideboard. First-time guests pleaded for the name of their cook and were disbelieving when Mary Frances offered her own recipes for the ragout and honey-baked pears she had served. The way she and Dillwyn lived, depending solely on the services of part-time help from the village, was a source of curiosity to guests and villagers alike.

At Le Paquis when the gardens were dormant and the *vendange* celebrated, Mary Frances wrote for her own pleasure, continuing her journals and drafting a few stories and articles. She also collaborated with Dillwyn on a strange novel about a woman who longs to have a child, which they called *Touch and Go* and published under the pseudonym Victoria Berne. Whether the book reflected an uneasiness about her own "limbo" state or not, Mary Frances's growing apprehension over rumors and friends' queries about her separation from Al precipitated a brief departure from Le Paquis.

At the end of 1937, Mary Frances returned home to tell her parents that she was divorcing Al. Whittier was still a small town of more or less conventional people, and the failure of Anne's marriage of five years and Mary Frances's of eight must have been somewhat embarrassing to Edith and Rex Kennedy. To her great relief, however, they supported her decision. She also visited Al's mother and sister to tell them of her intention to make her separation from him final, and then she filed the necessary papers.

Returning to Europe aboard the *Ile de France*, she was acutely conscious of the conversations about Laval, Blum, and the possible fall of France, but she resolutely put the fact that Europe would soon be engulfed in war out of her thoughts. Le Paquis was a safe haven that soon would be filled with budding vines and meadows colored with violets, primulas, crocuses, and wildflowers that grew waist high. The house would expand, as it had the summer before, with visiting relatives and friends. Dillwyn's sister Anne planned to stay for weeks. Mary Frances's brother, David, and sister Norah decided to combine study with their summer vacation in Switzerland.

It was during a weekend in Bern with Anne, David, and Norah in July 1938 that Dillwyn experienced an embolism in his leg that necessitated two operations and eventually amputation. In a frantic search for relief from pain and a more precise diagnosis of the degenerative circulatory disease that afflicted him, Dillwyn and Mary Frances spent almost six months in hospitals and sanatoriums in Bern and Adelboden. But very little help was forthcoming except in the form of drugs to ease the pain. When Dillwyn became more ambulatory, he and Mary Frances returned to Le Paquis to put their affairs in order. Each day brought evidence that war was becoming more and more a reality, and they decided to sail to the States as soon as possible.

At the end of January 1939, Mary Frances's divorce was granted. Although she doubted that a piece of paper could alter her relationship with Dillwyn in any way, for obvious legal reasons she married him in a civil ceremony at City Hall in Riverside, California. The Parrishes also bought ninety acres of apparently worthless land southeast of Hemet, California, planning to renovate the five-room pine-board house formerly owned by a "degraded government Indian trader" who had been found shot to death there. They then sailed back to France on the *Normandy* to sell Le Paquis and arrange for the shipment of their belongings.

Mobilization and grim signs of war were abundant as they crossed the border from France into Switzerland. It was a sad journey, and Mary Frances wrote, "The world seeped in. We were not two ghosts, safe in our own immunity from the pain of the living. Chexbres was a man with one leg gone, the other and the two arms soon to go. . . . And I was a woman condemned, plucked at by demons, watching her love die too slowly." Less than a half year later, they boarded the *Normandy* again, bound for New York and points west.

During the many months of ministering to Dillwyn, Mary Frances did little writing, but she did complete a bibliography for a Wine and Food Society chapbook that she had promised the prominent Los Angeles bookseller Jake Zeitlin she would do. The bibliography and the accompanying letter that Mary Frances wrote to Zeitlin reveal her continued respect for books like "Mrs. Simon Kander's oil-cloth covered masterpiece" and "the greatest book on gastronomy, Brillat-Savarin's *Physiologie du Goût*," as well as her preference for "a constantly shifting and permanently surprising library." "I should keep it small," she advised. "An important part of it would be scrap-books; and I am convinced that it should include information not only about the physiology of taste, but of digestion: and one or two good text-books on the human body in relation to food." She divided her bibliography into four sections: Gastronomy, Practical Cookery, Not Practical Cookery, and Wine. And she listed about seventy-five books, at least half of which were French.

The following year's New York World's Fair focused attention on many of her selections. The French Pavilion offered buyers an impressive array of culinary books from Escoffier to Brillat-Savarin. And while French cookbooks were not yet a part of the culinary libraries of most American households, interest in the pleasures of the table was growing, and there were many occasions for the collector of books about wine and food to range internationally. What Mary Frances had learned firsthand by living in France and Switzerland and by delving into culinary history catapulted her into a position of authority in a field that was gaining popularity in America.

Sometime between signing the contract for *Serve It Forth* and the Parrishes' relocation in California in 1939, a New York literary agent, Mary Leonard Pritchett, acquired M. F. K. Fisher (Mary Frances also used the name M. F. K. Parrish professionally at this time) as a client. Although Pritchett handled books and plays, she specialized in placing material in quality magazines, and through

her efforts Mary Frances was well published from the beginning of
her professional career. Two pieces from *Serve It Forth* appeared in
Harper's Magazine in 1937. A third piece, "I Was Really Very
Hungry," was printed in its original version in *Atlantic Monthly* the
same year. In a letter dated February 13, 1940, Pritchett indicated
that she was involved in placing two more articles, advising, "I
wonder if it might not be a very good idea to interpolate several of
the unusual recipes [in 'Come the Substantials']. This might aid us
in putting across a sale."

To occupy her time during the renovation of the house on the
ranch in Hemet, Mary Frances began to write to various people she
knew about the cookbooks in their personal collections. "I am
especially interested in what good cooks consider their minimum
kitchen libraries . . . if any, and whether they keep records of their
own happier inventions, and whether they all use one or two
standbys like Mrs. Simon Kander or Fannie Farmer and then a
changing collection of less sturdy recipes," she wrote to Mrs. Lewis
Gannett at *Life* magazine. And in a letter to her mother she said,
"Dearest Edie, This is a business letter. I am working on a series of
articles which will probably turn into another *Serve It Forth*, but
better, I hope, and am writing to several people who are known as
gourmets and good cooks, to ask what they think about cookbooks."

Although the answers to her many letters were interesting, Mary
Frances never developed the information into a book. Events were
simply happening too fast, and her time with Dillwyn was too
fleeting. Since their return from France, he had sustained two more
unsuccessful operations in Wilmington, Delaware. And after they
were settled on the ranch they called Bareacres, at Dillwyn's sister's
urging they went to the Mayo Clinic for more tests and consulta-
tions. It was there that they learned that Dillwyn had Buerger's
disease, a kind of chronic phlebitis for which there was no cure and
no relief.

During the two years of Dillwyn's debilitating illness (including
three transatlantic crossings), Mary Frances lived with his pain and
his dependence on painkillers; she also knew that the disease would
eventually necessitate the amputation of his other leg. To distract
him, she began a little book about oysters. She called it *Consider the*

Oyster, "an odd book without foreword or conclusion," but actually it is a small treasury of witty tales and anecdotes about the "indecisively sexed bivalve" that has one of the most fascinating histories in gastronomical lore and legend.

The book includes chapters on the androgynous life and ill-fated death of this mysterious mollusk, its aphrodisiac attributions, and its role in banqueting, along with recipes that are comforting, exotic, and sometimes purely fanciful. Through the stories, the reader becomes so caught up in the masterly way the thin young man behind the bar of the Doylestown Inn concocted a famous oyster stew that he wants to know exactly how to make one himself. The reader also follows the author's quizzical ramblings through recipes found in *The New England Cookbook* and *Brown's Country Cookbook,* with a formula for Butter Crackers from *Common Sense in the Household* added for good measure. By the time he has finished the last page of "A Supper to Sleep On," the reader identifies with the preferences of the author so completely that oyster stew is forever a part of his culinary vocabulary.

So confident was she of the power of her subject to sustain the reader's attention that Mary Frances blended oyster lore and subjective experience with abandon, reaching back several thousand years to consider the Chinese method of making oyster sauce, then drawing on a recent trip she and her husband had enjoyed in New Orleans. From speculation about the recipe for Oysters Rockefeller, she moves from the Roosevelt Bar in New York to the Old Port of Marseille, from East Coast to West (Chincoteague to Olympia), and from Oyster Stuffing to the French Creamed Oysters served at the Hotel Pierre. Without any hesitation, the author-heroine travels in time from the oyster stew suppers of her childhood to brief interludes in New York, France, the Delaware River Valley, and New Orleans, and a longer residence in California. She shares her stories, her memories of stories told to her, and her recipes the same way she would share a tureen of oyster soup, ladling out aromatic spoonfuls in a generous way—"a lusty bit of nourishment."

Duell, Sloan and Pearce published *Consider the Oyster* late in the summer of 1941, just days after Dillwyn Parrish shot himself under the scraggy cottonwoods in a remote area of Bareacres as he had planned to do if and when the pain became unbearable. In reminiscing about the arrival of the book, Mary Frances said, "I remember that I wrote a sad little criticism to my new editor, Sam Sloan, about how I wished that I'd been notified earlier when the book would be published, because neither Timmy [her nickname for Dillwyn] nor I knew about it and I very mistakenly felt, for a few minutes anyway, that he might have put off dying, if he'd known the publication date. As it was, he never saw the book, which was small and short. I dedicated the book to him, and I began to realize then that I must always write toward somebody I love, to make it seem real."

Dillwyn Parrish had been her lover, mentor, and inspiration for almost a decade, and the place that they had created together on ninety barren acres of arid land near Hemet now became her refuge, as did her work. After Dillwyn's death, her mother and sister Anne stayed with Mary Frances, and she spent some time at her parents' home in Whittier, but she knew that she was essentially alone. Dillwyn had taught her how to live and how to love, and when the time was right she wanted to write about the beginning and tragic end of "my fifteen minutes of marriage" to Dillwyn Parrish.

At her mother's urging, Mary Frances visited her brother, David, and sister Norah in Mexico for two months; then she returned to California to begin another book at Bareacres. Pacing back and forth in Dillwyn's studio, she dictated *How to Cook a Wolf* to her sister and completed the book in little more than a month's time. In many ways, the writing of this third book reconfigured both the joyful and the tragic experiences of the past two years.

With the constraints of wartime Europe quite vivid in her mind's eye, and more than a little dismayed by the advice given to patriotic American housewives by popular "home magazines," she recommends strategies for those who were still intent on living agreeably in a world full of an increasing number of disagreeable surprises. This is a practical book, advocating not the balanced meals devised by home economists but a proposed daily menu that includes "willy-nilly" fruits, vegetables, starches, and proteins. Heaps of toast for breakfast; an all-vegetable lunch of salad, casserole, or soup; steak or a cheese soufflé for dinner; and juice and fruit for midmorning pickups might startle guests, but, she maintains, "palates will awaken to new pleasures, or remember old ones."

In this marvelously titled book, every chapter is a "How to"—how to greet the spring, make a great show, comfort sorrow, be cheerful though starving—and is complete with recipes. And there are a few "How not tos": how not to boil an egg or be an earthworm (during blackouts or in bomb shelters), and how not to starve. She draws on memories of her mother's gingerbread, French food, and canned food, and arranges the anecdotes and recipes into traditional cookbook categories. Taking her cue from those old standbys Isabella Beeton and Marion Harland, she also recommends tips to ensure the survival of Butch the dog and Blackberry the cat during wartime shortages.

Published by Duell, Sloan and Pearce early in 1942, *How to Cook a Wolf* was reviewed as "lively and amusing and intelligent and a real cook book too." Its popularity prompted Clifton Fadiman, star of *Information Please* and literary critic of the *The New Yorker*, to say in his review: "M. F. K. Fisher writes about food as others do about love, only better." Its sage advice about menu planning, cooking, and baking, the inclusion of seventy-three recipes, and the phenomenal success of the book identified M. F. K. Fisher as a food writer, albeit an unconventional one. She dedicated the book to Larry Paul Bachman, an old friend from Occidental College, "who gave me its very catchy title one time when he was trying to convince me that I should not live alone on my empty ranch." His advice eventually convinced Mary Frances to leave Bareacres for a time and seek employment in Hollywood.

Executives at Paramount Studios so admired a picture of her that accompanied a review of the book that they sent a talent scout to sign her on as an actress. When she demurred, the studio offered her a seven-year contract as a "junior writer," with a starting salary of seventy-five dollars a week. While she was not on her way to stardom, she attracted attention as one of a group of career women emerging on the American scene. In a July 1942 issue of *Look* magazine, M. F. K. Fisher was featured, in "Hollywood-goddess" style, hand-grinding coffee, doing her own shopping, growing grapes on her ranch, discussing a script with a well-known actor, and revising a manuscript in a negligee with a glass of sherry in hand. She was thirty-five years old, divorced and widowed, and one of America's successful career women.

In the midst of the "Garden of Allah" crowd of actors, musicians, and scriptwriters, Mary Frances made lasting friendships, had two or three "good affairs," and became pregnant, but she felt that the work at Paramount was unrewarding: "I was unknown and also unskilled. I did little bits and pieces . . . worked on one full script aimed at a Helen Hayes return-to-the-screen, which never came off. I quit because I could not stand it any longer . . . the sterile creative life, living rather like a literary starlet, going to the right parties and so on." She broke her contract after a year, got caught in a struggle between the Screen Writers Guild and the studio, and left Paramount in May 1943.

Perhaps her closest friends knew that she was pregnant; her parents did not, and it is not clear how she managed to keep the birth of her child on August 15, 1943, a secret. She gave her daughter the name Anne Kennedy Parrish and indicated to one and all that she had adopted her. Mary Frances never revealed the name of the father of her first child.

Between her departure from Paramount and the birth of her daughter, she wrote The Gastronomical Me. In an effort to put the past into some kind of context before assuming the responsibilities of a single parent, she had to journey into that past and chart more precisely the future course of her writing career. Using a quote from Santayana, "To be happy you must have taken the measure of your powers, tasted the fruits of your passion, and learned your place in the world," Mary Frances chose the title "The Measure of My Powers" for eleven of the twenty-seven sketches and stories that re-created her earliest memories.

The characters in the book are the people "with me then, [with] their other deeper needs for love and happiness." Grandmother Holbrook skimming "froth" from the kettle of strawberry jam, Father serving peach pie and cream to his two small daughters on their way home from their aunt's ranch, Al Fisher and Mary Frances celebrating their "first month" anniversary at Racouchot's restaurant, and Dillwyn Parrish and Mary Frances enjoying captain's dinners aboard ship while war clouds gathered. These episodes reveal a more complex emotional terrain than she had explored before. Mary Frances explains that in writing about hunger, "I am really writing about love and the hunger for it." Taste experiences, furthermore, are always evocative. A young girl's gastronomical coming of age, symbolized by eating a first oyster at boarding school, leads to a consideration of boarding school crushes and lesbianism. And a young man drinking dark beer and eating enchiladas while listening to Juanito sing "La Malagueña" in a Guadalajara beer hall is as much a foreshadowing of tragedy as an evolving scene of hunger being unsatisfied.

The Gastronomical Me is possibly M. F. K. Fisher's most personal book, as it is also the most oblique. Years later Patricia Storace wrote: "Here are meals as seductions, educations, diplomacies, communions. Unique among the classics of gastronomic writing, with its glamorous settings, its wartime drama and its powerful love story, [it] is a book about adult loss, survival, and love." The sunny days of childhood and romantic days of honeymooning and studying in France pass to more complicated relationships and tragic events. The waiters, chefs, peasants, innkeepers, and ship's captains who half fall in love with the author-heroine fade in and out of focus when attention centers on the Al Fisher, Dillwyn Parrish (Chexbres), and Mary Frances ménage à trois, the idyllic year at Le Paquis, the illness and death of Chexbres, and her brother David's inability to function normally in what he considered a mad world. Each memory is presented separately, in the form of a self-contained sketch or story, but in the end they are all one. Through the sequence of shared happy and sad events, the author-heroine has "learned her place in the world."

But Mary Frances was still finding hers, and the desire to write fiction often conflicted with the "hot literary cook stove of gastronomical comment." Although Clifton Fadiman had praised *The Gastronomical Me* and suggested "that Mrs. Fisher was born to write novels and that it's about time that she did," Mary Frances was not only sustaining her reputation as a journalist but enhancing it by writing regularly for *Atlantic Monthly, Coronet, Esquire,* and *Gourmet.* When Mary Pritchett negotiated a contract for a regular monthly column in *House Beautiful* for 1944–45, Mary Frances was hailed as a different kind of food columnist.

As far as Mary Frances was concerned, this work was "hack stuff," honest sit-down-at-the-typewriter writing to support herself, her daughter, and her ninety-acre ranch. Like Colette, a writer and woman she much admired, she produced the magazine material quickly and wrote almost continuously, and her agent moved quickly to collect her published articles into books. But there were other voices—family, and old friends like Larry Bachman, who cautioned, "Please try not to write any more about food, if you can help it in a book. And don't write any more about yourself. I am highly dubious and suspicious of people who do—dubious as to their growth as writers. Suspicious as to their imagination and ability to project their minds to other subjects. Look at Thomas Wolfe."

Necessity, however, dictated another course. Seasonal, catchily titled, and completely different from the "molded salad" school of culinary writing, the *House Beautiful* articles broke new ground in culinary journalism. When the feature premiered in June 1944, the editor of the magazine promised that "she [M. F. K. Fisher] has the gift of creating moods around food as other writers create them about life and love. Her wisdom of the art of good living imbues even a recipe for apple pie with the fascination of a mystery novel," and the introduction to the series was accompanied by a photograph of M. F. K. Fisher taken by George Hurrell. Her menus included stuffed oysters, *coquilles aux crevettes*, and new potatoes aux fines herbes, and while her recipes could hardly be called models of exactitude ("as for the roast leg of lamb, the best thing to do is read a few books about it"), most of them were clear and helpful and occasionally witty. She listed ingredients in the order of use and took a reader's intelligence for granted. The introductions that she wrote to the Fourth of July, Thanksgiving, Christmas, Valentine's Day, and spring's arrival were filled with the insights that personal experience of the holidays at home and abroad provided. And she included ways to substitute ingredients and adapt recipes to personal preferences, adding suggestions about appropriate wines.

What is amazing about the curious blend of sophistication and lighthearted banter that distinguished the *House Beautiful* series is the fact that Mary Frances was so emotionally conflicted during the writing of it. The bittersweet pattern of intense happiness and grief that dominated the years she had spent with Dillwyn Parrish continued to influence her days. Only a few months before the birth of her daughter, her brother, David, had committed suicide, a tragedy that profoundly affected Mary Frances and her family. In less than a year, David's death was followed by that of her editor, Sam Sloan. It seemed that privately and professionally there was no respite from loss. And in early 1945, the death of President Franklin D. Roosevelt after more than twelve years in office seemed to climax what she considered to be the pervasiveness of death over the past four years of her life. Mary Frances became so despondent that many of her friends advised a change of scene. Taking Elsa Purdy, a neighbor who had helped her in various roles since she and Dillwyn had purchased Bareacres, and her two-year-old daughter with her, she went to stay in a friend's empty apartment next to the Third Avenue El stop in Manhattan.

The second night she was there, she met Donald Friede at a dinner party in Greenwich Village. Although Mary Frances had been introduced to him at one or two cocktail parties in Hollywood during her year at Paramount, she knew little more about him than his association with the Hollywood agent Myron Selznick and his earlier role in the meteoric team of Covici-Friede, publishers of Nobel Prize winners John Steinbeck and François Mauriac and of controversial works like Radclyffe Hall's *Well of Loneliness* until their company was taken over by creditors in 1938. She also knew his history of failed marriages and frequent career changes.

Intelligent, urbane, and cosmopolitan, Donald Friede was the sort of man whose company she enjoyed. They began to meet frequently for lunch and dinner and decided to make the relationship permanent. Their decision to marry on May 19, 1945, was extraordinarily precipitous and virtually doomed from the start; furthermore, it affected both of their lives profoundly.

After a brief wedding trip to Atlantic City, they settled into New York's social-literary scene. Mary Frances wrote, "It was fun, the summer of 1945 in New York, to meet all the people of the various publishing sets as a callow Westerner. . . . It was just after the war, a strange time indeed, and New York was filled with glittering bitter refugees. I promised to do a book for Pat Covici about a similar time in Switzerland, when Geneva and all the little villages around the lake swarmed with brilliant refugees from France. Mme. Récamier and Mme. de Staël had their salons, then, and Brillat-Savarin flitted around the edges before he headed for the more golden shores of America."

The similarities were unmistakable. Mary Frances had earlier taken refuge in Dijon and then in Vevey on the shores of Lake Geneva with a man she loved at the time. During the summer of 1945, New York became her refuge, a duplex on Bank Street in Greenwich Village was her salon, and Donald Friede was becoming an important figure in her life and a major influence in the direction of her work.

Just as Dillwyn Parrish had a kind of genius for inspiring Mary Frances to write, Donald Friede had a genius for urging her to produce one book after another. As a first step in "managing" her career, he broke her existing contracts and signed her with Viking Press, where his former partner, Pat Covici, became her editor. He also introduced her to Henry Volkening, a literary agent whom he thought could advantageously represent her.

During the summer months after she was married, Mary Frances worked on an anthology of gastronomical literature. While Friede continued to move in publishing circles in one capacity or another, she researched the book in the New York Public Library, and they met for cocktails in the garden of the Museum of Modern Art at the end of the day. In early fall, Friede wanted to leave New York, and he thought that Mary Frances, who was expecting her second child, would be more comfortable if they returned to California and settled into Bareacres.

Once there Mary Frances was off on a frenzied race against commitments. Shortly before the premature birth of her second daughter, Mary Kennedy Friede, on March 12, 1946, she finished *Here Let Us Feast*. Because it was probably one of the few collections of excerpts from world literature concerned with eating and drinking, the book was heralded as another "first," and reviewers were quick to point out that M. F. K. Fisher's readers would be delighted to find "almost more Fisher than selections."

And then Mary Frances changed course. Encouraged by Pat Covici and Donald Friede, she wrote a novel, *Not Now But Now*, with movie rights in mind. She also began a translation of Brillat-Savarin's *Physiology of Taste*, which her husband had signed her to do for the Limited Editions Club. The novel, however, had poor sales and was not destined to make money in Hollywood. With two small children to raise and a husband who was, at the moment, trying to pursue a writing career himself, Mary Frances continued to write short pieces and articles for magazines to keep the wolf from the door. But debts mounted. In 1947 they moved to Beverly Hills, where Friede signed on as a story editor for Ralph Blum, but the whole scheme proved to be short-lived, and they returned to Bareacres after six months. Friede's failures were beginning to put a serious strain on their marriage.

The first day of 1948, Mary Frances finished her translation of Brillat-Savarin's seminal masterpiece after almost eighteen months of work, and she considered it one of her finest achievements: "I did this extremely arduous and rewarding task for money, but with all the honesty and admiration I am capable of. I am very proud of it, and am fully aware of the enormous amount I learned about English from doing it." It was a beautiful and expensive book done for the Limited Editions Club with a lower-priced edition printed for the Heritage Book Club.

The satisfaction of publishing this work, however, was also short-lived. Some attending difficulties over an alleged breach of contract suit incurred by Mary Pritchett because had she arranged for the publication of excerpts from the translation precipitated Mary Frances's decision to engage Henry Volkening as her agent.

In spite of all the royalties earned by her hard work, the lifestyle that Friede thought desirable for his family was a continual drain on their financial resources, and most of Mary Frances's savings were depleted. During the first five months of 1948, she finished a series of twenty-six articles based on the alphabet, which were scheduled to run consecutively in *Gourmet* magazine beginning with the November issue. She wrote the series under great pressure and noted, "The more hastily and more carelessly I write stuff for magazines, the more quickly it is snapped up and paid for. This does not add to my respect for the present state of The Written Word." When Pat Covici at Viking agreed to publish the series as a book, she enlarged the articles and added more notes.

An *Alphabet for Gourmets* provides a kaleidoscopic view of the experiences and influences that dominated Mary Frances's life in the mid-1940s. From "A Is for Dining Alone," a replay of living in Hollywood, to "Z Is for Zakuski," which draws on the memories of "a man [Donald Friede] I know who spent his boyhood in St. Petersburg," meals savored, recipes that range from scrambled eggs to kasha, and bits of Brillat-Savarin's sage advice strangely come together. *Kirkus Reviews* hailed it as "a merry, sometimes biting, often passionate defense of the lover's approach to food—any kind of food," and a philosophical chat about eating and drinking. The *San Francisco Chronicle* observed that it was "no cookbook in spite of the recipes it contains"; instead, it was a book filled with shrewd observations and luscious memories.

Casting about for another project and the leisure to complete it without the financial considerations that usually accompanied her writing commitments, Mary Frances applied for a Guggenheim Foundation grant. She listed her achievements and stated that she "had established [herself] in a limited, and, fortunately for [her] a sparsely inhabited field of upper-class comment on the pleasures of the table." And she set forth her plans to do a "highly personal portrait" of Madame Juliette Récamier as "the archetype of intellectual-cum-sexual refugee," considering in the same light the comparable refugee mind of the postwar world. She wanted to turn her back on obligations, forget contracts and commitments, and descriptions of "perfect buffet-luncheons"; more to the point, she wanted some ease from the tyranny of her checkbook balance. But the grant was not awarded to her. Discouraged and in a state of almost chronic fatigue, she sought help from those around her but could not find it.

By the fall of 1948, her mother's health problems, considerably more acute since David's suicide, had worsened, and Friede, unhappy and depressed over his inability to cope with family obligations, was under doctor's care and in and out of hospitals and sanatoriums. Having experienced the suffering of Dillwyn Parrish for almost three years, and having witnessed her mother's illness during the past seven years, Mary Frances was unable to cope with her husband's near psychotic state. After fifteen months of unsuccessful treatment, he sought help in the East while she recovered alone from the death of her mother in June 1949.

Never one to admit failure, Mary Frances analyzed her relationship with Donald Friede and concluded that there was simply too much pain, too many problems, and too much fear over the possible effect of all this turmoil on her daughters. Her savings were virtually gone, she had accepted generous advances on future books from Viking, which were also spent, and her own health was in a precarious state. In an agonizing decision to make the separation from Friede permanent, Mary Frances and her two daughters left Bareacres to live with her widowed father in Whittier in November 1949.

Living in her father's home, managing the house, which often expanded to accommodate her sisters and their families, and chauffeuring her daughters to preschool and grade school was not the respite she had envisioned. There simply wasn't any time to write, and she felt less and less inclined to do so. Although she had a deadline with Viking for the Madame Récamier book that she had described in the application for the Guggenheim grant, she was literally unable to work on the biography.

Personally and professionally, 1949 to 1951 were watershed years in the life of M. F. K. Fisher. She acknowledged that filing for her divorce from Donald Friede was an admission of failure, but juggling being a wife to a talented but totally self-centered man and raising her children in a peaceful environment seemed impossible. She refused Friede's repeated requests for a reconciliation and was granted a divorce on August 4, 1950. For the sake of the children, whom Donald Friede loved in his own fashion, Mary Frances was determined to be as gracious as possible to both Friede and her successor as his wife, Eleanor Kask. She also continued to value her former husband's advice about her professional choices. The financial arrangements of the divorce, subsidized by Friede's mother's estate, also helped, in part, to cancel some of the debts that she and her husband had incurred during their five years of marriage.

Although Mary Frances did not write and publish another book for the next twelve years, the process of revising, collecting, and anthologizing her works had been under way since the early 1940s, when Clifton Fadiman had included one of her stories in his *Reading I Have Liked*. And stories from *Serve It Forth*, *Consider the Oyster*, and *The Gastronomical Me* were reprinted in at least seven anthologies, from textbooks to the *Best Short Stories of 1948*.

To everyone's surprise during the summer of 1950, Mary Frances began revising *How to Cook a Wolf*, writing a new nonwar or Cold War introduction and adding marginal notes, footnotes, and a section of additional recipes. It was, however, only the prelude to the issuing of her first five gastronomical books in one volume called *The Art of Eating*, which Donald Friede, who had joined Eleanor Kask at World Books, published in 1954, with an introduction by Clifton Fadiman in the American edition.

The Art of Eating was sold first to Macmillan and then later to Vintage. To anyone unfamiliar with M. F. K. Fisher, J. H. Jackson wrote in the *San Francisco Chronicle*, the collection introduced "one of the *haute cuisine* gastronomes of our time, and perhaps the shrewdest and wittiest commentator of the refinements of subsistence since Brillat-Savarin laid down his quill and his larding-needle." And reviewers from the *New York Herald Tribune* and the *San Francisco Chronicle* were quick to distinguish her works from "today's welter of cutie-pie cookery-chatter," adding, "The conversations of M. F. K. Fisher on the art of eating are like a refreshing breeze flowing from the twin sources of sense and sensibility. She writes as one intelligent adult to another—practically, often profoundly, and always beautifully."

The most insightful comments about M. F. K. Fisher's contribution to gastronomical writing, however, were written by W. H. Auden in the introduction to the British edition, published in 1963. Noting that she was as talented a writer as she was a cook, he said, "I do not know of anyone in the United States today who writes better prose." Proof, if anyone wanted it, he said, could be found in *An Alphabet for Gourmets*, and he directed readers to the first three pages of "I Is for Innocence."

Auden then theorized about women who developed a passion for cooking, maintaining that their animus, or unconscious masculine side, was stronger than normal. And, although he did not write extensively about M. F. K. Fisher in this context, he did suggest that her preoccupation with wine and food was cerebral as well as creative: "There is nothing of the 'Little Woman' about her. . . . Of her many stories and anecdotes, some are hilarious, some macabre, some tragic. If most of them are bitter-sweet, she is never saccharine nor acid. *The Art of Eating* is a book which I think Colette would have loved and wished she had written."

The five books collected in *The Art of Eating* were the core of M. F. K. Fisher's gastronomical works, the benchmarks against which she wrote. To her great regret, she never quite caught the magic of those early books again, or, perhaps, forces within and without militated against recapturing the "innocence" that had inspired them. They were all written for someone she loved, but time and events had conspired to deny her "a significant other."

In addition to her gastronomical writings, however, Mary Frances continued to write fiction. When Donald Friede read the short story "Legend of Love" in the *Ladies' Home Journal* in the early 1950s, he wrote, "I have always felt that you are a deeply rich and untapped well of wonderful fiction, and if you can keep yourself away from the hot literary stove for a while, you will be wise to do it. It is quite obvious, in reading magazines, looking at the publishers' lists, checking the book-stores, that the for-sale professionals have taken over the field that you almost pioneered."

The story in question had a deeper significance. Mary Frances responded to her former husband's letter by saying, "I discovered an odd thing about writing that story. It was the first thing I've ever written simply to *write*. Always before, without any exception, I've written for *someone*. That explains my almost abnormal disinterest in reputation and 'public' and so on. I imagine all I've ever wanted was the approval and encouragement and interest of a *person*. Well . . . I can't indulge in writing to please myself, the children are still too young to be an audience. So, I think I must putz along on hack stuff."

Sustaining book-length projects or even articles while she juggled all her duties on the ranch in Whittier became increasingly difficult. There were continuing demands on her time—pinch hitting at *The News*, helping her father with accounts and paperwork, and, when his health declined dramatically, caring for him. Domestic help was unreliable, the old twelve-room ranch house needed attention, and Mary Frances did most of the cooking herself between driving her daughters to their respective schools at different times of the day. She told her editor and friend Pat Covici that the only possible time for writing was between 8:30 P.M. and 6:30 A.M., and she could not risk "growing nervous or over-tired and resultingly cross and inadequate as a mother. Right now the children are more important than Modern American Literature, at least to me."

And indeed during the next ten years, she resolutely gave more time and energy to her daughters than she did to her career. When her father died on June 2, 1953, Anne was almost ten years old and Mary was seven. Mary Frances was keenly aware that the father figure they had grown accustomed to and depended upon was now absent from their lives. And while she thought seriously about remaining in Whittier, she and her sisters decided otherwise. The family ranch was sold, and declining her father's wish that she take over *The Whittier News,* Mary Frances and her sisters also sold the paper that had been closely identified with the Kennedy family for over forty years. She and her daughters moved to wine country in the Napa Valley, where she purchased a large Victorian house in St. Helena. But there were other places she wanted them to experience, and her share of her father's estate provided the means to live in France for a year in 1954 and then in Italy and France for more than two years from 1959 to 1961. "Being the girls' mother is so fleeting" echoes like a motif in her letters to family and friends, and even though the experience of living in Aix-en-Provence and revisiting the villages and cities associated with her own coming of age would provide material for books at a later time, she published very little during the 1950s.

Writing books "in her head" sustained her. At one point she was tempted to turn her attention to translating a part or perhaps all of Colette's works. But she postponed her plan, knowing that living in Aix with her daughters would strengthen her already considerable command of the French language. She also continued to collect material for what she called her "Old Age" project, although both her editor and agent were noncommittal on the subject. And the Récamier biography remained in a kind of limbo until 1957, when she simply pronounced it "dead" and felt it was "not the time either in my life or in history to worry the question of whether or not a silly woman slept with Napoleon!"

In the late 1950s, while her daughters spent long hours in school, she wrote to her friends that she had three books, in addition to her

"Old Age" project, in progress. She wanted to expand a series of five articles called "Modern American Drinking" that she had written for *Harper's Bazaar* into a book. The story of Peter Cartwright, a nineteenth-century frontier minister whom Mary Frances considered to be "one of the ingenuous accidental giants of our whole American culture," had fascinated her during her Hollywood days and began to take shape as a biography. She also planned a book on the subject "Some of the Men in My Life," with sketches of Brillat-Savarin, Peter Cartwright, Sherlock Holmes, Nero Wolfe, and Maigret. But neither the times nor the circumstances of her life were conducive to the completion of the projects.

The works in progress she had outlined, however, provide an insight into the way Mary Frances worked. From the earliest days in Whittier to the most recent trip abroad, she had always jotted down words, names, people, and happenings that were unusual or quirky or poignant. Returning to France in the 1950s, she saw firsthand the ravages of war; she renewed old acquaintances and heard incredible tales. Postwar Aix, especially, was peopled with dignified matrons without steady or adequate incomes, waiters with tales to tell, beggars, gypsies, and maimed outcasts whose stories would eventually mingle with her own experiences of time and place. And, of course, since her days of researching old cookbooks at the Los Angeles Public Library, she had kept letters, jottings, notes, and clippings that had caught her attention so that an odd collection of fact and fiction mysteriously worked its way into an article, story, or book. She was committed to every scrap of paper.

A wonderful example of the kind of collecting that Mary Frances called her "careless compulsion" was the transformation of odd notes and clippings that she gathered during her residence in Aix-en-Provence with her daughters in 1959. While preparing *A Cordiall Water: A Garland of Odd & Old Receipts to Assuage the Ills of Man & Beast*, she drew on "phisical receipts" from old cookery books, labels from pillboxes, family remedies, and cures and herbs that animals instinctively use and humans *believe* will heal. And she translated the odd restoratives and remedies into ways we can "comfort or strengthen Nature." Published in 1961, the little book reintroduced M. F. K. Fisher to her small but select audience.

Answering an interviewer's question about the best book M. F. K. Fisher had ever written, Mary Frances designated *A Cordiall Water*, after her translation of Brillat-Savarin, as "the pick of the litter," a choice dictated by the "purity of language" found therein. It was a quality she had sensed and admired in Joseph Conrad and Vladimir Nabokov and other writers who thought in two languages. As she said, "For a few hours, while I was writing about horny cats and aching bones and nosebleeds, and all that clutter of life, I was stripped of banality, and I wrote simply in my native tongue, because I was temporarily detached from it and thus more aware." Although it did not sell well, the little book written on the fifth floor of the Hôtel de Provence above the rooftops of Aix "tidied some mental drawers about folk medicine," even as it introduced the theme of healing, which from then on was woven into the fabric of M. F. K. Fisher's writing. The months in Aix, the second residence there in less than six years, also proved a "cordiall water," a comfort against the separations—some temporary, some permanent—that would occur when Mary Frances and her daughters returned to the States.

In the fall of 1961, Anne went to New York to study acting, and Mary Frances temporarily left St. Helena and rented a small apartment in Berkeley to be closer to her younger daughter, Mary, who was a five-day boarder at a private school. With time and excellent research libraries at her disposal, she agreed to write the text for *The Story of Wine in California*, which the University of California Press planned to publish. Using color and black-and-white photographs by Max Yavno, the oversize book presents the "story of wine from the planting of the vines to the moment when the consummate product of human skill and technical knowledge is poured into the glass." Beginning with wine's religious symbolism and its use as healer, tonic, and enjoyment, Mary Frances draws upon her background in viticulture and her love for her "adopted" state of California to write an appreciation of both.

Mary Kennedy Friede's graduation in 1963, and her decision to enroll in a premed program at Russell Sage College in Troy, New York, marked the end of Mary Frances's immediate domestic responsibilities "to keep the house pleasant and all four of us animals [including a dog and cat] fed and warm." Anne had opted for an acting career in New York City; Mary chose a school close to her father and stepmother. Declining to settle into an "empty nest," Mary Frances decided to volunteer as a teacher in a Black school in Piney Woods, Mississippi, in the fall of 1964, believing that she could contribute something to the civil rights movement. It was, however, a short-lived experiment. By the end of the first semester, she felt that the goals of the eighty-year-old founder of the school were being subverted by the current administration, and she knew that despite personal success with her students she would not be invited to complete the school year. Behind her casual comments about being "fired," there was a sense of frustration that her efforts had accomplished so little.

The experience did, however, reinforce the conviction that the times were changing perhaps faster than she realized. Movements, whether for civil rights or feminist consciousness, were gathering momentum. And on a different level, the early 1960s had ushered in *une frénésie culinaire*. Food became one of America's main performing arts with the success of Julia Child's *French Chef* TV series, and cookbooks became the reading of choice for all those following James Beard to the backyard grill and Craig Claiborne to Le Pavillon. The number of cookbooks published was escalating every year, and their quality was so varied that even *The New Yorker* allocated space to cookbook reviews and sought out M. F. K. Fisher to write them.

During her semester of volunteer teaching at Piney Woods, Mary Frances had begun to receive review copies of the wave of cookbooks inundating the market. Although her time was limited, she read them with interest and wrote to Donald Friede, who had joined Doubleday that year, "I am even more revolted by most of them than I planned to be. And I am shocked to reflect on their cost. Most of them, even if they were any good which they are not, are simply impossible to pick up, if one by some idiotic coincidence ever planned to look for a recipe. Now and then there is a beauty, like the Larousse, which has just as much right as the Bible to be too big and too heavy. The rest are pretentious prestige-symbols." And she suggested that Friede use his innate good taste to publish a book to bring out the real connection between the kitchen and the parlor. Illustrate recipes with Man Ray's photographs or appropriate reproductions from the Museum of Modern Art, she advised, or use artworks like Brancusi's *Bird in Flight* and add recipes for roasted quail and *poulet de Bresse truffé*. "If these idiots are going to pay $22.50 for useless poorly written prestige-cookeries which are an offense to everything but the publisher's budget, why not combine business with pleasure and do a GOOD book to catch the super-snobs with their Braques down?" It was a lighthearted plan, although the cookbook editor at Doubleday saw real possibilities in it if only Friede could persuade Mary Frances to write it. He was not successful; she had already started a book about Aix-en-Provence.

During the early months of 1965, Mary Frances received a "catch up on family matters" letter from Eleanor Friede that raised other, and ultimately more significant, issues than Donald's latest diet, her cooking classes with James Beard, and her neighbor Truman Capote's anxieties. Eleanor wrote, "I think I do know what you mean about not being able to just concentrate on your writing . . . perhaps you have gotten into the mental habit of considering your writing something you do 'on the side,' or when it happens, and that the essential life is bringing up two little girls, or teaching youngsters how to articulate. But you could, perhaps, start thinking in the other direction—that the writing . . . is the essential, and what you must devise is some satisfying filler for the time, lots of it, when you can't be at the typewriter. A matter of reversing the balance. . . . It is *wrong* to neglect *now* the very special talent you have, and anything less than putting IT in first place is neglect. Or evasion." And she went on to suggest satisfying time fillers—the house in St. Helena, activities at the Wine Library, and a bit tougher discipline on the good dropping-in neighbors.

The advice echoed similar words from Mary Frances's agent, Henry Volkening, and she knew the balance would have to be reversed, but she concluded, "I think the main trouble is that I don't think there is any importance, AT ALL, in anything I write. I write pleasingly, and sometimes well. But so what? I have known a lot of writers, and have always been basically amused by their frantic insistence upon being WRITERS. I don't think I have the right attitude. I mean this. I don't know who could ever convince me that it would matter one toot-in-Hell whether I wrote an article for *Holiday* or not. So, yes, I have come to consider what I write 'on the side' . . . and suddenly there is now more of that. And what is left?''

Meanwhile, her book on Aix, *Map of Another Town: A Memoir of Provence*, was being published by Little, Brown rather than Viking because her editor and friend Pat Covici had become terminally ill. And Volkening negotiated a more substantial writing contract with *The New Yorker*. By July 1965, however, only one of the pieces on current cookbooks had been published, and Rachel MacKenzie, her editor at *The New Yorker*, had rejected more than three stories. Mary Frances confessed to being completely at sea with the magazine, and told Eleanor Friede, "She [Rachel MacKenzie] liked the things but they didn't get past the boys . . . too far out, too vague, perhaps a tiny-winy bit sentimental . . . these were the thumbs down on three." Clearly, the lure of fiction writing continued to be stronger than "writing about cookbooks and food the way I used to," she wrote, but she seemed destined for more "cookery bookery."

After Donald Friede's death in the summer of 1965, the projected photographs-plus-text cookbook he wanted Mary Frances to write for Doubleday was not pursued by either his successor or the cookbook editor. During the same year, however, a suggestion from William Targ, an editor at G. P. Putnam's Sons, that Mary Frances compile a book of her own recipes seemed to challenge her at a time when she was aware of "too many and futile attempts" at writing definitive cookbooks. At first, she thought of it as an offbeat collection of "dated dishes," but when she went through her recipe file, she was pleasantly surprised with the jottings on preserves and pastries that had been so intimately linked to the kitchen in Whittier and the recipes she had often used in the various kitchens of her adult life.

She submitted a plan for three or four main sections with recipes from a "tight but fairly eclectic file of personal cooking, old tried-and-trues." And she expressed a wish "to bow firmly and openly to a list of perhaps five easily procurable and completely standard texts . . . Rombauer's *Joy of Eating*, *The Boston*, *Larousse Gastronomique*, Escoffier's *Cook Book*, and perhaps that near-classic by Julia Child and her associates about French cooking 'made easy' . . . it is used increasingly by amateur cooks, who are my main readers, I suspect." It was an honest gesture, one not usually found in cookbooks that were labeled definitive, and she thought that it would win her editor praise from cookbook collectors and serious cooks. Above all, it emphasized the fact that her cookbook would be about meals, recipes, and cookbooks that were personal and meaningful to her, for she had always believed that probably "not a single recipe I ever used has sprung virgin from my brain."

The four years between the signing of her contract with Putnam's and the eventual publication in 1969 of the recipe collection (titled *With Bold Knife and Fork*) were extraordinarily productive for Mary Frances. Many of the pieces for the book had been published first in *The New Yorker*. She agreed to do a series of eight two-hour lectures, called "Menus of Mankind," for the University of California Extension Center in January 1966, a project that involved more research than she had anticipated. And in spring when the lecture series was over, Richard Williams of Time-Life offered her a contract to write the text for the pilot volume in the Foods of the World series of books. It meant a trip to her "second homeland," almost two months in Paris and Provence, and an opportunity to meet Michael Field and Julia Child, who were both consulting editors for the first volume, which was to be called *The Cooking of Provincial France*.

Doors that she had not walked through before were opening due in no small measure to the efforts of Henry Volkening, but a growing demand for her writing was also possible because of a virtual renaissance of social and diplomatic dining. Mary Frances wrote, "Thanks to hostesses like Jacqueline Kennedy in Washington, dining has been simplified, but this demands an even greater knowledge of textures, flavors, and so on, than a twelve-course meal. I want to talk about the inter-relations of foods . . . and inevitably something of their reasons for being." And, of course, during the 1960s, Julia Child's TV series provided audiences across the country with an instant education in French culinary technique. Her name and names like James Beard, Craig Claiborne, Dione Lucas, Albert Stöckli, Michael Field, and Richard

Olney were in the vanguard of culinary luminaries that soon would include M. F. K. Fisher. And Mary Frances's small cult of avid readers would gradually expand to include insurance salesmen as well as food and wine connoisseurs as she went about her business of turning language into something special—a stew or a story.

CHAPTER THREE

D*E*A*R
F*R*I*E*N*D

*I am glad and strongly relieved to
know that you and Paul seem to feel
all right about my being so suddenly
and firmly a friend. These things
do not happen often, and when they
do they can be rather scary. But
me, everything is rosy. Since your
letter that is. Before I simply had
to wait and guess.*

M. F. K. FISHER

The story of how the salutations "Dear Mrs. Child" and "Dear Mrs. Fisher" changed to "Dear Julia" and "Dear Mary Frances" and then to "D*E*A*R F*R*I*E*N*D" is not a tale oft told. M. F. K. Fisher wrote about life, travel, food, and drink in a small town on the West Coast; Julia Child was a culinary celebrity on the East Coast. Their paths crossed only when they, along with Michael Field, were hired by Richard Williams to launch Time-Life's Foods of the World series with a book dedicated to the cooking of provincial France, and a new chapter in M. F. K. Fisher's life began.

It was the first time Mary Frances had agreed to write to someone else's specifications, or, as she described it, "for hire," and the one and only time she signed on to be a member of a team with a definite production schedule. Beginning in early June 1966, Williams arranged to have Mary Frances fly to Paris to work with a photographer on a typical French family lifestyle sequence before she went on to Provence to concentrate on regional specialties. She was responsible for writing the final text. Michael Field, accompanied by his wife, Frances, went directly to the south of France and by invitation made Julia's house, La Pitchoune, on Simone Beck's property in Plascassier his base for gathering recipes. Back in New York, it would be Field's job to test and select the recipes for the book. Julia remained at her home in Cambridge, Massachusetts, taking occasional trips to New York City to consult with the project's food photographers and interpret the photos and texts being sent to New York from France. Her remaining role was to read and comment on the manuscript. On paper it was an interesting arrangement, staffed with researchers, a test kitchen manager, and copy editors galore. As Julia wrote to Mary Frances, "What an enormous operation that Time-Life, Inc., turns out to be. The only limit to the excellence of these cookbooks is the limitation inherent in people, as all the equipment, and every imaginable resource from printing to distribution to money are all there in abundance."

Neither the decision to begin a series on the foods of the world with the cooking of the French provinces nor the choice of Julia Child as consultant and M. F. K. Fisher as author was lightly made by the series's editor. Both women had lived in France and had translated that experience into an American idiom. They shared an appreciation of fine wine and food, and an abhorrence for the word *gourmet* (pronounced "goremay"), and they both had made a substantial contribution to the reappraisal of "the pleasures of the table." Michael Field's reputation, although stellar, was far less grounded in the French experience, but his enthusiasm for the book was infectious.

Seen through the eyes of Julia's friend and coauthor, Simca, the curious trio housed in La Pitchoune was somewhat puzzling, but she often accompanied the Fields and Mary Frances to many of the two- and three-star restaurants scattered along the Côte d'Azur because Michael Field thought the experience was important for his understanding of French cuisine. Simca also extended her legendary hospitality to the three Americans, inviting them to lunch and dinner in her home, Le Mas Vieux, which was beautifully situated on the property. Mary Frances, though not always enthusiastic about Michael Field's restaurant hopping, happily revisited this sun-filled corner of France, which encompassed the glamour of Nice, Cannes, and Saint-Tropez as well as the hillside villages of the Alpes de Haute-Provence.

Not only had she long admired the authors of the monumental *Mastering the Art of French Cooking* but she was becoming acquainted with Julia Child as a person by living in her home, drinking coffee in her kitchen, and sitting on her patio looking out over the meadows that stretched toward Grasse. She had even written several notes to "Dear Mrs. Child" about plane, bus, and train schedules.

But none of these experiences really prepared her for the first firm handshake with the Cantabridgian in tennis shoes who towered over most of the other people meeting Mary Frances's flight from Paris to Boston's Logan International Airport on August 3, 1966. Julia recalled, "I so well remember meeting you at the airport, and we were expecting a diminutive creature, but you were a nice big girl." It was friendship at first sight, and in retrospect Mary Frances remembered that at the time she was both relieved and overwhelmed with the feeling that she would be the Childs' friend for life "even if we seldom met again and you did not care."

What each woman brought to this first meeting was considerable. *Mastering the Art of French Cooking* and the *French Chef* television series had established Julia Child as a "chef," writer, and teacher. In 1966, Julia's career was on an arrow-straight course. Volume II of *Mastering* was under contract, and her name lent more than a little authority to recipes and magazine articles. M. F. K. Fisher had a much smaller audience, although she had a solid literary reputation based on her ten books, the translation of Brillat-Savarin's *Physiology of Taste*, and an impressive record of magazine stories and articles. But both personally and professionally she sensed that many changes were coming. "For the first time in my so-called adult life I seem to be on largely uncharted courses," she confided to Julia over a light supper of *jambon persillé* accompanied by one of Paul Child's fine wines. They were sitting in the shade of the back garden of the Childs' large clapboard home on Irving Street in Cambridge, dining al fresco with the Childs' friend Avis DeVoto and sharing memories of France, which were considerably enhanced by photographs taken by Paul Child over the years.

When they met with Richard Williams the next morning, he indicated that he and his staff were pleased with the progress of the volume, although, he thought, it would be helpful if Mary Frances could arrange to stop over in New York before she returned to California. Shortly after the meeting with Williams, Mary Frances drove to Maine with the Childs. For weeks she had planned to visit with her daughter at the Kennebunkport Playhouse before returning to St. Helena. As it was en route to their summer cabin in Bernard, Julia and Paul invited her to accompany them. Driving north, Julia was shocked to learn that the New England landscape was totally unfamiliar to Mary Frances, and she enthusiastically urged her to join them the next year, with promises of blueberrying, lobster boils, and a trip to the Bread Loaf Writers' Conference. At least, she said, it was something for Mary Frances to think about.

In a "bread and butter" letter written from the Hotel Dorset in New York City a few days later, Mary Frances addressed Julia and Paul as her "Cher Nouveau Amis," and she thanked them for an interlude which she valued as a mysterious reward of some kind, following as it did a most unusual month in Plascassier. She also noted that New England was a revelation, an extremely pleasant experience, and she was looking forward to seeing it with the Childs someday. Although she was not much of a sailor or bather, she was a good looker at scenery. But for the moment, she was eager to return to St. Helena and finish her part of the Time-Life project, which seemed to be growing more complicated each day.

During Mary Frances's stopover in New York, she met with the editorial board of the series and learned that they were proposing that the first draft of the introduction she had written in France be divided into a shorter general introduction and several "chapter" introductions. In a state of limbo, she returned to California and awaited word about the new organization of the material. When she received it, she rewrote the text in less than a month's time and sent the manuscript to Williams in early October. A series of memos, letters, and editorial corrections followed.

While Waverley Root, who had been hired to review the first draft, concentrated his comments on small but important details, Julia's comments were far more substantive. She wrote directly to Mary Frances, telling her that she would send all the material that she had annotated to the general editor at Time-Life for forwarding, and she went out of her way to mention, "I have read and written as though you were not O*U*R F*R*I*E*N*D, which seems the only sensible thing to do." She thought that Mary Frances's text was "poetic" and "evocative," but she added, "I have an overall feeling that the French are over-romanticized and the Americans underestimated, as though France were seen with loving pre-war eyes, and America viewed from the super highways with every once in a while a meal with the TV-dinner set."

Using the photogenic Boulats, selected by the Paris Time-Life bureau as an exemplary French family, Mary Frances had written about Annie Boulat's Parisian kitchen overlooking the boulevard Montparnasse and about her kitchen in the family's remodeled *mas* about forty miles south of Paris. Marketing at the outdoor stalls on the rue Mouffetard or picking fresh produce at the farm of her neighbor in the country, this French wife and mother selected what was in season and what would help her create either a fine meal for her guests or an outdoor dinner for her family. As portrayed by Mary Frances, this one-of-many French housewives could handle a *mousse au chocolat* and a *potée* with skill.

Not so, said Julia. Always a Yankee in the court of the Fifth Republic, she had few illusions about the culinary expertise of French housewives. Years earlier she had subscribed to Simca's view that in France cooking was regarded either as a profession or as something menial associated with a rather unglamorous domesticity. French people either entertained or dined in restaurants, ate dishes procured from readily available charcuteries, or employed their own cooks.

At issue was an impression of France that each woman had formed under very different circumstances, different times of residence, and different needs. But Julia made a strong case for groups of people in this country who were dedicated to good cooking and eating and who might learn much from this book if they did not feel "chided" by it. She emphasized that American families knew their way around the kitchen far better than most French did, and American kitchens were much easier to work in.

Julia loved Mary Frances's stories and anecdotes, but she took a dim view of any comment that "degraded the red-blooded American way of life." She preferred instead a tone of urging on, an avoidance of the digs about folkways, gelatin salads, squeezy-fresh bread, and inferior grandmothers. "Not all people have been so unfortunate in this country," she wrote. "My grandmother and my Aunt Annie, too, were wonderful hen cookers and I have only the most delicious memories."

Mary Frances probably responded with a "Ho Hum and Ah Well" in imitation of her mother's reaction to cosmic upheavals, but she also became increasingly aware that what she had written was being cut and pasted into a constantly evolving book. And it was this reason along with persistent and occasionally conflicting requests for revisions from Williams that prompted her offer to resign from the project on October 31, 1966. In a letter to Williams, she asked to withdraw and withhold her name from the book. She would expect no further remuneration, and the editorial staff could salvage the 38,000 words of text she had supplied to them, "depersonalized," of course, in order to arrive at a suitable text. Mary Frances wrote to Julia the same day, thanking her for her help and encouragement, and hoping that she had not let her down in any way. She felt that she was not really the right one for the job but added that she had been immeasurably enriched: "I have met you both, and Michael and Frances Field, and the fascinating family of the fascinating Simca." She concluded that she was very much in debt to the Luce empire.

Between scrambling to shape the book into a cohesive whole, pairing photographs and recipes, and supervising test kitchen activities, Richard Williams and his assistant Irene Saint managed to incorporate the M. F. K. Fisher text into the book with as little rewriting as possible. And when Williams showed her the revised manuscript at her home in St. Helena in December, Mary Frances agreed to have her name appear on the book. Over the course of the controversy, Mary Frances had become more than a little uncomfortable with the fact that some jobs at Time-Life depended upon her association with the book. In addition, there had been a bit of minor "blackmail" on both sides, but being acknowledged as the author of the book would prove more professionally advantageous to Mary Frances than she realized at the time.

She confided to Henry Volkening, "The most surprising people, *nice* people, even dear good friends, are saying and writing to me the damnedest stuff about the glossy publicity in the Time-Life throwaway. I feel as if they actually had no conception of what I have been trying to do since I was nine or so: be a good writer. They call me long distance and scream happily at me, 'MF, you're *in*! You've *made* it!!!' . . . just because of a hammy toothy shot in the

subscription gimmick. . . . Actually it hurts me. You can add this
to your file on the Sensitive Soul Syndrome. Or am I simply being
peevish? Or snobbish, perhaps? I suppose if some obscure reviewer
had linked my name, referring to one of my books pre-doomed to
complete nonentity, with someone like Colette or V. Woolf or or
or, I'd feel happy as a fat cricket."

Because Mary Frances was in many ways her own best critic,
when she submitted a manuscript, she considered it an "honest"
piece of work that required very little editing. The publishing
process, therefore, was not without frequent "dustups." When she
signed on "to write a nice quiet book about my recipe file," William Targ wanted her to submit the manuscript chapter by chapter.
She sent one or two pieces to indicate that she was working but
refused to send any more material until the manuscript was complete because she "didn't work that way." And she had exacerbated
the situation at Time-Life by rejecting any editorial changes in word
choice or style. Sentence structure, punctuation, and a sophisticated vocabulary were her stock-in-trade, and she had little respect for editors who "tinkered" with her prose, and even less
respect if they questioned her judgment. In all these matters, she
relied on the advice of Henry Volkening. As a literary agent and as
a friend and confidant, he served her well.

At this time in her life, particularly, what had always been an
activity as necessary as breathing gradually became more than what
she did every day; the act of writing became a refuge as well. While
working away at an article or a story in the attic or basement of her
home in St. Helena, Mary Frances insulated herself from any problems her daughters were experiencing. With deadlines to meet, she
spun out articles about soups and sauces, casseroles and puddings
with so much gusto that "Mr. Shawn [of The New Yorker] himself
is reported to have said, 'Dang blast it'—or whatever expletive such
a godlike figure might use—'The woman can make even tripe
sound edible.' " She was not inured to that kind of flattery.

Julia's comments notwithstanding, the year between the resolution of the "dustup" at Time-Life and the publication of The
Cooking of Provincial France in January 1968 brought a deepening of
the relationship between Mary Frances and the Childs. Since their
first meeting, invitations to get together and even to meet each

other's friends were improvised, often in an indirect way. Julia was eager for Mary Frances to meet James Beard; she wrote, "[He] will be in San Francisco around the middle of September [1966], and I do hope you meet. We are extremely fond of him, and he was unbelievably generous and kind to Simca, Paul and me when we first arrived in New York with our great unknown selves and cookbook. I think he has done much to set the tone of friendliness among cooking types, which is so different from that sniping and back-biting that goes on in France."

In an effort to get Mary Frances into the "establishment," Julia went a step farther. She wrote, "Judith Jones of Knopf will possibly get in touch with you. She is our editor, and we love to work with her. She said she 'wanted to feel you out,' I believe. No harm in that!" Judith Jones had read several of Mary Frances's essays and reviews in *The New Yorker*. They became perfect introductions: "Reading your recent essay in *The New Yorker* on the anatomy of a recipe, particularly your look at the Aresty book [*The Delectable Past; The Joys of the Table from Rome to the Renaissance from Queen Elizabeth I to Mrs. Beeton*]," she wrote, "set me to brooding again on how much we need a delightful, informal sort of social history of food that would romp through the ages, picking up all sorts of telling bits about the whys and wherefores of eating habits . . . my own thoughts keep revolving around you." In response, Mary Frances mentioned the "Menus of Mankind" series she had given at U Cal; and she alluded to a project about her childhood days in Whittier. Under her contract *The New Yorker* had the right of first refusal, but perhaps Knopf would be interested if and when.

More introductions were arranged on both sides of the Atlantic. When Julia and Paul were in Plascassier early in 1967, Mary Frances urged her friends Eda Lord and Sybille Bedford to contact the Childs at La Pitchoune. Both women were writers of some repute who lived in England and Provence, and they were connoisseurs of fine wine and food. Eda Lord was also a good friend of the painter and food writer Richard Olney, who had left the States in the early 1960s and taken up residence at Solliès-Toucas in the hill country north of Toulon. Largely because of this friendship, Mary Frances, the Childs, Simca, and other culinary luminaries met and dined with Olney and were introduced to his bountiful table and justly praised wine *cave*.

Toward the end of February 1967, Mary Frances told Julia that she had missed meeting James Beard on at least two occasions. She was unable to see him in San Francisco, and she was away in Los Angeles when he was the guest of honor at a "blessing" of Robert Mondavi's new winery in Napa. But she informed Julia that plans were already being made for a get-together with the Fields and James Beard at her friend Eleanor Friede's home in New York at Eastertime. The eventual meeting was a great success, and she described the Easter Eve dinner in great detail, including the fact that Beard said, " 'Now all we need is to have Julia and Paul here . . . The Big Four!' (He was being polite about me, for I am not *in any way* in your class, except now and then with a snippet of Deathless Prose.)"

Stories about their mutual friends and acquaintances along with a schedule of comings and goings filled their letters, but they also wrote extensively about their work. Julia and Paul spent many months and over 200 pounds of flour perfecting the recipe for French bread for the second volume of *Mastering*, experimenting with nasal sprayers and soaked dust brooms to get the right amount of moisture into the oven to brown the bread. Mary Frances read the five-and-a-half-page recipe that Paul had included in one of his letters with much amusement.

Mary Frances wrote to Julia about chopping away at her recipe collection for Putnam's, now long overdue. She also mentioned that she was writing some things about Provence for *The New Yorker* and repeated her wish to write the text for a book of Paul Child's photographs of places and people in the south of France, which she had seen when she was in Cambridge. She told him that she had been "rocked" by the experience because she felt that the view of Provence captured through the lens of his camera was the view behind all of her experiences in that mysterious country: "I am limited and would have to do an approach to your work through myself . . . people . . . the senses. I don't know if this would be right, perhaps too simple." It was an invitation to collaborate on a book that she would extend to Paul many times over the years.

As scheduled, the first cookbook in the Foods of the World

series was published in January 1968, and Time-Life planned a huge party at The Four Seasons restaurant for the event. Julia was enthusiastic and wrote to Mary Frances, "On the whole I think things are pretty good. I am most anxious to see it, aren't you? I am sure it will be most swish and handsome."

The day of the Time-Life book party was precisely the day the *New York Times* ran Craig Claiborne's review of *The Cooking of Provincial France*. Incisive, authoritative, and selectively damaging, Claiborne's comments left M. F. K. Fisher's contribution unscathed: "Mrs. Fisher knows whereof she speaks, and she knows how to say it. . . . She has authority, experience, memory and a pen to admire and envy." He gave Julia Child a tap on the wrist for not correcting the egregious errors of the "former concert pianist," who clearly failed to make a serious distinction between the recipes savored in the provinces and those developed under the aegis of haute cuisine. "What naïveté makes anyone include fillets of sole bonne femme in a volume on provincial French cooking . . . [or] coquilles Saint-Jacques à la Parisienne with its sauce Parisienne? One suspects that these recipes were in somebody's files and were—in their opinion—too good to resist including." The implied culprit, of course, was Michael Field; the review was a dismissal of the first book in a series "that could have been a grail-like monument to good taste."

The success of the Time-Life cookbooks (Claiborne's review notwithstanding) was guaranteed by the 500,000 subscribers to the eighteen-book series. And even Mary Frances thought that the first book was "a pleasant surprise. . . . I decided," she said, "to let the whole slick series come along . . . the Italian book does have some nice pictures in it, and I have hopes for the one on Japan. As for anything on Haute Cuisine directed by Michael, I shudder (as I did to learn that his current cooking course is on la cuisine provençale)."

Comments like "throwing down the gauntlet" and "a meringue not a soufflé on the cover" were parried by the food famous at The Four Seasons on February 19, 1968, and controversy continued to plague the first volume in the series. More to the point, however, the battle lines were drawn in the volatile world of culinary journalism. Nora Ephron, in an article in *New York* magazine about the

current culinary "world of self-generating hysteria," used the controversy to expose the "ins" and the "outs." Could the culinary
world be any more ingrown than the theater world and the music
world? Of course, it could and it was. "The food world is smaller.
Much more self-involved," she wrote, "and people in the theatre
and in music are part of a culture that has been popularly accepted
for centuries; people in the food world are riding the crest of a
trend that began less than 20 years ago."

Brandishing names and gossip with abandon, Ephron discussed
at length the two wings of the Food Establishment. On the one side
were the home economists, writers, and magazine editors who,
industry-oriented and mindful of the needs of the average housewife, lined up on the side of shortcuts, kitchen gadgets, and convenience foods. The other group were the purists or traditionalists
who championed the merits of haute cuisine and worked tirelessly
to develop taste. "The Big Four of the Food Establishment are all
purists—James Beard, Julia Child, Michael Field, and Craig Claiborne. They are virtual celebrities. Their names conjure up a sense
of style and taste; their appearance at a benefit can mean thousands
of dollars for hospitals, charities, and politicians."

Julia sent a copy of "Critics in the World of the Rising Soufflé
(Or Is It the Rising Meringue?)" to Mary Frances with the comment
that she and James Beard found the article hilarious: "I don't think
we would if we didn't come off mostly unscathed—although the
remark about my Bavarian Cream hurts—it was not that but an
orange soufflé in orange cups—now fixed, but it will always pain
me. There is always some truth in these things!"

Mary Frances thought that the Ephron article was "delicious,"
especially so because she knew many of the individuals involved.
And she added, "I have not met Craig Claiborne, but for years he
has sent me books and I have exchanged little notes with him and
he has invited me to Long Island and so on." A few years earlier,
Stein and Day had approached Mary Frances about writing a biography of Claiborne, and she had declined, not because she did not
regard him highly but because she considered a biography about a
living subject simply too difficult, if not impossible, to write. Still,
all this gossip about the Food Establishment offered no end of
amusement to Mary Frances, who deliberately lived in a little town

in the Napa Valley and did not publish a cookbook a year or endorse the newest can opener or create recipes for the Northwest Pear Association. At the time, M. F. K. Fisher was not even considered one of the "Big Four."

Julia was not as far removed from the internecine quarrels of the food world as Mary Frances was, although living in Cambridge and Plascassier insulated her to some extent from New York City's Balducci–Bloomingdale's–Coach House circuit. She was also known to be scrupulous about avoiding endorsements of any kind. She directed her considerable energies to her television series and, especially during this period, concentrated on "cookery-bookery," being madly busy, "panting over stove and typewriter." She often wrote to Mary Frances about reading through reams of clippings and going into the kitchen to refine instructions in order to get a recipe just the way she wanted it. And she shared her concerns: "I see the grave danger of everyone doing the same thing, clipping out every interesting recipe from everywhere including la Belle France, and then making a little change here or there, and publishing it as one's own. This is a terrible problem, as some recipes, such as Le Quatre-Quarts Modernisé . . . I just intend to use—having made some improvements of my own and some fuller explanations. Perhaps what one must do is to say in one's introduction that one has made free, ruthlessly, with every published idea one has run across (I shall abandon 'one' for 'I/me/we' 'one' can entrap) but that when something has gone through our mill it has come out in another form; however to give credit where it is due. For instance, *Joy of Cooking* gave me the great hint on Pommes Anna. You have given me a great idea on pea cooking, a simplified 'à la Francaise.' What are your feelings on this knotty question?"

In response, Mary Frances bluntly criticized the growing practice of lifting countless recipes from both bad and good cookbooks and fobbing them off as original the way so many second-rate cookbooks did. She was convinced that "rarely like a great planet, comes a BOOK: Mrs. Beeton's, Mrs. Rombauer's, Montagne's, *yours*. Willy-nilly, they are enough. But I'll tell you, because I know I can, that even in yours I have adapted a couple of things because of local tastes." She explained how she cut and adjusted the quantity of mustard in a mustard sauce for roasting lamb. "But I sure-as-

Hell would not fob that off as my recipe. Nor would I write for permission from your publisher and then go on to tell what I did with it. I would straddle the problem if it ever came up, by saying, 'This is the way I learned it from Child, with a couple of minor changes.' Do you think that is all right?'' Mary Frances followed the same practice with the other "greats" on her working cookbook shelf. Escoffier used truffles; she substituted local mushrooms. If she made gingersnaps, she simply quadrupled the amount of ginger Rombauer listed. And Larousse's recipe for *petits pois à la française*, she felt, could successfully be made with frozen peas and Los Angeles lettuce. That there is really no such thing as an original dish was her basic belief, and even the greatest dishes are adaptations.

On the stylistic use of "one," Mary Frances was just as emphatic: "I agree with you about the over-use of 'one' . . . especially in such a book as yours. The introduction must be J. *Child* eye to eye with the millions of adoring readers." From jaded college professors to teenagers, people were on a first-name basis with Julia. And Mary Frances added with more than a little mischief that several women had discovered that their husbands could not keep their eyes off Julia and that because of her they loved to think about good cooking: "I mean that they are amazed that they do not mind losing their husbands to you because they are already in your thrall, themselves."

While Julia kept working on the second volume of *Mastering*, *The Cooking of Provincial France* had been translated (apparently poorly) into French, and the Time-Life book had not been received kindly in French culinary circles. Mary Frances sent a clipping in which French cookbook author Robert Courtine dismissed certain things in the text as errors. It served to crystallize something that Julia had been dimly aware of for some time, and she repeated it to Mary Frances: "Every Frenchman is convinced he is a connoisseur who has nothing to learn from experts." In a nugget, it was the very thing that had been "bugging" her in her collaboration: "I don't know why I have been so dumb, but it is something one can hear, but not feel viscerally because how can anyone (but the French) have such arrogant non-sense as to live by that conception. Eh bien."

Mary Frances herself was about to embark on a joint venture with a Frenchman, and she would soon have occasion to remember Julia's words. In November she told Julia about secret plans being worked out by Eleanor Friede to have Mary Frances translate into English an autobiographical picture book by Maurice Chevalier called *Mon Paris*. "From Brillat-Savarin to *L'Homme a Cheveux Blancs*," she wrote, "in one quick happy jump!" It would mean, among other things, that she would travel to Paris to meet with Chevalier in the spring, and she wondered if the Childs would be in residence at La Pitchoune in April or May. If so, it would be a wonderful opportunity to meet in Aix or Plascassier—something to look forward to in the new year.

Before the end of 1969, however, the book Mary Frances had started four years earlier for Putnam's was published. *With Bold Knife and Fork* collected more than 140 recipes, some "doable," some not, and to the reader they seem delectable or avoidable depending on the author's enjoyment or lack thereof. "This book is about how I like to cook, most of the time, for people in my world, and it gives some of the reasons," Mary Frances wrote. Subliminally she relied upon recipes to re-create meaningful experiences in her life. Using "boiled dressing" from Grandmother's old and stained recipe book, her mother's "dark, heady broth," which cured a bout of flu, Sevruga caviar shared at the Café de la Paix, and Madame Bonamour (Rigoulot)'s cheese soufflé savored in Dijon, she pulled the strands of her life together. *With Bold Knife and Fork* also contained Mary Frances's tribute to Julia Child as the "culinary arbiter of at least this much of our century," plus a glowing account of Julia's "five months of work, 200 bakings, and use of 250 pounds of flour" to achieve an infallible recipe for French bread. Julia returned the compliment by saying in a newspaper interview that *With Bold Knife and Fork* was her favorite 1969 cookbook. It would also be Mary Frances's last "formal" cookbook.

When the plan to forge ahead with the Chevalier book encountered some difficulties, Mary Frances spent the first three months of 1970 working on a book about growing up in the midst of a Quaker community. She literally isolated herself, first in Eleanor Friede's summer house in Bridgehampton, Long Island, and then, when the weather grew too stormy, in a rented room in nearby Sag Harbor to re-create the Whittier experience. Icebound and completely alone, she wrote day and night on a book that she regarded as the "hardest work I'd ever done. . . . It was hard as Hell itself to strip down all the wishful dreams of what had really happened." As a straightforward, if chronologically limited, narrative, the episodes reveal the security of living in the Kennedy home when other homes were closed to her, the influence of literate and culturally sophisticated parents, and the attraction of a dining room where the convictions and needs of Grandmother Holbrook and the propensities of Edith Kennedy were often sharply contrasted. When most of the individual stories were accepted by *The New Yorker* and a contract signed with Knopf to publish the sequence as a book called *Among Friends*, Mary Frances felt that she "had cleaned [her] own inner air" but also that the book was not as forceful as she had wanted it to be. Like Colette, she had returned to "her mother's house" and drawn upon childhood reminiscences to conceal as well as reveal present feelings. Childhood, too, was its own kind of refuge.

During the winter months of 1970, Julia spent most of her time completing the second volume of *Mastering* in Cambridge. As meticulously detailed as the first volume, the second book proved to be a greater drain on her time and energy than she had anticipated. And, as a result, the plans for a new "color" series of *The French Chef* continually competed for her attention. At long last the Childs went to France in spring, when they were joined by a crew to photograph and film various local scenes for the forthcoming TV series. Visiting the markets and local merchants was fascinating, Julia wrote, but she and Paul both sensed that they were experiencing the end of an era, with handwork in the kitchen and dining room increasingly difficult to find and three-star restaurants becoming big business, well-managed but not the gastronomic temples of old. "We went to four of the 'greatest' (Véfour, where Paul got food poisoning for the third (and last) time, Bocuse, Troisgros, Oasis.) NON. I have eaten every bit as well in New York—in fact, they are all much the same now."

Mary Frances, on the other hand, had postponed her trip to France in order to correct the page proofs of *Among Friends* and to celebrate the hundredth anniversary of her house in St. Helena. "Say we shall not miss again," Julia wrote in August. With eight TV shows in the "can," she and Paul planned to work exclusively on the series until December, then go to La Pitchoune and stay through most of January. "How much more fun the TV is than doing a book is" was becoming a kind of refrain in her letters.

The possibility that both the Childs and Mary Frances would celebrate the end of the year in Plascassier grew substantially over the summer months. Mary Frances began to think long and hard about selling her large home in St. Helena. With both of her daughters married and many of her good friends in poor health, she realized that she should probably plan a refuge for a "singularly solitary old age," or risk what she considered the very real possibility of being found dead on the kitchen floor with a half-eaten pear in her hand. Consequently, when British architect and preservationist David Bouverie offered to build a house to her specifications on his ranch in that part of Glen Ellen known as the Valley of the Moon, she accepted.

After she sold her home in St. Helena, Mary Frances and her sister Norah decided to visit France in September while Mary Frances's new home was being built. Selecting a vigorous itinerary, they planned to take a boat trip along the Burgundian canal, spend some time at Porquerolles, then rent a little flat across from Eda Lord and Sybille Bedford in La Roquette-sur-Siagne during the month of November and possibly longer. "One reason we are friends is that we both understand the acceptance of NOW," Mary Frances wrote to Julia. "There is all the imprisonment of nostalgia, but with so many wide windows. . . . It would be wonderful if you were at La Pitchoune when I was there . . . just around a corner or two."

The Childs arrived in Plascassier early in December, and the guest list for the holidays at La Pitchoune changed and grew daily. When Mary Frances arrived for dinner on December 10, she was welcomed by James Beard as well as the Childs. The foursome had a whirl of traveling around the countryside, dining at small country inns, visiting Richard Olney, and just relaxing on the terrace until a week before Christmas, when Beard and Mary Frances left the Côte d'Azur to go their separate ways. They were replaced by eight

more people who had favorably responded to the Childs' invitation to spend the holidays in Plascassier. "Christmas here has been
on the wild side," Julia wrote. "We have Paul's twin brother and
his wife, Judith and Evan Jones, an English couple, and two other
friends. I did go a bit wild on food-buying, but it is far better to
have a bit too much than too little, n'est-ce pas?"

With her sister Norah already in transit to California and her
house in Glen Ellen still under construction, Mary Frances decided
to revisit Arles at Christmastime, stop in Avignon, and return to
Marseille before even considering leaving France. She found Arles
bound in the first days of what was to be one of the coldest and
windiest sieges in years. Avignon was even colder, and the port of
Marseille was almost paralyzed for the first two weeks of the new
year. It proved to be a winter view of a part of Provence that had
always been sunny and pleasant for her, and it provided material
for yet another story, "About Looking Alone at a Place," which
would become a part of a book on "other places." But finally even
the ambience of the Hôtel Beauvau could not compensate for the
frozen desolation of the Vieux Port. Hoping to see the Childs once
more before they left Plascassier, Mary Frances tried to persuade
them to join her in Marseille with her vivid accounts of delicious
meals at the Jambon de Parme, the Miramar, and the New York,
but weather problems and lack of time prevented another get-
together. And so the Childs and Mary Frances returned to homes,
old and new, via different routes.

Although the interior details in the house on the Bouverie Ranch
were not completely finished, Mary Frances began the difficult task
of sorting out, packing, and moving her belongings from St. Helena
to her new home. By intent and design, the two-and-a-half-room
palazzino accommodated many of the memories of her past. Dillwyn Parrish's paintings were hung. Her vast library of books was
shelved according to subject, from mysteries to witchcraft, from a
marvelous collection of old cookbooks to contemporary ones.
Antique furniture and treasures from former homes including her
father's revolving bookcase and her mother's teacups made the
"newness" of her home less apparent. She slept, wrote, read in one
room, prepared meals and entertained in the other. A large, elaborate bathroom separated the two rooms. And she had the added

security of various members of the Bouverie household and staff when she needed them. After some getting used to, she wrote to Julia, her new home would be a perfect place in which to work.

While she had been in France, Mary Frances's book *The Art of Eating* had been reissued by Vintage Books with an introduction by James Beard. In the midst of taping shows on French bread, pressed duck, and flaming fishes, and in the throes of remodeling the house on Irving Street, Julia wrote, "Just love that appreciation by Jim Beard. I think that is one of the most charming bits of JAB I've read, full of love and warmth and so deftly said. He does sound better in the several telephone calls we've had—more spirited, and relieved." She also added some news from New York. A big to-do about who would be appointed food editor of the *New York Times* was the talk of the town. Craig Claiborne wanted Michael Field, but Field was working at such a hectic pace writing cookbooks and promoting his own cooking school that he thought the job too limiting.

James Beard's health and his jovial filtering of the ever-evolving culinary scene had always been a point of reference in Julia and Mary Frances's exchange of letters, but as his health problems grew more erratic, his name, and more particularly the state of his health, wove in and out of their letters with greater insistence. When Mary Frances visited him in New York on her way to New Orleans on a job for *Playboy*, she told Julia that he had flown in from his current job in San Francisco the night before their breakfast together, and that he was scheduled to leave for Philadelphia right after their visit. "Quelle vie!" she wrote, "on se demande *pourquoi*."

Why, in fact, became a more and more insistent question. In May 1971 Michael Field, who had been teaching, writing, and demonstrating at a feverish pitch, had a brain hemorrhage and died. Julia and Paul were at La Pitchoune at the time and wrote to Mary Frances that they had talked two or three times with Michael's wife, Frances, after her husband's death. And they remarked on the conspicuous silence that had accompanied his untimely end: "He seems to have dropped into a well—boom-plop, and that was the end of him. . . . I think that his downfall began when he took that Time-Life job, and that summer right here at Pitchoune. That alone would have been most people's complete job."

Whether Field actually was one of the "Big Four" in the 1960s culinary establishment is open to question, but there is no doubt that M. F. K. Fisher soon became one of their number. Her name attracted attention from coast to coast, and her increasingly solitary lifestyle invited curiosity. "Here is the way to drive up from San Francisco" was not just a point of information in her letters; the directions also became a "must have" for journalists and culinary novices. And as more national attention centered on the excellence of California wines and produce and on a new breed of dedicated restaurateurs, more people included a visit to M. F. K. Fisher and the home she called Last House as a part of their itineraries.

Occasionally, however, it became a question of your place or mine. James Beard frequently traveled to San Francisco, either on book tours or to demonstrate some new kitchen item for his good friend Chuck Williams. They often invited Mary Frances to dine at a favorite San Francisco restaurant with them. Jim Nassikas, president of the Stanford Court Hotel, and his wife, Helen, also graciously provided a home away from home for Mary Frances at the hotel, where she could invite friends and host private dinners. And whenever Craig Claiborne and other luminaries of New York's publishing circles stayed at the hotel, she was included in the list of guests. It was a chance to see and be seen in the city, although she really preferred to entertain at Last House, where her original menus were often ballyhooed by her guests.

Julia and Paul Child visited Mary Frances there for the first time early in December 1971, during a trip dedicated to seeing friends in the Los Angeles area and Julia's sister in Sausalito. In anticipation, Mary Frances resolutely kept friends and acquaintances who were JWs (Julia Watchers) away from her door. Because one of the adjacent houses on the ranch was vacant at the time, Julia and Paul stayed there, and, of course, they were introduced to David Bouverie. Mary Frances served her favorite Sonoma wines, sourdough bread, and Teleme Jack cheese; she also prepared a special tripe dish in their honor. But seeing Mary Frances surrounded by her books and paintings in the *palazzino* that had been built for her was probably the most interesting aspect of the Childs' visit because it reinforced Julia's impression of Mary Frances as a deep person, an intellectual who had lived life to the fullest. And Julia could not help noticing that *Mastering the Art of French Cooking, Volume I* had a prominent place on Mary Frances's working cookbook shelf next to the refrigerator. After spending a few days with her, the Childs returned to Cambridge and more work on the TV series in progress.

During the five years since Mary Frances had first met Julia and Paul in Boston, they had drawn each other into an ever-widening circle of friends and acquaintances. Mary Frances wrote, "It is very nice and amusing that as we develop our friendship, it criss-crosses with so many others that are older and just as promising. . . . Jim [Beard] will be here on the 11th, and of course we'll talk about you. . . . I love your description of getting the shows on the road. And I do hope I get a chance to see some re-telecasts." Although through the years Mary Frances resolutely avoided owning a television set, Julia's "Bon appétit," caught on the screen in a motel room that she had checked into after one of her U Cal lectures was an experience she loved to relate. And because she was often invited to serve as hostess at various events in Bouverie's home, she did occasionally go there for the specific purpose of seeing one of Julia's shows.

As might be expected, references to food and cooking dominated their correspondence. Mary Frances told Julia that she saw the show on zucchini and loved it, being hooked on the vegetable as well as the lady doing the show. And she described making a grated version *à la crème* (but without the flour) for a finicky Italian friend who lapped it up, with a little Parmesan on the side. For the most part, Mary Frances was a great improviser, and she passed along dishes that particularly pleased her. She told Julia about a combination of equal parts of bread crumbs, Parmesan, and grated almonds that was used in all the gratinéed dishes in her favorite Marseille restaurant. She wondered if Julia had ever prepared a gratin that way.

Julia, on the other hand, enjoyed the tried-and-trues. When she and Paul were in Paris in the spring of 1972, Julia wrote about the "striving" quality of the starred establishments: "They must have green peppercorns to be chic this year. The little places remain the most pleasant to us, where they have 10–12 tables, and are not

trying so hard to be chic." Julia's most dramatic culinary comments, however, revolved around her show: "We are over-
goosed—I smell like a goose, and of onions, and rendered goose fat
and we've been among them all week. Eight (8!) geese—all cut up
for RAGOUT OF GOOSE yesterday on the French Chef. Anyway, it was fun." And it was infectious. There seemed to be no
aspect of menu planning, shopping, preparing, and presenting food
that didn't interest her or that wasn't improved upon in the letters
that she wrote to Mary Frances.

During the early months of 1973, Julia was under considerable
pressure to do another cookbook based on the just completed
French Chef color series. With the two volumes of *Mastering* and
her collaborative work with Simca behind her, Judith Jones
thought that it was time for Julia to concentrate on the entire
spectrum of cooking done in *her* kitchen because her cooking
vocabulary now included American dishes as well as ingredients
easily obtained in the supermarket. Her editor also urged her to
write the sequel to *The French Chef Cookbook*, which was based on
her first TV series, and to write it in a style that was as personal as
possible. In 1972 Simone Beck had come into her own, so to speak,
by publishing a well-received cookbook at Knopf called *Simca's
Cuisine*. And now it seemed appropriate that Julia write a cookbook that would reflect the personable style of her TV series.

It was not long before Julia wrote to Mary Frances about the
great difficulty of being personal and informal in her books. Mary
Frances advised her not to try: "You are one of the most 'personal'
people in the world, on TV, but it would not sound right to have
you change your *written* style/manner/approach." And she suggested, "Why not Paul??? Several million people know that he is an
intrinsic part of the shows and the books . . . and he can write
superbly in any way he chooses . . . and he could do 'footnotes'
about you that readers would love and that you could not possibly
do, yourself." It was an intriguing idea, a way to personalize a
recipe by remembering the time or place or some unusual circum-
stance associated with a dish, but Mary Frances's suggestion was
not adopted.

Meanwhile, Mary Frances and her sister Norah returned to the
south of France to work on their respective writing projects and

possibly to visit with the Childs, who would also be in Provence that spring. Mary Frances loved Marseille and wanted to spend most of their time in France there, writing about the city as it had been when she visited it earlier. When Norah's research on the Mary Magdalene legend, which had started as a hobby of sorts, yielded more and more fascinating information, the time that she spent in churches and libraries gathering facts grew considerably. Before they realized it, it was almost time to return to the States, and a visit to Plascassier became impossible. Because of their busy schedule, the Childs were not able to visit Mary Frances and Norah in Marseille. So during the spring of 1973 they relied, instead, on letters and elaborate descriptions of all the comings and goings at La Pitchoune.

By the mid-1970s in subtle and not so subtle ways, Paul Child's health problems were beginning to interfere with traveling plans and visits. Although the Childs spent the summer of 1974 doing a week of demonstrations in Venice and resting in Plascassier, their return to Cambridge was not worry free. Having experienced chest cramps intermittently during the weeks before their return, Paul had a series of tests that indicated that there was some blockage in his heart vessels. Usually communicative about physical problems, Julia was cautiously silent about Paul's imminent surgery. Mary Frances only learned of his condition indirectly from Simca, who was in Napa conducting a series of cooking classes in the fall of 1974.

Although sworn to secrecy, Simca could not hide her concern about Paul's condition and the strain the forthcoming operation was putting on Julia. To make matters worse, she told Mary Frances, James Beard was also hospitalized. "I send you waves-thoughts-vibrations of real love, now as always," Mary Frances immediately wrote to Julia. "I hate it that things have not gone well. I wish I could show you how much I pray, in my own fashion, that you both stay strong."

Paul underwent double bypass surgery on October 18, 1974. Although he had always enjoyed good health, the gravity of the operation and his slow recovery proved difficult. In early January 1975 Julia wrote, "Paul is coming slowly along. He's up and about, but still weak and groggy. It's been 2½ months since his operation,

and they all say it takes 6, which I now believe. The doctor says he
should, in a few weeks, begin feeling a surge forward, an appetite
for food, and an energy—we are waiting. I've finished my big book
[based on the color TV series and called *From Julia Child's Kitchen*],
and find I have little more to say about anything. I'm writ out,
wrote dry."

Paul recuperated slowly, spent spring in Bermuda, and gained
enough strength to help Julia promote her new book in September.
Julia wrote to Mary Frances, "My enormous and endless book is
finally out . . . we are about to launch it in New York. We do comic
chicken demonstrations in five Bloomingdale stores and one Alt-
mans, a half-hour on the 'AM-America' show and various other
things. Anything to sell a book (well, almost anything), is my
motto." And she reported that Paul was doing very well except for
some "aphasia" troubles, which resembled dyslexia because numbers and letters seemed to get mixed up. Although it might be
permanent, she was grateful that otherwise he functioned remark-
ably. The Childs planned to combine a book tour in San Francisco
with the celebration of Thanksgiving at the home of Julia's sister
and brother-in-law in Sausalito. Then they planned to drive north
for a visit to Last House. They both thought that it had been much
too long since their last visit.

While Mary Frances, Julia, and Paul drank wine in the late
autumn sunshine, Provence wove in and out of their conversation.
The Childs wanted to spend the holidays at La Pitchoune. And
Mary Frances, who was in the middle of her book on Marseille,
again spoke enthusiastically about Paul's photographs of some of
the places she was writing about. Ever since she had seen them on
her visit to the Childs in 1966, she had wanted Paul to consider
publishing the photographs in a book accompanied by a text that
she would write. Now, admittedly, it would be difficult for Paul.
And Julia thought that even if he could assemble all of them, the
sheer cost of publishing such a book might be too prohibitive, but,
"with your name and his, it might have great appeal."

Although Paul never regained the health of his preoperation
days, and Mary Frances experienced some difficulty of movement
as a result of rheumatoid arthritis and was afflicted by eye and
throat problems, France drew the three friends back as often as

possible and always with the possibility of meeting there. In the spring of 1976, Mary Frances and her sister rented a housekeeping flat on the rue Brueys in Aix-en-Provence. Its location, which unfortunately included the "constant scream and mutter of too many cars-motorbikes-people-sirens-TV-sets," only served to intensify her feeling "that everything, inside and out of one's self, is more intense in Provence than anyplace else I know or know about. Salt is almost dangerously saltier. Foods that grow from the earth taste stronger, or subtler, or stranger. If a person feels unwell, he is usually more miserable there than he would be in Sussex or Mendocino County, and if he is exhilarated and happy, it is immeasurably better than it could be anyplace else."

Paul and Julia joined Mary Frances in Aix, visiting in a café along the Cours Mirabeau, where they decided to petition the mayor to set limits on the number of motorbikes. Some time later they met in Marseille and dined at the Calypso. And Mary Frances and Norah drank Champagne on the terrace at La Pitchoune. Letters written to each other while they all were in Provence invariably closed with the wish "have a lovely last few days in this blessed land, and may we soon meet again."

They did meet with more frequency, but in California rather than in the south of France. Glen Ellen became the crossroads of the culinary great and not so great. Mary Frances enjoyed telling stories about journalists who got halfway to the San Francisco airport before they discovered that her cat had hidden in the backseat of their rented car. And when the notable French chefs Jean and Pierre Troisgros, Roger Vergé, and Michel Guérard sought out the Sonoma Sourdough Bakery and asked for one roll, she reported to Julia that Mme. Guerra, the owner's wife, thought that they were four more Frenchmen who'd stopped up the street at a couple of bars. Only her daughter, who had studied in France the year before, knew the identity and reputation of the men who stood on the sidewalk outside the bakery eating the roll in nibbles, nodding and smiling. She stared at them in disbelief while her mother nonchalantly waited on customers. Mary Frances hoped that Julia would enjoy that story.

Chuck Williams, another Sonoma notable who had launched a successful cookware business in town, was a good friend to Mary

Frances and a frequent visitor, often accompanied on his visits to
the ranch by James Beard. Early in January 1977 the two men
joined the Childs at Last House for what a *Los Angeles Times*
reporter called a conclave of cooks. When questioned about the
event, Mary Frances told her interviewer, "They brought up some
Dungeness crab. We were going to have a simple meal of cracked
crab and plenty of good bread and sweet butter and that's about it.
Chuck and Jim and Julia were all standing at that sink working on
the crab and Paul, who is a great photographer, took several shots.
The three behinds were so funny. Afterward, we sat at the table
with great mounds of marvelous crab . . . it took about five hours
to eat and, of course, there was good white wine." Another of
Julia's longtime friends and associates, Rosemary Manell, became
a part of Mary Frances's circle of friends and acquaintances. And
when she conducted cooking classes in Sonoma, she often stopped
by the ranch with tastings of one kind or another, or accompanied
the Childs on their visits.

Since Mary Frances met the Childs, her circle of friends had
expanded into the world of culinary professionals and journalists.
And their letters and visits both filled her days at Last House and
distracted her from the loss of people who had always been her
mainstays. When Henry Volkening died in 1972, she had lost a
good friend as well as an agent, but he had placed her work well.
Articles by her were in demand at *McCall's, Esquire, Travel &
Leisure, Bon Appétit,* and *Vogue.* She was also secure in Judith
Jones's "stable" at Knopf, where *A Considerable Town* was pub-
lished in 1978. And when Robert Lescher became her agent that
year, he opened new doors for her. At the age of seventy, M. F. K.
Fisher was a prolific writer, still able to work anywhere, "whether
I feel like it or not."

To be sure, failing eyesight necessitated certain changes in her
daily activities. She gave up driving altogether and began to dictate
letters rather than type them herself. But she continued to meet
deadlines before, during, and after two cataract operations, which
she underwent in 1978. Despite the discomfort and changes in her
work schedule, she went on entertaining family, friends, and all her
"good-dropping-by" neighbors and took advantage of the reprieve
gained by the operations. And when she learned that she was to be

honored by Les Dames d'Escoffier in New York on April 29, 1978, she began to make plans to travel to France, using New York as a convenient stopover. Accompanied by Norah, she intended to revisit Marseille, Aix, and Le Tholonet.

During the forty-five days that Mary Frances and Norah were in Provence, they visited the Childs twice at La Pitchoune, where Julia was relaxing after taping the *Julia Child and Company* TV series. They found Plascassier bathed in sunshine; the grasses in the meadow were green and lush, and the roses that grew beyond the shaded terrace were in bloom. It was a perfect backdrop for the midday meals that Julia served every day. She prepared zucchini blossoms dipped in the "Beard–Child Beer Batter," boned and stuffed chicken, *mesclun* salad, cheese, and crisp white wine. In the absence of deadlines, meals lasted well into the afternoon. In the easy exchange of ideas, Julia confessed that *A Considerable Town* was not altogether to her liking, not her own impression of Marseille. And Mary Frances agreed that they were bound to have seen and felt the city in completely different ways. It was the same with Paul's canvases; Mary Frances preferred some more than others, but they were all impressive, with a new warmth and happiness in the later ones. The visit was, as Julia said, most familial and as it should be.

Julia and Mary Frances were adept at holding their own and were so confident of their judgments that they could easily accommodate differences of opinion. Julia never varied, however, in her belief that Mary Frances was their "Monumental Friend," and, as Jean Strouse phrased it, "a national treasure." She had a crafty and witty way of writing about her eclectic tastes and often outrageous recipes, but she was above all a writer. Mary Frances, on the other hand, thought of Julia as a teacher and a very good one. The two volumes of *Mastering* were, in her opinion, "near classic." And other people felt the same way. At one time Mary Frances had written to Julia, "Last night I went to dinner with about eleven people who know a lot about wines and good food and about cooking, and they started talking about Julia Child and how she changed their lives and so on. . . . One man said that he simply could not grasp how to cook until he started reading your directions. A woman who teaches and runs kitchens at the Chateau St.

Jean winery said her students are required to read the proper procedures of preparing any dish in the world from your Vols.1 & 2." That, Mary Frances felt, was no small praise.

By the end of the 1970s, Julia had published six cookbooks and had literally created a market for a number of other cookbooks devoted to French food and wine. Richard Olney's *French Menu Cookbook* (1970) and *Simple French Food* (1974), Madeleine Kamman's *Making of a Cook* (1971), Jacques Pépin's *A French Chef Cooks at Home* (1975), and the translated works of French celebrity chefs—Paul Bocuse, Michel Guérard, Raymond Oliver, Jean and Pierre Troisgros, and Roger Vergé—contributed to an almost insatiable appetite for the latest trends in French cooking.

The interest in cooking, moreover, extended beyond France to other shores. Beginning with Time-Life's series The Foods of the World, the general reader had been initiated into the array of dishes that could be prepared by American cooks if more exotic ingredients were understood and made available. In the 1970s highly specialized cookbooks written by professionals who were devoted to the cuisines of various countries expanded culinary boundaries even further. Diana Kennedy's *Cuisines of Mexico* (1972), Madhur Jaffrey's *Invitation to Indian Cooking* (1973), Paula Wolfert's *Couscous and Other Good Food from Morocco* (1973), Elizabeth David's *English Bread and Yeast Cookery* (1977), and Giuliano Bugialli's *Fine Art of Italian Cooking* (1977) all served to translate poblano chilies, tandoori-style chicken, Bisteeya, Chelsea buns, and osso buco alla novese into the American vocabulary.

But translating, with its attendant widening of experience, did not exclusively focus food preferences. The sixties and seventies produced other movements, including those protesting the commercial packaging of American food. Multigrain breads baked in communal ovens, organically grown produce, and vegetarian recipe development emphasizing tofu, yogurt, and herbs encouraged a number of cookbooks reflecting renewed interest in health and ecotopia. Living in the midst of the excellent regional ingredients found in such abundance in California, Mary Frances eyed the market baskets of the long-haired, hippie-type shoppers at Shone's Market at the crossroads known as Glen Ellen. And they looked into hers. Unsalted butter, wheat germ, olive oil, Teleme Jack cheese, fresh coriander, tarragon, and dill proved that she had been enjoying the fruits of the earth many years before her fellow shoppers and would continue to do so for many years to come. Shopping at the Marché aux Herbes in Aix had given her an education in the best ingredients imaginable.

Meanwhile, Julia focused her attention on American ingredients and dishes and on American entertaining as well in her new television episodes. The *Company* and *More Company* sequences featured whole menus that stressed what goes with what rather than the presentation of a single dish or subject. And time constraints necessitated a book for audiences to consult while they viewed the show. Because she could not tape the show and write the recipes and instructions at the same time, Julia had to enlarge her staff into a group which lightheartedly came to be called "Harmony Inc. Complete Food Productions," a handpicked team that included many cooking assistants and a collaborator charged with writing the accompanying book. Julia was in her element, and her letters to Mary Frances were enthusiastic accounts of good times cooking *for* company *in* company.

She told Mary Frances that she had never used a writer before, but that she liked it very much: Although Mary Frances had complimented Julia on the first *Company* book, praising the large, handsome format, she had reservations about how well it represented her friend. When she read *Julia Child and More Company* a year later, she felt more comfortable with the finished product: "1,000% better *in every way* . . . more pure class . . . more true spirit of Julia's own spirit," she wrote. "The language is better. The subtitles have caught the way JC talks. The hand-pictures show supple knowing hands, and the methods are perfect. The shots are fine. In other words, it looks like an impeccable job to me, and I feel really happy and reassured and excited about it."

In the fall of 1978 Mary Frances expanded her own culinary horizons further when she agreed to write an introduction to Shizuo Tsuji's classic volume *Japanese Cooking: A Simple Art*. To prepare for the assignment, she accepted the publisher's offer of a two-week trip to Japan to sample the cuisine of that country and observe its preparation. Her host, Shizuo Tsuji, was an acquaintance of many years and someone Mary Frances had entertained in her own home, but she never expected the one-step-below-the-imperial-family hospitality which he lavished upon her and her sister. She wrote to Julia, "If I could eat the unprocurable things that Tsuji managed to present to us as lessons in what present Japanese cooking is based on, I would gladly eat nothing else for the rest of my life. I would forego every subtle dish I had ever tasted in the past seventy years. This is a shattering statement to make, and, of course, there is absolutely no risk of its ever happening, but it is *true*."

Within weeks after her return to the States, Mary Frances was hospitalized for what she called a surgical caper to remove some "lover's knots" that had been found wrapped around a 1941 adhesion. Although she made light of the operation, she did not quickly recover, and she missed seeing the Childs when they were in the San Francisco area, although they did visit with her sister Norah. Julia and Paul, on the other hand, traveled from coast to coast with abandon, from Cambridge to Provence with ease. Mary Frances wrote that she envied them because, she felt, they were "a breed apart," like the Marseillais. "It's because you love what you're doing, of course, but there's more to it than that. Probably the main thing is that you are *together*. And you've built up a superb supply of extra strength." And, indeed, the Childs clocked more air miles than even their good friend James Beard, who was having his own continuing problems with poor health, and Simca, who was a favorite on the cooking class circuit.

With increasing interest in the quality of culinary education in the States, Julia actively worked for greater professionalism in the culinary community. In 1978 she was the driving force behind the establishment of the Women's Culinary Guild of New England, which, in her words, "turned out to be a great deal of fun and a great success—130 members, and going only a year, and all members professionally concerned with food or wine in some gainful or business way." Her interest inspired many women to establish catering businesses and join the ranks of professional chefs.

Mary Frances acknowledged news about the culinary group as heartwarming, but, more important, she thought it was an example of how attitudes toward eating and cooking had changed. She also wrote that up and down the Napa Valley, at Yountville for in-

stance, there were very decent places where they could get com-
mendable, fresh, and intelligent food when the Childs visited her
after their Thanksgiving in Sausalito. It was something of a miracle,
she felt, thanks in large part to a few people like Julia.

Before leaving Cambridge for the West Coast, Julia wrote, "Everyone and his brother, mother, and cousin is having a cookbook
out this season. Claiborne, Mimi Sheraton, Pépin, and so on and
so forth. Including your friend and great admirer Bert Greene—
who came last night for supper (baked beans, pork chops, slightly
burned carrots, and ice cream with Chocolate sauce). He *adores*
you. I like his new book—interesting recipes, original ones." It
was not an endorsement but an observation meant for Mary
Frances only.

During the winter she stayed in Sag Harbor on Long Island
writing *Among Friends*, Mary Frances had met Bert Greene. He was
another of the cookbook and culinary writers who corresponded
with her, interviewed her, and visited her at Last House. There was
something about his robust appearance and humor that she liked,
and although she did not write formal introductions to his cookbooks, she generously allowed him to quote her in order to publicize them. Knowing only too well that he would do it again, she
even scolded him for playing fast and loose with her recipes in an
article from his syndicated column called "Bert Greene's Kitchen."
"Now I must chide you about using recipes as if they were my
versions when really they are *yours*," she told him. He had made
reference to M. F. K. Fisher's "Cool Collected Celery," "Simple
Vinaigrette Sauce," and "Slow-Cooked Spinach Tart," and she
denied ever writing or entitling any of the above. Any self-
respecting cook will make his own changes, she maintained; however, she wrote, "if I call it by the name of the original after my own
changes have been added, I am dishonest. Once I have transposed
his original order of usage, and have added one cup instead of 3/4
cup, or have changed the way of baking or cooking, I must say that
it is *my* version, and that I have adapted it."

Unlike Julia, and perhaps a little unwisely, Mary Frances had for
years lent the authority of her name to other authors' books. They
simply asked, and she obliged whenever it was possible. There was
seldom a pattern of author or subject to the more than twenty

introductions that she had written since 1952. Sometimes the subject—tea, Japanese cooking, California food and wine—caught her
attention. Sometimes the author—Angelo Pellegrini, Alice B. Tok-
las, Judith Clancy—captured her interest. Her association with
Knopf also brought many cookbooks to her attention, usually in
galley form, and she was forthright in her comments: "I really
galloped happily through the Edna Lewis book. It's a loverly
[sic]. . . . It must remain nostalgic," she wrote to Judith Jones. And
in the same letter, she referred to Raymond Sokolov's *Saucier's
Apprentice* as "a mixture of modern commonsense and 19th Century romanticism," its author "a blushing newcomer, an amateur
fumbling his way toward the sauce pots . . . the Woody Allen of
la haute cuisine."

With Escoffier's motto *Fais simple* as a rule of thumb, and only
five or six cookbooks, including *Mastering*, on her "working"
shelf, Mary Frances questioned the value of every new cookbook
that came her way either to review or to endorse. And her preferences were usually on the side of authenticity, her praise reserved
for authors who had something important to say and knew how to
say it. As early as 1966, she had set the standards by which she
would consider the merit of a cookbook by dismissing promo-
tional gimmickry: "Self-styled cookbooks, often of dubious value,
do not hesitate to call themselves things like *definitive, wonderful,
dazzling, exciting, excellent,* and even *superb. Unique* is another favorite adjective that is bound to raise my hackles as well as my
deep-seated suspicions." She simply thought that very few, in fact,
almost none, deserved the praise implicit in those modifiers. Julia
Child's invariably did, but during the next ten years she set about
reconsidering the various introductions that she had written.

Endorsement in its many forms and guises, name recognition in
all its glory, and the razor-sharp line between encouragement and
compromise posed problems. Julia took the indisputable high road
and withheld her name from endorsements of any kind, refusing to
name products and declining the hospitality of restaurateurs she
patronized. James Beard, often to his friends' chagrin, came to be
considered "one of the worst offenders." Mary Frances told an
interviewer, "I remember one time I almost threw up because I
opened a women's magazine in a dentist's office and there was a

full-page ad with Jim with a silly crown on his head, and he was King for a Week of the American Sauerkraut Society! And, I thought, 'He should not do this!' "

Clearly, there was no unanimity of opinion, and the matter was not even discussed between Julia and Mary Frances, except for the latter's observation that "I seem to be in a period of knowing lively, attractive, ambitious (ruthless) women who write about gastronomy in general, and most of them have been influenced by Julia Child . . . followed you around when last you were in San Francisco . . . stayed one week with Simca [enrolled in her cooking classes in Plascassier], etc." A few words from Mary Frances about their current projects often brought the desired results from editors and publishers. And she welcomed them into her home, sometimes with the uncomfortable feeling that she was being used. For the most part, Julia was insulated from aspirants by the team who worked indefatigably for and with her. And professionals knew of her firm resolve not to lend her name. Her understandable hesitancy and Mary Frances's sometimes uncritical availability were simply another manifestation of the many differences between these two friends.

What is so memorable about the letters that crossed from Cambridge or Plascassier to Glen Ellen during the late 1970s is the ease with which the correspondents wrote about such a variety of subjects, thanks in no small measure to mutual friends and Mary Frances's developing popularity within the culinary community. While in Paris, Julia visited La Varenne, Anne Willan's new cooking school, and described its great potential; Mary Frances already knew of it because one of James Beard's friends had told her about taking classes there. Mary Frances discussed the problems that some friends encountered while preparing California ducks; Julia sympathized but expressed her own views about how tired she was of being polite and servile about those ducks—burned outside, spongy raw inside. She certainly adored wild duck, but she wanted to cook it her way. Their friend Sybille Bedford wrote a book about Huxley; Mary Frances and Julia sent reviews of the book to each other and discussed the perceptual problems of using footnotes. When Simca and her assistant conducted cooking classes in the Napa Valley, Mary Frances reported details about the classes and the publicity that swirled around them. Distances seemed to

disappear. Food, family, friends, and, above all, Provence were so
important to each woman that they became the warp and woof of
their correspondence during the years that seemed to hold poor
health and illness precariously at bay.

As the last day of the last month of the 1970s drew near, Mary
Frances sent greetings and happy landings to the Childs wherever
they were—Plascassier, Cambridge, or perhaps California visiting
relatives. For her part, there were many things to think about as the
bell in the tower of the Bouverie Ranch tolled in the new year and
the 1980s. She now knew that when she had seen the Childs at La
Pitchoune in the late spring of 1978 she had probably visited Provence for the last time. She also felt that the trip to Japan had been
her last long-distance flight and that an occasional trip to San
Francisco, though difficult, would become one of her only "es-
capes." Diagnosed with Parkinson's disease in late 1979, she realized that she would have to rely more and more on a tape recorder
and dictation to her secretary in lieu of typing first drafts herself.
What she did not or could not anticipate this New Year's Eve was
a hip replacement operation that would even more severely limit
her mobility and necessitate a live-in companion, with the conse-
quent loss of privacy. There would be weeks, even months spent
in hospitals and in convalescence; rooms whose solitude she loved
would suddenly be overcrowded; and familiar scenes would not be
seen again. She became increasingly aware, moreover, that Paul's
gradual but steady decline would soon either prevent or seriously
curtail her friends' frequent visits to Provence.

Perhaps to compensate, the Childs gradually gravitated toward
California, where the prospect of a warm winter lured them to
Santa Barbara and precipitated the purchase of a third home in
Montecito Shores. Previously, book tours and demonstrations had
often brought them to the West Coast and, when possible, to Glen
Ellen, but now, at least for the wintry months of the year, they
planned to make their home in California.

While illness prevented Mary Frances from the kind of writing
schedule she wanted to keep, the momentum of Julia's career never
waned. After a visit between the two friends during the filming of the
Dinner at Julia's TV series, Mary Frances wrote, "You seem to have
a wonderful gift for staying in focus. I suppose it is part of what used
to be called being real troupers. You know that you must go on stage

again tomorrow, broken leg or not, and it does something magical to your adrenals. . . . I remember something that was almost a peripheral thing I heard when we were sitting at the table [during one of their last visits to Last House]. You said casually that of course you were not a writer. I cannot agree with this at all. You write correctly, of course because you are well educated and articulate, but there is much more, because you write in a simple unaffected honest way, without any affectation or deliberate attempt to be 'literary.' In other words, you are a good writer, in my mind anyway. I look forward to reading a book by you, and before long . . . write something that is completely for *you* without any editorial demands except your own and Paul's. End of presumptuous and unsolicited opinion." And Mary Frances urged her to follow the example of James Beard's *Delights and Prejudices* and Craig Claiborne's *Feast Made for Laughter* and write an autobiographical book.

But Julia could not be persuaded to embark upon another "big book" in the early 1980s, preferring instead to be in the vanguard of groups dedicated to raising America's gastronomical consciousness. And although her efforts were not always fully realized, they were soon rewarded in various ways. In 1981 Beard's disciple Peter Kump had organized a testimonial dinner in honor of his mentor. Because of the success of the event and the attention it focused on the luminaries of the culinary world, the New York Association of Cooking Teachers, spearheaded by Kump, planned to turn the celebration into a yearly event, naming Julia Child the 1982 honoree.

Intending the highlight of the evening to be the presentation of a leather-bound volume of letters from the people who had played a part in Julia's career, Kump contacted Mary Frances with a request for a letter. Her response was immediate, and the letter was a tribute to more than fifteen years of friendship:

13935 Sonoma Highway
Glen Ellen
CA 95442

7.ix.82
Dear Julia and Paul, T*R*E*S C*H*E*R*S A*M*I*S:
  This is a special *note! I feel very honored to be invited to add to*

your book of admiring and respectful and loving messages . . . and all I can think of is that the first time I met you, I knew I would be your friend for life, even if we seldom met again and you did not care. I was infinitely fortunate, because you liked me too, and we've managed to meet much more often than seldom.

That was about twenty years ago, I think. Julia met my plane in Boston. I'd been staying in La Pitchoune with the Michael Fields, purportedly to work on the try-cake book about provincial French food for Time-Life, and it felt strange to be in the house of people I'd never met, so that I was more than usually shy about seeing you. And there you were, standing at the bleak airport gate like a familiar warm beacon . . . old tennis shoes, a soft cotton shirt-maker . . . tall boarding school teenager from Pasadena! We'd met before, not in this life but somewhere. I went happily along with you, and felt home again.

And I still do . . . Plascassier, Nice, Glen Ellen, Marseille.

That night in Cambridge, in a big cool house that was like ones I'd always known in Southern California, an editor from Time-Life dined with us, and was puzzled at how little the summer's work seemed to matter to anything but his project. We ate jambon persillé you were experimenting with. And the next morning Paul and I walked on the Commons, and watched Watusi visitors throw fris-bies and then float after them in the sun and shadow. We talked about e e cummings and Dos Passos and my husband as if they too were there again.

And the next day there was a roadside picnic (cold sliced steak . . .), as we headed for Kennebunkport where you would leave me on your way to the Island off Maine. . . .

It is all part of my life . . . the real part, the best. You welcomed me, at the Boston gate and on the Commons, as if we'd all been there before and would be again, and I am very thankful.

My love to you both as always . . .
Mary Frances

This may or may not be the kind of letter you want, she told Peter Kump, but it is just the way I always write to Julia and Paul.

That same year, winemaker Richard Graff enlisted Julia's help as well as Robert Mondavi's in organizing a group called the American Institute of Wine and Food. Mary Frances took a dim view of the effort, and only through the urging of her friend Alice Waters and Jeremiah Tower finally agreed to write an article for the group's *Journal of Gastronomy*. She wrote to Julia, who was in Provence at the time, "I hate to be rather blasé and once-bitten-twice-shy about such ventures, but I am." And only with reluctance did she allow her name to appear on the advisory board of the institute. Instinctively, Mary Frances seemed more concerned about Julia's influence being abused than she was about her own role in the organization. And it was the first sign of a kind of protectiveness that she extended to her friend, a fear that a more subtle kind of "using" could endanger Julia's reputation.

Meanwhile, Mary Frances published a collection of essays about "other places" that Knopf titled *As They Were*. Beginning with a brief introduction to the neighbors and friends who were inextricably bound to her childhood in Whittier, the people who contributed to her self-image as a "child of an inner ghetto," and ending with a description of Last House in the Sonoma Valley, the "other places" of her life assume a deeper meaning and become points of reference. Ice cream parlors in Los Angeles, Burgundian inns, kitchens in Provence, Laguna Beach, a solitary Christmas in Arles, the Gare de Lyon, and a fierce winter storm in a Bridgehampton summer house are vested with different levels of meaning because they are scenes transmogrified by the writer's imagination and, in some cases, by her palate. She recalls the sensual thrill of the "Easter Special," composed of several kinds of ice creams, sauces, and chopped nuts. She explains the feeling of being "generous, warm, floaty" after a breakfast of French bread, butter, Parma ham, and brut champagne in the Gare de Lyon. She shares a wealth of simple experiences made complicated by life as it must be lived and then much later reflected upon. Taken together, they outline a portrait and present a kaleidoscope of secret palaces, private ghettoes, Provençal kitchens, and enticing places that were intensely memorable to her.

In 1982 Mary Frances also terminated her contract with *The New Yorker*, preferring instead to write occasional articles for *Bon Appétit*, *Food & Wine*, and *Westways*. Learning that Julia had also given

up her *McCall's* monthly column in order to contribute articles
and recipes to the syndicated newspaper magazine *Parade*, Mary
Frances commented, "Isn't it fun to get out from under an editorial
umbrella. When I decided I was truly fed up with the *niceness* of
writing in a certain pattern for the NYer, and agreed to do some
little pieces for a friend of mine who was then editor of *Westways*,
it was strangely like getting out of jail." With growing detachment,
she collected what she wanted from the past and discarded whatever proved cumbersome.

During a long convalescence after her first hip replacement operation in 1983, Mary Frances returned to and completed a project
that she had started more than thirty years earlier, gathering up the
sketches and stories for a volume called *Sister Age*. Like it or not,
she confided to Julia, "it is not always easy for us lesser people to
accept gracefully the inevitable visits of a nagging harpy without a
saint's guidance." In many of the stories, Mary Frances explores
the theme of human strength in the inevitable encounter with the
end of life. And in her letters variations on the same theme persist.
"I am bowing very realistically to instructions from both Mother
Nature and the medicos," she wrote and acknowledged that she
would sit tight and change a few of her habits. Having sustained
lens transplants in both eyes and a hip replacement all in one year,
she adjusted to long periods of immobility. She also vicariously
experienced the publicity trips and demonstrations Julia described
in detail in her letters and imaginatively relived the weeks the
Childs enjoyed living in Provence. "How can I be in Plascassier and
here too?" she asked. "It's one of the rewards perhaps??? But I am
there, even taking a shower in the guest-room . . . looking across
at the hill village and then back to Paul's ever lovely sightings."

Julia's activities, and particularly the way that she wrote about
them, were a continuing source of amusement to Mary Frances.
But now that they emanated from California and involved the
collaboration of Rosemary Manell to a greater extent than ever
before, Mary Frances became more personally involved. She liked
Rosemary and had often told Julia that to have had such a depend-
able close friend for thirty-nine years was probably one of the
greatest blessings on earth. And now that Rosemary Manell had
also befriended Mary Frances, she was keenly interested in what

both of them were doing. Send the latest *Parade* articles, she wrote, because she already knew about many of the recipes that they were testing and thought Julia's style in presenting them was very effective. And the recipes initiated more correspondence between the two friends, including what came to be known as the "corned beef" exchange. Mary Frances had followed Julia's instructions to the letter, aging the brisket for days as directed, only to find that the meat was tough when she prepared it. Julia retreated into her kitchen, retested, and rewrote the recipe with apologies to her readers.

Mary Frances also watched with interest when Julia ventured into commercial TV as the star of the *Good Morning America* show and the hostess of the Polaroid-sponsored series *Dinner at Julia's*, which showcased American chefs and California wines. She was not alone, however, in preferring the Julia of the earlier shows, who came into the kitchen in her simple blouse and apron and threw wonderful clusters of words together and was interested simply in good cooking and good food. But cooking shows were proliferating, and Julia expressed fear that just straight cooking wasn't sufficient for prime time. And, after spending all that time, effort, and money, if the program was not aired on prime time, it was not worth it. Nevertheless, if there was going to be another series, Julia hoped it would be less "campy" and more informative than *Dinner at Julia's*. She loved working with friends; "bookery was so damned solitary."

Mary Frances agreed with her friend's appraisal of writing, but the solitude, which had always been so welcome to her, had given way to a household staff that included a cleaning woman, a companion, and two young people whom Mary Frances called her amanuenses. It was in spite of and because of these good distractions and the attentions of relatives, friends, and neighbors, however, that she managed to do the thing she most wanted to do. When she lacked the energy to sustain a lengthy piece, she published her annotations to Mrs. Plagemann's *Fine Preserving*. Objecting to what she considered a monopoly in magazine publishing, Mary Frances refused to write articles for the Condé Nast "empire." She did, however, plan to write new introductions to the introductions she had written for her own and others' books, reconfiguring the M. F. K. Fisher persona. "I feel rather sorry for [editor Judith Jones], with you working on your end and me on mine and God Knows how many wordy souls in between," she wrote to Julia.

With reluctance, Julia had finally agreed to write another cookbook to survey the past "forty years sashaying between stove and typewriter." It had been twenty-five years since the publication of the first volume of *Mastering,* and during those years radically new equipment had changed procedures for making everything from fish mousse to soufflés. Because those years had also popularized fast food consumption and unleashed a growing fear of certain foods, she felt the necessity of formulating her nutritional manifesto.

From 1984 to 1988, Julia's letters reflect her enthusiasm about using a word processor to get ideas down on paper quickly and efficiently. "I can, in a flash, re-edit anything on a disk," she wrote to Mary Frances, "because I must get my new how-to book out PDQ." But, word processor notwithstanding, she did not meet her 1986 deadline, and she continued to work steadily on the manuscript until December 1988. Along with the difficulty of condensing material, she said that at times she simply did not know enough and had to try something out again. But she was happy to have her never-ending work, especially in the light of Paul's steady decline. "It's sad to see that happen, but at 85 . . ." There was no need to finish the sentence, and Mary Frances was quick to reply with a letter telling Julia, "I am sorry that PC is withdrawing from us all. I'm very happy indeed to have known him for so long a time now. I salute him with deep respect and real love. As for you, I know you will come through all this."

When James Beard died in 1985, and the Childs were unable to travel to La Pitchoune any longer because of Paul's "slow decline that started in earnest" in the fall of 1987, the subjects Mary Frances and Julia had explored in their earlier letters were no longer pertinent, but their interest in each other's work and general well-being never wavered. Postcards and the refrains "Thank you for calling" and "Your voice sounds strong and well" gradually replaced the often lengthy letters that had been the brick and mortar of their friendship. But as in all letters, what was often most important was not what was written about. And that was the continuing *amitié* between one woman whose very existence was to write and another woman whose mission was to teach. Despite their many differences, both believed that food is an art form, a delightful part of civilized life, and they continued to communicate that belief.

With cookbooks proliferating in unbelievable numbers, cooking schools—both professional and dilettantish—registering students for two years or two days, culinary guilds and societies flourishing, and wine tours and tastings the "in" thing to do in the eighties, Mary Frances's books were apotheosized. From 1981 until 1989, North Point Press reprinted ten of M. F. K. Fisher's books, including the five compiled in *The Art of Eating*, in handsome paper-bound editions with striking photographs of the author by Man Ray, George Hurrell, and John Engstead. In the wake of such publicity, Mary Frances was introduced as the "doyenne" of America's culinary writers. Her views on everything from secret indulgences to microwave ovens were sought, and interviewers from publications as diverse as *W* and *Ms.* knocked on her door. Recognition, so long in coming, was hers.

On the eve of Mary Frances's eightieth birthday, *Dubious Honors*, a selective story of her writing career, was published. Using twenty of her introductions to other people's books as well as the introductions and revised introductions to her own books as a framework, she writes of her pleasure and even reluctance in lending her name to others' work, reconsidering these to have been dubious honors. And because the introductions to introductions are arranged chronologically, they incidentally reflect her changing attitudes on a range of subjects. It is in the introduction to Part Two, her own introductions, however, that she traces her development as a writer and acknowledges her debt to the agents, editors, publishers, family, and friends who served her well. In these pages she provides necessary background and, in many cases, interprets her own work. Mary Frances becomes the ultimate critic of M. F. K. Fisher. And, although she parted company with Judith Jones at Knopf over the advisability of publishing this kind of book, her judgment prevailed: "A writing cook and a cooking writer must be bold, at the desk as well as the stove."

"Almost every gastronomer has some kind of literary predilection," she had written in 1949. M. F. K. Fisher's election to the American Academy and National Institute of Arts and Letters in 1991 honored that predilection and secured her literary reputation. But what of the "hot literary cookstove of culinary comment"? In her refusal to be labeled a cookbook writer and her insistence on the pleasures of the table, she stood apart from the mainstream of culinary writers while remaining their avatar. That note of nostalgia or longing for an ideal past that can be symbolically repossessed by familiar foods—a note that pervades the most meaningful cookbooks—has certainly been given it fullest expression by her distinctive first-person style. And the unremitting use of gastronomy as a kind of surrogate to ease human longings found its most varied expression in the scenes she re-created. From a piece as fundamental as "The Anatomy of a Recipe" (to date, the most compelling directive for clarity in culinary prose) to stories like "The Kitchen Allegory," with its overlay of metaphorical meaning, Mary Frances wrote of the pleasures of the table like no other writer in the tradition of American letters.

Several years ago she shared with Eleanor Friede her thoughts about why it is important for some women to work, describing "an above-average feeling that we must justify our existence, . . . should pay our way, sing for our supper, justify breathing all this air and drinking all this wine. I have absolutely no illusions about the importance in the world of anything I have written. But I think that it is important that because I *am* in the world I *do* write."

But the fact that Mary Frances wrote so elegantly and distinctively about the art of eating and "willy-nilly" became a more involved and visible member of the culinary establishment during the last twenty-five years of her life was a result, in part, of *The Cooking of Provincial France*. That she found friendship, encouragement, amusement, and even a surrogate family in that establishment was, in large measure, because of Julia and Paul Child. "Perhaps I should light a little candle to Henry Luce," Mary Frances often wrote to them. *The Cooking of Provincial France* was, after all, the beginning. And there seems to be no end.

Memorialized in poetry, prose, and film since her death on June 22, 1992, M. F. K. Fisher continues to influence the way food is thought about and written about. And "as the most poetic voice of the working woman in the 20th century," she speaks posthumously, turning language into an evocation of her life in *To Begin Again: Stories and Memoirs, 1908–1929* (1992) and *Stay Me, Oh Comfort Me: Journals and Stories, 1933–1941* (1993).

She may have, as Julia is wont to say, "slipped off the raft," but she remains the Childs' "Monumental Friend." And the narrative of a friendship, like friendship itself, really has no end.

CHAPTER FOUR

In Julia's Kitchen

Both as a hobby and as a professional
necessity, I spend a great deal of my
life in the kitchen.

JULIA CHILD

Kitchens have not always been Julia Child's mise-en-scène. In fact, her recollections of the one in the big, brown-shingled house on South Pasadena Avenue where she grew up in the 1920s remain as faded as the taken-for-granted meals of overcooked beef, gray lamb, and Sunday codfish balls prepared and served by the family's maid. Not even her mother's baking powder biscuits and white sauce, made on the cook's Thursday night off, attracted much of Julia's attention. She simply liked most things and was usually very hungry. The oldest child in a happy upper-middle-class family, Julia, along with her siblings, ate as much as she wanted with the same gusto with which she played ball and swam at the beach house in Santa Barbara. During the years of her growing up, the kitchen held very little, if any, attraction to the woman who would years later commandeer her own and television's "set" kitchens as America's "French Chef."

But this is not to say that good cooking was not a part of Julia's inheritance. Proud of her "pioneer background," Julia relished stories about her Grandfather McWilliams, a Scots immigrant who went west from Odell, a small town near Joliet, Illinois. And she often cites her Grandmother McWilliams, who, besides being a "good hen cooker" made doughnuts and crullers that were memorable. Time and affluence, however, modified the McWilliams' lifestyle, and by the time their son, Princeton graduate John McWilliams, married Smith graduate Carolyn Weston, his experi-

ments in rice farming in Arkansas and land development in California had opened the door to genteel domesticity. Carolyn Weston
McWilliams, a New Englander who had never been farther west
than Chicago, left the Berkshires behind her and went to live in
California, where maids and housekeepers were an integral part of
her life and her daughters were enrolled in Smith College on the
day they were born.

On the day of her birth, therefore, on August 15, 1912, Julia
Carolyn McWilliams inherited a double legacy: an idyllic childhood in California and a promise that she would also live in New
England and know firsthand the scenes of her mother's coming of
age. Inherited also was the pioneer spirit of the McWilliamses,
their sheer physical stamina, and a longevity that enabled them to
live well into their eighties. In her mother's carefully annotated
Baby's Happy Days, special note was taken of Julia as a typical
McWilliams baby. She was so long that her feet were usually not
covered by her crib robes. And she grew to be a tall child, who
towered over her younger brother, John, and little sister, Dorothy,
although they eventually caught up to and even surpassed her.
Somewhat amused, Carolyn McWilliams often repeated to friends
and relatives that she had produced at least eighteen feet of children. It would be fair to say that she also bequeathed something of
her quirky humor and her generosity (she was a member of a family
of ten brothers and sisters) to her eldest child as well.

Despite disclaimers from Julia's younger sister, Dorothy, that
their growing up in Pasadena was singularly uneventful, family
photo albums preserve pictures that portray an active and fun-filled
childhood in a conservative household. Julia at two, fetchingly
dressed in white bloomers and smock with matching hat and shoes,
sitting on a garden stone with a cookie held tightly in each hand,
presented a serious and somewhat skeptical face to the camera. A
few years later, pictures show a youngster with freckles on her face,
wavy light brown hair, and long legs, clowning around on top of a
birdbath. And in a later album, assuming a half debutante, half
madcap air, she lounges in a lawn chair with a cold drink in her
hand, rides horses at Ojai, skies in Sun Valley, sails off the shore
of La Jolla, and enjoys a barbecue with friends at a ranch in Red-
ding, California.

There were also other telling scenes from what Henry James called "the visitable past." Although Julia studied piano, bugle, ukelele, and accordion, she was, according to her sister, not a particularly accomplished musician. So when she knew that her elderly relatives were coming for lunch, she would close the piano, drape it in a large Spanish shawl, and position a bouquet of roses on top of it. But inevitably after a long meal enjoyed by the various guests, who on many occasions ranged in years from seven to ninety, Julia would be asked to play, "and then off would come the bouquet and the Spanish shawl and Julia would open the piano and struggle through a piece." Performing, however, was not always painful. Because her reveilles woke up everyone in the morning, Julia's penchant for playing the bugle usually produced an uproar.

Childhood trips were memories of a different kind. To this day, Julia cannot explain exactly why a certain foray south of the border with her parents in 1925 remains as vivid as it does. It might have been because her parents were "wildly excited" about having lunch at Caesar Cardini's restaurant, or perhaps because it was one of her earliest remembrances of a restaurant that provided beer, cocktails, mariachi bands, and various other extravagances absent from its American Prohibition-bound competitors. But more than likely it was the sheer drama of the tableside preparation of the famous salad by none other than Caesar himself. At thirteen, Julia watched the tossing of the romaine lettuce in a large wooden bowl with complete fascination, and when Caesar broke two eggs over the greens and rolled them in so that the eggs went all creamy over the romaine, she experienced a thrill she would never forget.

And a few years later, as a high school student at the Katharine Branson School near San Francisco, she wrote of another travel adventure, probably one of her trips back to Pasadena from school. She begins the short narrative, which she titled "A Woman of Affairs," for the school's literary publication, The Blue Print, with this observation, "The idea of going down alone was not at all unpleasant to me, it gave me a sense of proprietorship over my soul which I seldom if ever feel. In short, I felt like a time-mellowed woman of the world." She relates the following experience in the dining car. Pretending to misread the steward's gesture toward a table for four with one unoccupied seat, she slips into a chair at a table for two, thus avoiding sharing a meal with a doting grand-mother, mother, and young child. Then, in an effort to economize, she orders a salad, a delectable concoction which arrives in a bowl "as big as a bathtub." Correctly spooning only a small portion onto her plate, she is horrified when the waiter "swoops down" and removes the partially filled salad bowl. "I couldn't protest because that would prove my verdant inexperience: so I had to content myself with a complacent, worldly smirk." The tale continues through the traumatic tipping scene, when she discovers that her only coins are a nickel and a fifty-cent piece. Although she leaves the latter for the one-dollar cost of the meal, she writes, "My Scotch ancestry shrieked a protest: my pocket book looked dis-mayed: but my pride and the waiter said, 'Thank you. Madam.'" Deciding that her worldly-wise reputation must not be compro-mised, she tips the porter at the end of her trip and hopes he doesn't see her miss a step when she leaves the train or when her suitcase opens accidentally.

Not quite as entertaining but perhaps more revealing is "A True Confession," which Julia submitted to *The Blue Print* a year later. "I am a rain cloud," she begins; then she explains that she came into the world with weak tear glands. Although she spent a some-what tearful childhood and frequently "let loose the flood-gates in a theatre," she insists that she is no "weak-glanded maiden with hot tears laden." In great detail she writes about her deficient gland with a thoroughgoing discussion of the various types of tears. Hers are purely mechanical, she says; I "in my innermost inner I am as hard as a nail."

Whether these literary activities escalated into the resolve to be a famous woman novelist before Julia attended Smith College or during her college career, while she was a contributor to the college *Tatler*, was never established, but she seems to have developed a broad and somewhat eclectic range of career choices, from writing novels to playing professional basketball, while she was at Smith. She also made lifelong friends. Her designated roommate, Mary Case, recognized a kindred spirit in Julia, and their clowning was infectious. Before long they decided that, in order to get any study-ing done, they would have to string a rope down the middle of their room and drape a rug over it. During the evening study period,

Julia, usually armed with a supply of jelly doughnuts from the local bakery, would inquire if Mary was hungry and then sail a doughnut over the makeshift wall. She devoured the rest of them herself while doing her assigned reading and then was ready for more fun.

Academically Julia apparently never excelled in any one course or subject, preferring instead to coast along with C's. According to her roommate, Julia "was the big picture type and didn't care much for details . . . nothing brilliant, nothing poor. She always did her work." And she seems never to have missed an opportunity to be a part of the high jinks on campus. She painted the toilet seats in Hubbard House red and beat tom-toms outside a faculty member's window. Occasionally she danced a tom-tom dance for people she knew because she had a "thing" about Indians and had learned to do the dance when she stopped off to visit an Indian reservation on her trips to and from college. She also had a great gift for mimicry. Of course, there were a few traces of vanity. Julia always wore stunning clothes and stood straight and tall. Her roommate remembers an occasion when her own future husband, Leon Warner (also over six feet tall), and Julia were walking down a sidewalk together, and Julia said, "Leon, aren't we magnificent?" Colorful herself, she didn't pay much attention to colorless people, but she was unfailingly kind to almost everyone and was "tremendously popular."

When her college days were over, she approached *The New Yorker* for a job, was turned down, and went to work in the advertising department of W. & J. Sloane, sharing an eighty-dollar-a-month apartment under the Queensboro Bridge with two other Smith graduates. Equipped with little more than a can opener and a hot plate, Julia's first kitchen was skimpy at best and thoroughly unphotographable. And when she spattered the walls with grease spots from her efforts to fry chicken, most of her attempts at home cooking ceased. Remembering or choosing not to remember those far-off days, Julia refers vaguely to eating like everybody else in 1934, probably cans of this and that.

After three years in New York City, she transferred to Sloane's store in Los Angeles and lived with her parents in Pasadena. When her mother, who had always been plagued by high blood pressure, became increasingly unable to manage the household, Julia left her position at Sloane's and continued living "a lovely butterfly life."

After her mother died in 1939, Julia divided her time between participating in the many activities of Pasadena's Junior League and being a hostess to family, friends, and her father's business associates until her younger sister returned from college and assumed that role.

Julia was twenty-nine years old when World War II began, and with genuine feelings of patriotism she decided to "turn her back on all *that*" (parties, dances, good times) and get a job in Washington and, hopefully, training in espionage work. For six months she plugged away at a typing job in a government agency nicknamed Mellet's Madhouse. But she quit soon after she accidentally dropped a box of meticulously filed index cards showing where all the VIPs were billeted in the city and was either unable or unwilling to extricate herself from the situation. She then joined the Office of Strategic Services, where she took charge of the files in General Donovan's office. But Washington was not as exciting as she had anticipated. In February 1943, when overseas duty became available, she put in for the Far East, assuming that she would be traveling to Europe on her own after the war.

Part of a diverse group that included the anthropologists Gregory Bateson and Cora Du Bois and an assortment of explosives experts, forgers, and missionaries who were returning to the Far East, she traveled by troop train across the United States and then by boat to Australia and on to Bombay. Some members of the group, Julia included, continued by train across the Indian subcontinent to Madras, and then to Kandy, Ceylon. She assumed charge of the Registry, the central exchange office in the China–Burma–India theater for signals going out to field operatives behind the Japanese lines as well as to Washington and other strategic areas. Between the time of her first assignment in Kandy and the end of the war, she was transferred to Kunming, then to Chungking, and back to Kunming—always in charge of the Registry.

Living in military quarters, dining in the mess hall, working long hours in a job of high responsibility certainly contributed to Julia's coming of age. Meeting Paul Child, chief presentation officer, OSS, dramatically changed her life. Having come to Kandy from New Delhi, where he had set up a war room for Lord Louis Mountbatten and General Wedemeyer, Paul Child had been involved with maintaining the war room for the general OSS staff for at least two months before Julia arrived. And it wasn't long before she noticed the visual presentation officer. Widely traveled, fluent in several languages, a self-taught artist and photographer, ten years her senior, and a bachelor, he represented what she had felt was lacking in her life. She confessed, "I was a real hayseed, having never been outside of the USA except to Tijuana." He was an intellectual, a man who could converse interestingly and amusingly on almost any subject, including gastronomy. So it was not surprising that in the absence of good food in the mess hall, cuisine became a major topic of conversation. And it was not long before Gregory Bateson, Cora Du Bois, the ornithologist Dillon Ripley, the journalist Theodore White, Paul Child, and Julia escaped bad army food and became passionate devotees of the many regional varieties of Chinese cuisine.

As the war progressed, Paul was sent to help set up other war rooms on the Chinese mainland, first at Chungking and then at Kunming, and Julia was also assigned to the Registry in both places at approximately the same time. The friendship that had begun in Kandy developed into something more serious when they began dining à deux in Kunming, with Julia beginning to feel "nesty" and Paul very much in admiration of her goodwill and good looks. Somewhat cautious because the war had, after all, created a succession of unusual situations, they both realized that they needed more time and a little distance. After the Japanese surrendered, Paul made his way home to the States by way of Peking. Julia's detachment was scheduled to move to Shanghai, but she opted to return to the States as well. With the war over, the unit's morale declined; and Julia felt they had lost something of their "purity of purpose." Being a self-declared Victorian woman at heart, she decided to go home, flying over the hump to Calcutta and then sailing for several weeks aboard a crowded troopship bound for California.

After reaching home, Julia and Paul carried out a sort of courtship by mail, followed by the decision to meet in Washington to look each other over in civilian clothes. The meeting was successful, and, with marriage definitely in the future, Julia went back to California, enrolled in a sewing course, then took classes in a cooking school to prepare for her next role. But the results were discouraging. Her younger sister remembered Julia showing her a white dress that she had made. When Dorothy laughed, Julia took it off and abruptly ended her sewing career. And cooking lessons were even more disastrous. Her béarnaise sauce congealed because she used lard instead of butter, and a duck caught fire in the oven because she failed to put it in a pan. Undaunted by accounts of these domestic mishaps, Paul traveled to California to meet Julia's father, stepmother, sister, and brother. Then the engaged couple proceeded to plan their wedding, not in Pasadena but in Pennsylvania, where Paul's twin brother, Charles, and other members of the Child family resided.

The long-awaited day in September 1946 was more than memorable. Just one day before the wedding, while the bridal couple drove from Washington to Lumberville, Pennsylvania, their car was struck by a truck without brakes. Julia was thrown through the windshield and had twenty-seven stitches in her head. And Paul's legs were so bruised that he had to use a cane. "We were married in stitches," Paul says, "me on a cane and Julia full of glass." After such an auspicious beginning, Mr. and Mrs. Paul Child started their married life in an apartment in Washington, D.C. As soon as they could afford to, they purchased a home at 2706 Olive Avenue in Georgetown, where they began the serious business of home-making.

Julia's first kitchen was on the garden level of their 150-year-old frame house. Featuring a twenty-five-year-old stove, the kitchen lacked many conveniences. Julia, however, determined to get this cooking thing right, soon filled the counters with current issues of Gourmet, Rombauer's Joy of Cooking, and other basic cookbooks and began to cook in earnest, sometimes with her sister-in-law, Freddie, at her side but more often than not alone. Thinking back on those early years, Paul remembered dinners served at nine or ten o'clock in the evening by his exhausted bride. But as time went by, Julia also managed cocktail parties, and the large foyer and living room on the first floor of their house accommodated friends and Paul's associates from the State Department, where he was engaged in exhibits work for the government because the Office of Strategic Services had been discontinued.

Early in 1948, by a stroke of good fortune, Paul was assigned to the United States Information Office in Paris. They were both pleased, but for very different reasons. For Paul the transfer meant a return to the city where as a young man he had known Hemingway, Gertrude Stein, and other expatriates who had gravitated to Paris in the twenties, a time when he eked out a living by selling woodcuts and making copies of the antique furniture on exhibit in the Cluny Museum. In sharp contrast, Julia's perception of the City of Light had been colored by reading *Harper's Bazaar*, and *Vogue*. Disembarking from the boat at Le Havre on November 3, 1948, "seeing all those beefy people," having lunch at La Couronne in Rouen, and driving into Paris at night when the lights illuminated the city, was, therefore, not only a revelation but a *coup de foudre*. "From the beginning I just fell in love with everything I saw," she said. "I didn't know very much about French food at that point. I hadn't started in on my career, and I'd never had such cooking in my life—I'd never had a fillet of sole with a white wine sauce."

What followed, of course, was a systematic immersion in *la cuisine française*, with mastering the language the first requirement. Soon after the Childs left temporary quarters at the Hôtel Pont Royal and settled into their at-a-former-time-elegant apartment on the third and fourth floors of 81 rue de l'Université, Julia began to take two lessons a day at Berlitz to shore up her college French. During Paul's long day at the embassy's offices on the rue du Faubourg St. Honoré, Julia studied French, and when she was not doing that she explored the narrow cobbled streets in the neighboring sixth arrondissement. Occasionally when the bells of St. Germain des Prés tolled, she watched the coming and going of bridal parties and funerals. Quite by accident one day, she joined the crowds of mourners at the funeral of Marshal Jean de Lattre de Tassigny and described it in detail, "in the rain, as befits state funerals, the widow in her weeds under a large black umbrella, the horse with its empty saddle, the Guarde Républicaine—the French do know how to do a great funeral." And from time to time she caught glimpses of Colette at Le Grand Véfour; Chanel and Schiaparelli in their fashionable shops.

What she enjoyed most, however, was taking the money that was

not designated for rent and current expenses and dining at a favorite restaurant with Paul. They came to know that L'Escargot served
wonderful fish dishes; *rognons de veau* were flambéed tableside at La
Grille, and the Restaurant des Artistes in Montmartre featured a
poulet sauté à l'estragon that they ordered whenever they dined
there. More frequently she prepared a meal in the service kitchen
on the top floor of their apartment, then sent it down to their Louis
XVI dining salon by way of the dumbwaiter, but both Julia and
Paul agreed that her cooking still left something to be desired.

Determined finally to do something about it, she enrolled in a
professional six-month course at the Cordon Bleu, joining twelve
ex-G.I.s who were going to the school on the G.I. Bill. She recalled,
"I would leave home at seven in the morning, cook all morning
with the G.I.s, and then rush home to make lunch for Paul. I'd give
him the béarnaise or the hollandaise sauce I'd just learned, or
something equally rich. In about a week we both got terribly bil-
ious." Her sister, Dorothy, who was visiting them at the time,
wrote that the unremitting diet of Julia's butter-soaked experiments literally sent her to the doctor, who prescribed a total change
of diet.

Julia was undaunted. In chef Max Bugnard, one of her favorite
teachers at the Cordon Bleu, she found a sympathetic and encouraging mentor. A pupil of Escoffier and former restaurateur in pre-
war Brussels, he excelled in stocks and sauces and was a marvelous
meat and fish chef. When he discovered that she was particularly
interested in his specialty, he gave her as much attention as he
could. Her other teacher was the pâtissier Claude Thillmont, a
former associate of Mme. Saint-Ange and for years the pastry chef
at the Café de Paris. Although both men were in their seventies,
their combined skills provided a sound foundation in the classic
repertoire. In the afternoons, the students at the Cordon Bleu also
attended demonstration classes conducted by Pierre Mangelatte, a
brilliant technician and owner of the Restaurant des Artistes. As
her French improved, Julia had little difficulty keeping up with the
instruction, and her enthusiasm for all aspects of French cuisine
soon knew no bounds. "Until I got into cooking," she once said,
"I was never *really* interested in anything."

Doing marketing, preparation work, cooking, and serving was, however, not typical of most of the Embassy wives or most of the Frenchwomen she met at various diplomatic functions. And Julia wanted to share her newfound expertise with people whose enthusiasms equaled her own. Looking back on her friendship and collaboration with Simone (Simca) Beck, Julia recalled how it all began, in 1949. George Artamonoff, the first president of Sears International, planned a cocktail party for more than a hundred people in his home in the suburb of Saint-Germain-en-Laye, and he promised Simca that he would introduce her to an American woman who might share her interest in food. Her name, he said, was Mrs. Paul Child, and it would be easy to find her because she was over six feet tall. When Simca introduced herself, she and Julia immediately began to discuss food and how to make "a valid professional project out of it." Julia invited Simca to her apartment the next day to continue their conversation. Julia also met Simca's friend Louisette Bertholle a few days later, and both Frenchwomen urged Julia to join Le Cercle des Gourmettes.

The exclusive club began in 1927 as the feminine counterpart to the all-male Club des Cent. But by the time Julia joined their ranks, most of the women were in their seventies and quite corpulent. Not particularly interested in the guest chefs' preparation of their elaborate luncheons of foie gras or lobster specialties, the ladies appeared just in time for the aperitif and meal. Julia, Simca, and Louisette, however, arrived at nine-thirty, assisted the chef, and enjoyed what could only be called a private lesson. The three women worked well together and soon became friends. And, more to the point, Julia discovered that there was much to be learned from the actual preparation of a meal together.

When a handful of her American friends who were on holiday in Paris asked her to teach them something about French cooking, Julia talked the idea over with Simca and Louisette. The two Frenchwomen had written a small book of recipes called *What's Cooking in France* at the urging of one of Louisette's American friends, and they planned to expand their recipes into a "big book" destined, like the first book, to be published by Ives Washburn Publishing Company in the States. Already very much involved in communicating the fundamentals of French cooking to American audiences, they quickly realized that teaching American students with Julia could be an ideal arrangement, not only because it presented an opportunity to refine their recipes but also because they needed an American partner to translate their recipes into acceptable English for an American market. A veritable cooking triumvirate was soon established and called L'Ecole des Trois Gourmandes.

The kitchen on the upper floor of Julia's apartment was the perfect place for the newly founded cooking school. Intended for the servants of the once affluent household, the room was large and airy, with windows looking out over the gardens and buildings of the Ministère de la Défense with the spires of the Basilique Sainte-Clotilde in the distance. Furthermore, the kitchen was well equipped. Since the days of her classes at the Cordon Bleu, Julia had systematically increased her "megalomaniacal" collecting of kitchenware from specialty shops like E. Dehillerin, near Les Halles. The kitchen, therefore, had the requisite *batterie de cuisine*, and the schedule of lessons opened the possibilities of inviting guest Cordon Bleu teachers like Max Bugnard and Claude Thillmont to teach the finer points of haute cuisine.

With the initiation of L'Ecole des Trois Gourmandes, Julia's kitchen lost its private character and became a schoolroom. At first there were only a few lessons a month given for friends or groups from the embassy, and there were never more than six American or occasionally French students in the class. It was planned as a practical cooking class, so the students could *mettre la main à la pâte* (get their hands on the dough). And after a morning of preparation and cooking, the dishes that they made were sent via the dumbwaiter to the dining room, where Paul was busy decanting the wine for the communal luncheon. The students were pleased with the results of their labors and frequently brought paying guests to the luncheon. Julia, Simca, and Louisette discovered that they were absolutely fascinated with teaching.

For Julia, especially, the early 1950s were heady days. She continued her association with Max Bugnard and Claude Thillmont, and Simca introduced her to renowned gourmets like Curnonsky and professional chefs like Aimée Cassiot. She and Paul were invited to the tastings of the Chevaliers du Tastevin de Bourgogne, and Paul's interest in wine complemented her own fascination with planning menus that paired wine and food beautifully. And, of course, they both came to know firsthand some of the best restaurants in Paris. In short, she was well on her way to a successful culinary career.

Though at first reluctant to join the cookbook project undertaken by her two French friends, Julia recognized that simply being American gave her an advantage, if only slight, in dealing with publishers on the other side of the Atlantic. By the fall of 1952, therefore, she began to question the wisdom of publishing the book with an editor named Sumner Putnam at Ives Washburn. *What's Cooking in France*, admittedly a trial balloon, had been entirely translated and largely rewritten by a food adviser named Helmut Ripperger, but Simca and Louisette saw nothing of the book until it appeared in print. Very little publicity was given to it, and shortly after it came out, Ripperger bowed out of the picture. There was no contract between Ives Washburn and Simca and Louisette, and no advance had been made on the more ambitious book, tentatively named *French Home Cooking*. When she agreed to collaborate with them, Julia insisted that the three authors carefully outline the book, discuss its scope, indicate that they expected it to be published in a sequence of five individual volumes, and obtain the services of an American lawyer, namely Paul's nephew Paul Sheeline, who would handle the legal aspects of all contractual arrangements. With the request that all the material already sent to Sumner Putnam be returned for translation and editing, Julia was literally beginning to organize the venture that nine years later would appear as *Mastering the Art of French Cooking*.

In February 1953 Paul was reassigned to the U.S. consulate in Marseille. Julia shared some of her feelings in her letters to Paul Sheeline: "We are up to the ears in good-byes and packing as you can imagine. My, I hate to leave Paris. It has been like a honeymoon these last four years. I don't expect to be fully satisfied living anywhere else. . . . It has been a continual enchantment. . . . My life has been enriched, my soul has been sweetened, and I shall be eternally grateful." Her priorities had also substantially changed. And when she and Paul went apartment hunting in Marseille, the suitability of the kitchen became the most important consideration.

In mid-March, she wrote to Simca, "Enfin, we are installed in our little apartment, and I am at this moment sitting in the dining-room work room, with a two masted schooner right in front of my nose, sea gulls flying about, fishing boats coming in and out, and a bright sun over all. It is heavenly. We do need one more room, however, for us to paint and write cookbooks in." They had rented the apartment from a Scandinavian civil servant because the view overlooking the Vieux Port was perfect, the furniture "modern" and spare, and the kitchen large enough to work in comfortably. But soon the lack of a proper worktable sent Julia out to purchase a sturdy piece of wood the size of a door to mount on two large trunks for a makeshift desk, and she asked Simca to go to Dehillerin's and buy some sturdy pots for her Marseille kitchen.

If there were such minor inconveniences, there were also advantages accompanying life in Marseille. Shopping in the big covered fish market, Julia discussed the names and varieties of the fish on display with the sellers before she purchased "une fraîcheur exquise baby rougets and dorades" for lunch. And she experimented with the Provençal "flavor base" of tomatoes, onions, garlic, and herbs, so different from the butter and cream of the Parisian palate.

At about the time the Childs moved to Marseille, Julia had read and then answered an article written by the historian Bernard DeVoto about the scarcity of good knives in the States and his continuing search for a carbon steel paring knife. Julia sent him one from France, and the initial correspondence developed into an interesting exchange of letters between Julia and his wife, Avis DeVoto, a freelance editor for some of the Boston publishing houses. When Julia concluded that the publishing agreement with Ives Washburn had become unfeasible because both publisher and authors had very different ideas about the scope of the book, she wrote to Avis, who gradually assumed the role of unpaid and unheralded literary agent. She put Julia in touch with an editor at Houghton Mifflin, and with the legal services of Paul Sheeline, the three women signed a contract with Houghton Mifflin in 1953 with the stipulation to finish the "big book" as soon as possible.

With the authors under pressure to complete the chapter on soups and gather more recipes for the ensuing chapters, letters went back and forth from Marseille to Paris once or twice a week, as Julia experimented with Simca's recipes, altering, refining, and sometimes completely changing them with a view to the American market. Often Louisette had what Julia considered nice little ideas about garnishes that were very much "L'esprit Américain." "They love novelties," Julia wrote to Simca. "You and I are more straight chef-type cooks, I think. We are really, I must say, a very good combination of personalities, as we do each complement the others."

Whether friends or relatives from the States or the consul general were guests at her table, Julia tested recipes, preparing as much as possible ahead of time. If a sauce broke, she was determined to find out why; if an electric blender could shorten the time and ease the tedium of making quenelles, she experimented endlessly. Soon Julia's reputation as a good cook preceded her in consulate circles, and the Childs entertained often. She was also drafted to participate in more elaborate parties, like the one for the 500 guests invited to the consulate's cocktail party to celebrate the Fourth of July. The Navy provided cans of ingredients, but Julia was the official "fixer-upper," mixing all sorts of things into the sardines, salmon, canned liver sausage, and cheese to produce finger food for the guests. "Difficult to make first-class things with third-class material—impossible in fact" was her motto, but she did manage to concoct truly delicious hors d'oeuvres. And, of course, the variety of fresh foodstuffs available in the Marseille market, the quality of wine that Paul liked to serve, and the array of cheeses available from the Provençal countryside contributed to the refinement of Julia's palate.

When she wasn't marketing, cooking, or deconstructing Simca's recipes, she was busy fixing up her kitchen, not with curtains and shelf papers but with cookware. Since her days at the Cordon Bleu, Paul had applied his former war room expertise to the task of hanging all her measuring cups and spoons, pots and pans, molds, forms, rings, and other utensils on a kind of pegged board, and, as they moved from one home to another, this mode of organization became the distinguishing feature of their kitchens. A day spent away from this most important of all rooms was a day that Julia considered lost. The only way she could justify an afternoon at a ladies' lunch or tea was if the occasion led to a request to teach someone how to make an omelette or soufflé. And when an acquaintance who had not been in the kitchen for years made a near perfect dish following Julia's instructions, she had renewed confidence in the recipe destined for inclusion in her book.

In mid-May 1954, when Julia and Paul were preparing for a two-month leave in the States, Paul received word that he would be assigned to Bonn, Germany, when their summer leave was over. Julia, who was in the midst of preparing a list of things to check out in the States, wrote to Simca, "If anyone can think of a sillier way than this to try and collaborate on a cookbook! It is particularly for you that I am upset as here you are slaving away and your colleague keeps putting up one delay after another. However, I think a personal survey of the US at this point is extremely necessary so there is some good in it at least." Julia was determined to find out specific differences in the cuts of meat, the sizes of chickens and turkeys, the availability of soft and hard wheat flours, and the extent to which frozen food had invaded the American market.

The trip back to the States was, indeed, enlightening. Julia found that there was much more interest in food and cooking since the war, but very little knowledge of how to cook in the French manner, with stocks, sauces, marinades, and the use of wine in cooking generally not accessible to the majority of people who did their own cooking. And she observed that eating was not a national sport in America as it was in France. Time to cook seemed to be an overwhelming problem. She concluded, therefore, that the recipes in the book would have to be not only tempting, but whenever possible, prepared, at least in part, ahead of time. The initial recipes also would have to be simple, with complex ones introduced gradually.

During the two and a half months that they were in the States, the Childs spent several days in Cambridge visiting with Avis DeVoto, who introduced Julia to some of the personnel at Houghton Mifflin. They also visited relatives in California and Pennsylvania before they returned to Washington, where Paul took German language lessons. Reflecting on the time they had spent in the States, Julia wrote about the difficulties readjusting to American life, to the pace of New York, and to the "large scale" of urban time-saving conveniences. What she did not fully realize were the changes that almost six years of living in France had brought about in her. Not only had living in Paris and Marseille broadened her horizons, but the experience had also propelled her into a purposeful career. Gathering up the fragments from the past—all the time she had spent in writing advertising copy for Sloane, the organizational skills she had developed working in the Registry, and the techniques she had learned at the Cordon Bleu and in the kitchen of L'Ecole des Trois Gourmandes—she had at her disposal the means to excel in the task at hand. And she turned every trip, every new experience, and each new home into an occasion to further her objectives.

After they settled into a newly constructed apartment in a big American housing development outside Bonn, Julia confided to Simca that in order to function at all properly as a *cuisinière* she would have to learn German. She would also have to adjust to the more than adequate electric stove that went with their comfortable, well-heated, and unimaginatively furnished apartment. "There are few distractions to keep me from my work, which is fine. But it is, nevertheless, lonely. I miss my friends, and I do miss La Belle France."

Living in what she considered little more than an American community located in Plittersdorf, Julia felt none of the excitement she had experienced living in Paris and Marseille. But she did find a situation that seemed to be about as American as possible outside the borders of the United States, and she decided to use the time in Germany, not to learn about the local cuisine but to adapt American ingredients to French recipes. The commissary resembled a big American supermarket, and it was stocked with cans of fruits and vegetables and a complete line of frozen foods. Cooking for the first time on an electric rather than a gas stove and using frozen chickens and vegetables, she tested the recipes that Simca forwarded to her, making adjustments for ingredients easily available to the American audience for whom the book was being written.

The German interlude also had other advantages. For one thing it removed Julia from the center of the storm brewing over Louisette's greatly diminished role in the evolution of the cookbook. Unlike Simca and Julia, Louisette did not view it as a thoroughgoing presentation of basic French culinary techniques, which involved testing and retesting each recipe for absolute accuracy. She would have liked a nice, little, charming "chez nous" type of book, very chic, very "la vie en rose." Instead she found herself in the middle of a magnum opus that required tedious writing and rewriting, and she simply demurred, raging one moment, weeping the next. Through the intervention of lawyers on both sides, she was ultimately persuaded to agree to a lesser amount of the royalties that would be generated by the book, but she insisted that her name appear as an equal collaborator. As far as Julia was concerned, the important thing was to publish the book, and she also felt that Simca and Louisette's relationship should be preserved at whatever cost. Distance from the role that each Frenchwoman was gradually assuming in Paris's culinary circles, moreover, had its advantages because Julia had some concerns closer to home.

Paul worked long hours arranging exhibits and trying to gain fluency in the German language, but both activities were proving difficult, and Julia tried to divert his attention from work to other things. After a quiet Christmas, they went on a short holiday to Nuremberg to celebrate the beginning of 1955. But Paul really disliked living in Germany and continued to be frustrated over his inability to express himself fluently in the language. As always Julia was his mainstay in a kind of humdrum existence in an American enclave where his neighbors washed their cars on Saturday mornings and followed sports events enthusiastically. She knew how to bridge the gap by roasting a turkey for the Christmas party in his office and by inviting neighbors and associates to their home for experimental "casserole sautées." She also used the lure of the countryside and the promise of good food to plan a series of weekends in Holland and Belgium, with a promise of a trip to Paris in the early spring. Paul more than once remarked that Julia was a "natural." She could converse with everyone from the ambassador to the local sausage maker with ease and good humor, and very few people could plan a trip with more enthusiasm than she.

Paul's work also dictated a certain amount of travel. They drove to Frankfurt for a modern art exhibit arranged by Paul and attended by Nelson Rockefeller and the director of the New York Museum of Modern Art. And they spent three weeks in Berlin while Paul organized Edward Steichen's photographic show "The Family of Man" and a clothing and textile show at the Berlin Fair. While Paul worked, Julia enjoyed being in a large city again. Putting aside the work she always took with her, she found Chinese restaurants and shopped for well-made woolen clothes. She told Simca that German food was far from interesting. Best to order only German things—sausages, sauerkraut, smoked pork, and the beer, which was always good. German wines, too, were wonderful, although for a good year from a good vineyard the cost was high. She concluded that there was simply no place like France to shop and enjoy food and wine.

The Childs' plan to welcome in 1956 in Paris was upset when a virus that had confined Paul to bed for over two weeks developed into infectious hepatitis. Ordered to remain in bed for a minimum of three more weeks and restricted to a fat-free diet for the next six months, Paul was responsible for at least one more variation in Julia's pot-au-feu and poule au pot recipes. "I am surprised how much one can do using no fats in cooking. If one can cook vegetables in stock, with a bit of shallot, that helps . . . I have also found to my surprise that I can grill meats and chicken with no fat . . . I usually put in a bit of salt and lemon juice," she wrote to Simca. But testing recipes for braised goose and duck confit was much more to her liking.

In February, after spending two weeks in Rome at his doctor's suggestion, Paul seemed fully recovered, although he was not permitted to drink wine until June, and he definitely had to be careful with his diet. Then it was Julia's turn at *les malheurs d'un certain âge*. She checked into the American clinic for treatment, and although she took her "ducks" with her on paper, staying at the clinic for three days interfered with her recipe testing. In a short time, however, she was entertaining house guests, preparing a buffet supper for twelve, and planning to spend Easter in Brussels with their Paris embassy friends Abe and Rosemary Manell.

Late spring brought news that Avis DeVoto, now widowed, would join the Childs in England in June, then travel with them to Paris to meet Simca and her husband, Jean Fischbacher. Julia planned every phase of the itinerary, including a visit to Rouen for a great duck dinner. Then they would stop in Amiens to pick up a *pâté de canard* for picnicking along the Seine en route to Paris, finally arriving in Paris via the Auto Route Bois de Boulogne, the avenue Foch, and the Champs-Elysées to the place de la Concorde. By this time, Avis was "godmother" to the book, and Julia wanted her advice about publishing it in sequential volumes, beginning with sections on sauces and poultry, then continuing on to soups and vegetables. After much thought and discussion, a consensus about the various volumes was reached in Paris, and when she returned to Germany, Julia wrote to Simca that the decision was a relief and a release: "I was beginning to feel it was all rather hope-less, I must say! Now I feel that things are going to be possible in our lifetime!" But there were unforeseen distractions ahead.

The Childs had anticipated at least two more years of duty in Germany when they learned of the strong possibility that Paul would be transferred to Washington after arranging for a major exhibit in Berlin in September. Julia's reaction to this latest change was mixed. While she regretted not having become acquainted with Germany, for the book the move would be a plus because she could clarify many of the details about ingredients that seemed impossible to do anyplace other than the States. Undoubtedly, the move would also signal a better job and promotion for Paul.

While they were in Berlin, Paul received definite word that he was assigned to Washington. Although there were still a few exhib-its he had to supervise in Bonn and Cologne, they planned to pack and leave Plittersdorf the third week in October, travel to Le Havre by way of Strasbourg and Paris, and arrive in the States the first week in November. After eight years, Julia knew that the house on Olive Avenue, rented during their absence, would need repairs, which, in turn, would mean further delay in getting the manuscript ready for Houghton Mifflin. Undaunted, she persuaded Simca to join them in Washington as soon as possible to work on the book and learn firsthand about the American "do-it-yourself" trend and the new interest in cooking that they had been reading about in the women's magazines.

Unable to move into their Georgetown home until after the first of the year, the Childs spent the Thanksgiving holidays in Cam-bridge with Avis DeVoto. They also conferred at length with their editor at Houghton Mifflin, Dorothy de Santillana, discussing the pros and cons of publishing the finished chapters in single volumes versus the advisability of waiting four or five years to complete the fish and meat sections and publish the entire book. Julia and Paul traveled to California to spend time with relatives and friends. Visiting some of the newer California vineyards, they were surprised and delighted at the quality of the wines. And although they felt that they did not compare with the full-bodied white and red Burgundies of France, the lighter red and white wines were quite acceptable. It was a promising sign that Americans were becoming discriminating in matters of food and wine.

After celebrating the Christmas holidays with Paul's twin brother and his family in Lumberville, Pennsylvania, the Childs returned to Georgetown to find their house in more serious need of repair than they had anticipated. Faced with a dangerously outmoded electrical system, a leaking roof, bathrooms requiring extensive plumbing work, and an antiquated kitchen, they decided to use the money that had accumulated during their eight years abroad to renovate the house. In spite of its condition, Julia loved the charming three-storied home and began planning the removal of a partition to enlarge the kitchen. And soon those plans included the installation of a professional-size gas stove with a grill and an electric oven with a rotary spit as well as a garbage disposal and a dishwasher.

Within two weeks she had cleared a space to work in one of the small bedrooms on the top floor. She also discovered what she described as those "great serve yourself markets where you buy everything from bread, creamery products, meat, fruit, mops, light bulbs and everything. . . . It is fine to be able to pick out each separate mushroom yourself, for instance, instead of having two bad ones thrust upon you when you buy a pound. Seems to me there is everything here that is necessary to allow a good French cook to operate." Passing through Washington, visiting in California, and cooking with her sister-in-law in Pennsylvania during the previous few years had failed to acquaint her adequately with the march of consumerism across America. And she was finding it great fun to be back.

Trying to work in the middle of renovation, however, was difficult. If she escaped to her top-floor workroom, either the electricians or the carpenters found her to ask questions or demand decisions. Compounding the problem was the arrival of the couple's books and personal belongings from Germany. As the work progressed, boxes and crates had to be moved again and again to make room for cabinetmaking or stair rebuilding. Julia's letters to Simca, however, were optimistic about getting the completed manuscript to Houghton Mifflin by February of the next year.

By the end of March, the house was finished, the workmen gone, and Julia was busy "entertaining like mad. [I] have done three turkeys, one lamb, an enormous steak, Coquilles St.-Jacques, Artichokes à la Grecque (using frozen ones). Also your Crêpes de Pommes de Terre aux Poireaux (delicious) . . . doing them I suddenly didn't have time to do them as crêpes, so piled them into a gratinée dish, sprinkled top with speck of cheese and dots of butter and heated them in the oven. Perfectly superb, and everybody loved them," she told Simca. "I can't wait for you to come here and to go shopping." Her enthusiasm was boundless; she made *pâte brisée* with at least three changes in the ratio of butter to Crisco, using the surplus dough for hors d'oeuvres at a cocktail party for Paul's associates.

And in May she began to give cooking lessons to a group of women who met every Monday to prepare lunch for themselves and their husbands. Her first menu was chicken suprêmes Florentine, risotto, and pommes à la Seville. Everything turned out extremely well, and, to Julia's amazement, the women said that it was the best meal they had ever eaten. One of the members was a friend of the editor of *Harper's Bazaar*, and Julia confided to Simca that this might just open the door to an article and some advance publicity for their book.

La vie was settling down into a good routine. Paul was rapidly becoming a passionate gardener, planting a two-foot border of flowers and shrubbery around the small brick patio accessible through the dining room's French doors. And Julia was busy gathering information about turkeys from the National Turkey Federation of America, experimenting with "l'oncle Ben's" rice, and anticipating their vacation in Maine at the end of August.

Each new day brought a realization that the America she had left eight years ago had changed, but she had also changed into a culinary professional, and looking at supermarkets, women's maga-zines, and what could only be called the zeitgeist of the late fifties through her eyes was revealing. She felt that American housewives had neither the time nor the inclination to prepare complicated dishes. To accommodate them, manufacturers were trying to make things as easy as possible with pre-prepared foods. On the other hand, the do-it-yourself creative urge was strong, and the markets were making good ingredients available. If their book could demys-tify French cooking and emphasize cuisine bourgeoise rather than haute cuisine, they might just tap into the existing interest in French food and provide the means to achieve the taste of that food by using blenders and time-saving procedures rather than tradi-tional mortars, sieves, and pilons.

Although Julia spent long hours in the kitchen, her particular blend of curiosity, efficiency, and love of good food made those hours pleasurable rather than tedious. One moment, she was a scientist in her laboratory experimenting with quantities, methods, and temperatures. The next moment, she was a hostess of no small repute devising menus. And at other times she was a teacher in a maze of students. While engaged in all of that no-nonsense culinary activity, however, she never neglected family and friends, writing letters, visiting, and enjoying holidays and vacations together.

Julia and Paul resumed a pattern established before their Euro-pean years when they joined his brother and sister-in-law that August on Mount Desert Island, Maine, where the twin brothers had built a log cabin using felled trees from the dense forest. With only a huge stone fireplace for heat, the cabin was primitive in every way until they gradually added a few modern conveniences and more rooms to accommodate their families. The isolation of the place, however, did not change nor did the bounty of the sea accessible just offshore. Mussels, periwinkles, clams, and lobster were there to be harvested, as were the blueberries, raspberries, and blackberries in the woods. And Julia's sister-in-law planted a sea-sonal garden, so there were always fresh herbs, string beans, cucumbers, and tomatoes in abundance. The time that Julia and Paul spent there always seemed too short.

During the fall of 1957, Julia became increasingly busy with manuscript preparation, and she was also caught up in a whirl of entertaining, teaching, and local events, only taking time out for special events like watching the parade (a passion) for the visiting queen of England. And, of course, she was involved with plans for Simca's visit in February. Trying to answer Simca's questions about Little Rock and the civil rights movement, Julia advised her to read *Time* magazine to get a feel for what was going on in the States. Meanwhile, the chapters on sauces and poultry were sent to a typist as soon as each was completed. Accompanied by Simca, Julia planned to deliver them to Houghton Mifflin herself.

Toasting in the new year, Julia anticipated the visit of her *chère amie* with absolutely no idea of the disappointments that 1958 would bring. As far as she was concerned, after sauces and poultry, eggs and vegetables would evolve, then either meat or soup and fish, followed by entrées, luncheon dishes, hors d'oeuvres, terrines and pâtés, on through pastries and desserts, each published at one- or two-year intervals. But in March, to her chagrin, Houghton Mifflin rejected the idea of the multivolume *French Cooking for the American Kitchen*, even though they praised the 850-page manuscript on sauces and poultry. They simply said that it was not the book they had contracted for, not the single volume that would tell the American housewife how to cook using French techniques.

Julia's first response was to return the $250 advance and end their association with Houghton Mifflin. But two days later, after discussing the matter with Simca at great length, she redrafted her letter to Dorothy de Santillana: "We well realize that the continuing trend in this country is toward speed and the elimination of work, and that our treatise on French Sauces and French Poultry furthers neither aspect of this American dream. We have therefore decided to shelve our own dream for the time being and propose to prepare you a short and snappy book directed to the somewhat sophisticated housewife/chauffeur. . . . Everything would be of the simpler sort, but nothing humdrum. The recipes would look short, and emphasis would always be on how to prepare ahead, and how to reheat. All the recipes we need are at hand and fully experimented upon, and within six months or less we could have a completed manuscript in your hands." And they proposed about 300 pages of recipes for soups, sauces, chicken, meat, fish, eggs, soufflés, vegetable dishes, and desserts. Houghton Mifflin approved the single-volume plan.

The rejection had been especially difficult for Julia, who felt responsible for "dragging" Simca into the magnum opus. But after a much needed vacation with her family in California, she became enthusiastic about the shorter book as their "introduction" to an American audience. "People must say of this book. A MARVELOUS BOOK. I've never been able to make cake before, but now I can. Or such and such." Letters went back and forth across the Atlantic covering everything from broken hollandaise to *crème Chantilly*, and Julia admitted that recipe rewriting, testing, and teaching were her mainstays in an otherwise not always satisfying world.

In mid-July Paul had been passed by for promotion to head the Exhibits Division. Getting into something else at fifty-six seemed improbable, but there was no doubt that the constraints of working in such a vast bureaucracy were beginning to take a heavy toll on his spirit. One moment he contemplated early retirement; at other times he considered requesting another assignment. When he was offered the post of cultural affairs officer in Oslo in August, therefore, he accepted, but with the stipulation that he remain in Washington for six months to acquire facility in speaking Norwegian.

Completing Julia's book before their departure was also of major importance, and she optimistically hoped that she would have it in Houghton Mifflin's hands by that time. But the pressure to do it and the thought of leaving her newly remodeled kitchen probably made this move less exciting than ever. And there was a nagging fear that if she had not been so involved in her work, she might have contributed more to Paul's career. She told Simca that she had decided to be more of a "diplomatic wife" when they moved to Oslo because the pressure of producing the cookbook manuscript would no longer be an excuse to avoid social activities. Good intentions notwithstanding, she could not resist asking, "What are we planning to do when it is done? Continue with our complete research for our complete and magnum opus, I imagine, with thoughts for another short book interspersed, and some magazine articles, in fact, quite a few magazine articles, so that we become known with authority."

Julia had found a niche in cooking, teaching, and writing, and for the moment the prospect of service in Oslo seemed to please Paul. They both knew, however, that the time would soon come to make plans that would reach beyond Norway. What they did not know was that at least one decision about their future would have to be made immediately. In early December, Avis DeVoto called to tell them that a very choice house was for sale in Cambridge and would have to be seen and purchased immediately because such properties rarely appeared on the market. Julia and Paul took the train to Boston the next day, found the former home of the Harvard philosopher Josiah Royce just perfect for their retirement needs, and purchased it by mortaging their Washington home. Reluctant entrepreneurs, they had no choice but to rent both houses for additional income during the time that they would be in Norway.

As March drew near, Paul managed to secure two more months of language study in Washington to enable Julia to finish the manuscript. But there were so many other things to be done before departure that time dedicated to the manuscript was continually compromised, despite her best efforts. She was so busy relaying chapters to the typist and in writing the explanatory material that she lightly referred to as the "blah-blahs" that she actually engaged a professional caterer for four de rigueur farewell cocktail parties. On a series of evenings, she entertained what she called a mixed bag, including upper office colleagues, then the art and culture crowd, followed by newspaper types and Democrats, and, at the last event, her social, business, and Republican guests. In addition to these social obligations, decisions about what to store and what to pack for Oslo had to be made, the house on Olive Avenue had to be made ready for tenants, and then it was time to go to New York and sail to France. Before they left the States, Julia mailed as much of the completed manuscript as possible to her editor at Houghton Mifflin with a promise that the rest would be forthcoming as soon as she was settled in Oslo.

After arriving at Le Havre on April 29, the Childs followed the familiar routine of claiming their luggage and car and driving to Rouen for lunch with Simca. Then Paris beckoned. Louisette planned to give a special class with Max Bugnard as guest, and Simca prevailed upon Le Cercle des Gourmettes to schedule a special lunch during the time of Julia's visit. There were lists of people to see, favorite small restaurants to revisit. In Paris days passed too quickly, and Julia always longed to be in her former kitchen there. On May 9, the Childs reluctantly left the City of Light and drove to Amsterdam to meet Paul's niece and her husband, who were touring Europe on their wedding trip.

After a pleasant visit, they traveled through Denmark, sailed up the Oslo fjord, and arrived in the city that would be their home. At first glance it seemed little different from any old and large American urban center, but on closer inspection they discovered that the low-lying hills ringing the city offered beautiful views of the fjords and the clean, crisp smell of spruce forests. Renting a home in the hills, therefore, seemed preferable to living in the midst of the city, and when they went house hunting Julia found the perfect place. A house that had been built by a recently deceased wealthy widower was available for rental while his estate was being settled. Perhaps it reminded her of their Washington home, although it was built on a larger scale, or the size of its kitchen and dining room might have been a factor, or simply the magnificence of the views from its windows made it the most desirable house for them. And because it was, they were willing to wait several weeks and pay a rental well above their allowance.

With the help of their niece, they moved in during the last week of June. After Julia arranged their bedroom and chose a room to use as her study, she enlisted Paul's help in hanging everything in the kitchen to make it "OUR kitchen." And an embassy friend soon took Julia on a tour of the shops. She found that vegetables were limited; chickens were, for the most part, broiler size; veal was only so-so, but the pork was fine. Some limitations in ingredients and a very small, old-fashioned electric stove caused Julia to be thankful that all the major cookbook testing was finished. But there were compensations—delicious fish and shellfish, good cream and butter, and a garden with flowering fruit trees, strawberries, and raspberries. When manuscript preparation became tedious, she spent a few hours in the strawberry patch or picked currants to make preserves for the much-anticipated venison dinners she planned to serve in winter.

On September 7, 1959, Julia sent off the completed manuscript of 785 pages to Houghton Mifflin and two weeks later was assured by her editor that it was "amazingly, startlingly accurate and inclusive." She had read it twice and told Julia that she had presented it to the business office for actual size estimates, costs, and all those details involved in the final decision on a project. With a cleared desk, Julia began to take Norwegian lessons at the university twice a week, and she became an active member of the American Women's Club of Oslo. Not really interested in ladies' luncheons, she volunteered to make sandwiches for bridge parties and cakes for special occasions. But she confided to Simca that she missed working on the book and missed her friends back in the States even though they were beautifully housed in Norway.

During the sixteen months that Julia and Simca had spent in revising their cookbook, there had been no hint that the enthusiasm and continued encouragement from their editor at Houghton Mifflin would lead to anything but publication. So they were completely unprepared for the letter of rejection that they received on November 13; it categorized the book as "a big, expensive cookbook of elaborate information that might well prove to be formidable to the American housewife." The news could not have been blacker, especially because Julia felt personally responsible for having raised Simca's expectations. Avis DeVoto got a fuller report from their disappointed editor, who also had to reconcile herself to the equation of probable costs against possible sales, which had determined the decision not to publish. Distressed because she was the one who had steered the authors to Houghton Mifflin, Avis immediately called William Koshland, a senior editor at Knopf. He had seen bits of the book when he visited her, Avis wrote to Julia, and had been interested in the project over the years because he was an enthusiastic cook himself. She thought that since he was a vice president at Knopf, he would be a persuasive voice to sponsor the book. When he agreed to read it, Avis asked Houghton Mifflin to forward it to Knopf directly.

Julia had said over and over again that she was not interested in a "gourmet" book that would merely add a touch of thyme or garlic to create an international dish. But with the rejection, she seriously wondered whether any publisher felt that there was enough interest to warrant the expense of publishing the kind of book they had written. The realities of publishing were discouraging, especially because she had spent years in mastering the techniques of French cooking, and she was not interested in writing a

book that really wouldn't contribute anything. She would rewrite
and cut where necessary, but, she said, "the basic principle of
teaching people how to cook correctly is the only thing which
interests me in this type of book. I don't think that is a very clear
statement . . . what I mean is that I like our basic approach and
don't want to go into Cuisine express . . . won't go into it." Given
the vagaries of the publishing world, there was nothing to do but
wait and see if the manuscript that had taken more than eight years
to produce would eventually be published.

November brought snow to Oslo, and Julia divided her time
between studying Norwegian, entertaining, and anticipating spending the Christmas holidays in Paris. Paul and Julia also planned to
celebrate *Réveillon* with Simca and her husband in their newly
acquired farmhouse, Le Mas Vieux, on a tract of land called Bramafam in Plascassier in the south of France. It was a vacation that she
looked forward to with pleasure and a certain amount of unease.
The holiday visit would be the first time the two collaborators
could actually discuss Houghton Mifflin's rejection of their manuscript. And when the discussion did take place, to their mutual
relief, they found that they were more determined than ever to see
the book in print. From the beginning of their friendship, Julia and
Simca had shared a passion for cooking that was not typical for
women in their respective social circles, and their culinary training
and hard work had professionalized that passion. When they
worked on a recipe, Simca's Gallic prejudices were balanced by
Julia's inventiveness. And when they shared the same kitchen,
there was an intensity of purpose, a will to experiment, and a
thoroughgoing give-and-take of criticism and good humor. It was
difficult to determine whether respect was the basis for the genuine
affection the two women felt for each other or whether their affection promoted mutual respect. But while Julia always credited the
Cordon Bleu for teaching her the techniques of French cooking,
she just as insistently acknowledged that Simca gave her finesse,
enlarged her culinary vocabulary, and taught her what could be
described only as a French attitude toward food.

Welcoming in the New Year of 1960 with Simca and her husband also introduced the Childs to a sunny, herb-scented corner of
Provence that would eventually be the site of La Pitchoune, their

retreat on the Fischbacher property. And the holiday celebration was certainly the foreshadowing of the Champagne toast sent from Oslo to Paris when Knopf offered them a contract for their book in May. William Koshland had sampled many of the recipes and turned the manuscript over to Judith Jones, a young editor who worked primarily on French literary translations but had lived in Paris and loved cooking. She thought that the manuscript was as good as and even better than taking a course at the Cordon Bleu, and she enlisted the opinion of Angus Cameron, an editor at Bobbs-Merrill during the publication of *The Joy of Cooking*, before presenting a strong case for publication to the Knopfs. When they agreed to publish the manuscript, she told Avis DeVoto that the book was unique, really French, and she knew from testing innumerable recipes that the authors' emphasis on technique would enhance other French cookery books. She concluded her letter with the observation that, "The enthusiasts around here are absolutely convinced that this book is revolutionary, and we intend to prove it and to make it a classic."

Again, there were legal issues to resolve regarding the collaboration. And to facilitate matters for Knopf, Julia was designated an agent for the other two authors. A new agreement had to be drawn up among the collaborators concerning expenses connected with the preparation of the manuscript and the distribution of royalties. Louisette disagreed about the percentage she would receive, which in turn created problems for the two collaborators who had actually written the book and were still involved in preparing the final text. Julia's work of editing the manuscript, especially, was far from over. When Judith Jones requested a few more hearty peasant dishes and an adjustment in proportions of ingredients to serving sizes, she complied. The recipe for cassoulet caused a flurry of letters between Simca and Julia because they could not agree on the necessity of goose in the dish. And by the time Julia had read the manuscript a second time, there were other potential dustups in the making. But now that the book was accepted, Julia assumed a surer tone with Simca, deferring to her expertise regarding correct French recipe titles but impatient with inconsistencies and unnecessarily complicated procedures.

As far as Louisette was concerned, Julia felt that there was more than a little preposterousness in her demands, but she concluded, in a letter to Simca, "I do not care too terribly, as I think your relationship with her is more important than anything else. . . . My feeling in general is that it is not at all fair that we do all the work and she gets a free ride, so to speak. And I do think that if she refuses to be reasonable in this affair, and if we must compromise with her, that this is the end of any joint authorship of the three of us (but not, bien entendu, with you, ma soeur, colleague, et plus grande amie)."

Simca's friendship with Louisette was a long and complicated relationship that had begun in the grim months immediately after the war, when Louisette returned to France from Detroit and relayed an American friend's suggestion that she write a cookbook about French cooking for an American audience. When she enlisted Simca's help, the suggestion literally catapulted Simca out of private life into the world of the Parisian "gourmettes," and her professional career began. So it was a combination of loyalty and sympathy because of Louisette's difficult marital situation, plus the involvement of each woman in giving cooking lessons, individually or in tandem, that provided strong reasons for Simca's tolerance. Julia maintained cordial, even friendly, ties with Louisette, although Paul was convinced that she was up to nothing short of a game of *chantage*.

Royalties and authorship were, of course, the basic issues posed by the tripart collaboration, but others arose as well. After the book was under contract with Knopf, Simca's proposal to publish menus and recipes in France's *Cuisine et Vins* was accepted, and the monthly articles carried the byline Les Trois Gourmandes. Simca and Julia continued the same procedures they had used in writing the book. They sent ideas for menus and dishes to each other; then Simca sent the actual working recipes to Julia for testing and writing. Louisette received 10 percent of the payment for the articles because her name was a part of Les Trois Gourmandes. And presumably she was entitled to use the special monogram that Simca had had designed for the Gourmandes as well.

A far less manageable issue involved teaching under the banner of L'Ecole des Trois Gourmandes. Julia had tried to copyright the name in the States but was unsuccessful, so there was no way to prevent Louisette from using it independently to publicize the cooking lessons she gave from time to time. Julia's concern that the practice might undermine the professionalism that both she and Simca were seeking to establish, however, was appeased during the 1960s, when Simca joined Louisette in offering an extensive program of classes under the name L'Ecole des Trois Gourmandes in Louisette's apartment on the avenue Victor Hugo.

For her part, wherever Julia found herself, she discovered either American women associated with the embassy or diplomats' wives who wanted lessons. In Marseille, Bonn, Washington, and Oslo a pattern developed. She usually taught a group of six or eight women in one of their kitchens. In some cases, after the preparation of three courses, there would be a luncheon for the students and their guests. At other times, the novice cooks prepared three courses, served the first course and dessert for lunch, and took the entrée home for dinner. It was always participatory, informal, and "fun." Planning and shopping for the lessons kept Julia busy on teaching days, and the hours spent with her students also kept her aware of what procedures worked and what didn't. In her correspondence with Simca, she continually focused on what could be learned if good students not only were taught good techniques but actually prepared the dishes and enjoyed them later. The important thing was to develop a critical sense of taste, and this was exactly what she had been doing herself during so many years abroad. When she revisited Paris, she dined in good, but not necessarily the most expensive, restaurants and noted the freshness of ingredients, the smoothness of sauces. When she and Paul occasionally ventured into a restaurant in Oslo, she was more often than not aware of the shortcomings of good ingredients prepared badly. Technique was essential, and teaching was the best way to communicate it—informally or under the aegis of L'Ecole des Trois Gourmandes.

Teaching, preparing the final text of the book, and continuing to exchange ideas and recipes with Simca for the *Cuisine et Vins* articles eventually occupied so much of Julia's time that she was unable to enjoy all the advantages of living in Oslo. But the views of the fjords and hills from her windows were a never-ending source of pleasure, and the sight of entire families spending their free time on skis tempted her into a modest skiing program of her own until the snow on the ground disappeared. Spring was long and cool, and in the early days of summer Paul was especially busy with Fulbright scholars and American students who were participants in one academic program or another. As August neared, Julia expected their usual flood of visitors, and when they arrived she prepared for them various local dishes—gravlax, grilled lamb, and babas garnished with blueberries from the garden. At the end of the month, her eighty-year-old father and her stepmother visited them on the first part of their trip to Germany and Portugal. After a three-day tour of the fjords with them, however, Julia was again at work on the revisions that seemed interminable.

The book in its final form slowly evolved during the fall months. Line drawings rather than color photographs of stylish dishes were chosen as illustrations. Paul's "over-the-shoulder" photos of Julia's hands performing various procedures from the perspective of the cook became the reference point for Sidonie Coryn's drawings. By the end of November, Judith Jones announced that the staff had finally selected a title, *Mastering the Art of French Cooking*, and Julia sent it along to Simca saying that it was perfectly all right with her if the salespeople thought it would sell books.

While Julia was busy going over the corrected manuscript from the copy editor, Paul was busy making plans of his own. With the reality of turning fifty-nine on January 15 only a month away, he decided that Norway would be his last tour of duty. Through the years the press of his work had left little opportunity for painting, photography, and writing, and he wished to devote much more time to all three activities. And he was keenly aware that Julia had made difficult moves at some rather disadvantageous times because of his career. Now, he decided, it was his turn to put her career first. Admittedly the prospect of settling into their Cambridge home after so many years of moving from place to place also had no small part to play in their mutual decision to leave Oslo in May 1961.

In February the manuscript of *Mastering the Art of French Cooking* went into print, and the succession of galleys sent to Oslo and then forwarded to Paris sorely strained Julia and Simca's working relationship. Simca didn't like the title, became upset with mistakes in the French recipe titles, and frequently questioned the ingredients she didn't remember she had incorporated into her original recipes. Julia simply could not believe the number of inconsistencies and omissions that had gone unnoticed from the manuscript to the galleys and had nightmares about not correcting them before the page proofs were printed.

Their second spring in Norway was particularly colorful, and Julia grew a bit nostalgic about leaving Oslo, with its magnificent scenery, the excellent theater they had grown accustomed to, and the friendly people. Especially touching was a gala farewell dinner prepared by her students featuring the various dishes she had taught them. The *mousselines de poissons*, coq au vin, and *choux à la crème* were perfect, and Julia was both pleased and gratified that the recipes she and Simca had so painstakingly worked out had been so easily learned. Although the Childs had planned to spend almost two weeks in the fjords and at least two more weeks in France before departing for the States, they decided to leave Norway and return directly to the States on May 27. "We have both decided that nothing shall stop this book—wars, revolutions, hurricanes, nothing," Julia wrote to Simca. "I think you would agree that the book is more important than anything." They planned to be in New York by June 5 in order to confer with Judith Jones before going on to Cambridge to correct page proofs with Avis DeVoto.

From June until August 15, the Childs worked on page proofs and prepared an index, which Julia felt had to be a great big index so that the reader would be psychologically prepared for a great big book. They then anticipated the book's debut in mid-September. Although Avis had made her Cambridge home available to them, they spent most of the summer at Paul's twin brother's home in Pennsylvania. The final three weeks of their transition they spent in Maine, before driving south to Cambridge on August 15.

When Julia and Paul entered the driveway of their home on Irving Street, the exterior of the house seemed a darker gray than they remembered, and the interior rather brown. The floors were in poor condition, the electricity old, and the apartment on the third floor needed a separate stairway and entrance. But the rooms, especially the kitchen, were large, and there were enough of them to accommodate their special interests. A few days later, when

Judith Jones told Julia that Craig Claiborne had seen the galleys of the book and wanted to interview and photograph Julia in her Cambridge kitchen, they decided to get the kitchen in order first. The professional gas stove was moved from their recently sold Georgetown home. But the lighting in the kitchen was poor, more windows were needed, and the butler's pantry and regular pantry would have to be remodeled into a pastry room and a multipurpose bar, open shelf, and cabinet area. Paul gingerly took charge of designing the room with the familiar arrangement of pots, pans, and cooking utensils mounted on pegged board, while Julia and Simca sent letters back and forth across the Atlantic planning their self-generated publicity campaign.

From the office of the vice president down to the publicity department, the people at Knopf were impressed with Mastering the Art of French Cooking, and with the first copy in hand, William Koshland called Avis on September 22 to thank her for steering it their way. Julia and her French collaborators were also pleased with the magnificence of the whole. Simca planned to fly to New York the third week of October to tour major cities with Julia, giving in-store cooking demonstrations and attending book signing parties arranged by friends and acquaintances.

The two months following the publication of Mastering the Art of French Cooking on October 16 were nothing short of a coup d'éclat. Craig Claiborne called it "probably the most comprehensive, laudable, and monumental work on the subject," written "without compromise or condescension." And Michael Field simply said that it surpassed every other American book on French cooking already in print. On October 22, Simca arrived in New York to a schedule of meetings and lunches arranged by Julia and Judith Jones. The editor of Vogue met them at the Cosmopolitan Club; they lunched with José Wilson of House & Garden magazine the next day to plan a six-page article; and the same day they were interviewed on the Martha Dean radio show. Before leaving for Boston and points west, they also met Dione Lucas, who offered to give them a book party at her own restaurant, the Egg Basket, before Simca returned to France in December, and they had lunch with James Beard at The Four Seasons.

The realization "We are in. Hooray!" propelled the two authors from New York to Boston, Detroit, San Francisco, Los Angeles, and Chicago, and then back to New York. Julia prepared their props long before Simca arrived. White aprons with the monogram of L'Ecole des Trois Gourmandes, French omelette pans, utensils, and sharp knives would be carried in what was to be the first of the many "sacred black bags." And she had made all the reservations for trains and planes. Whenever possible, they stayed with friends and Julia's relatives because the trip was strictly do-it-yourself, not subsidized by Knopf. Visiting prominent department stores, they started at 10:30 A.M. and continued nonstop all day preparing Roquefort quiche, sole in white wine, and chocolate madeleines, and they baked *Reine de Saba* cakes in the test kitchens of big-city newspapers as a part of their interviews. Sometimes the facilities were so unsuitable for cooking demonstrations that their pots and pans had to be washed in the ladies' room. But Simca, Julia, and Paul had found their stride.

Arrangements for the party at the Egg Basket were made long-distance between California and New York. Although the actual party was a tremendous success and the authors met a veritable who's who of culinary celebrities, the effort to stage it all became more memorable in many ways than the event itself. By arrangement, the Childs and Simca were to be responsible for the invitations and some of the dishes. But in Dione Lucas's charming but somewhat quirky way, many of the other arrangements simply were not made. When they arrived in New York, Simca, Julia, and Paul realized that tables and chairs had to be rented and wine procured, and the "stuffed lamb" entrée would have to be prepared in the studio apartment of Paul's niece. Cases of good wine appeared when Simca contacted an old family friend. Paul supervised the printing of the menu, juggled the seating arrangements, and served as porter, diplomat, and general indispensable factotum. With Dione's fish course and dessert, the dinner came off in grand style. It was a fitting tribute to the book that Dione thought was an excellent contribution to the cuisine she had in her own inimitable way popularized in *The Cordon Bleu Cook Book* in 1947.

Before leaving New York, Simca and Julia accepted John Chancellor's invitation to appear on the *Today* show. They both agreed that Simca should demonstrate how to make an omelette, and toward that end Julia and Paul coached her in the now familiar apartment of Paul's niece. "With panache, Simca," Julia coaxed. "Toss that omelette! Ham it up, and make it visual fun for the audience." And, of course, she did. Not only was it a foreshadowing of things to come, but the TV appearance also established the link between the book and the cook in action. It was not lost on Julia. That teaching and cookbook writing were interconnected had been demonstrated in *Mastering*. In the spirit of the sixties, it was only a short step from the interaction in the kitchen on the top floor of 81 rue d l'Université or the apartment overlooking the Vieux Port or the dining room of the house on Irving Street to the studios of Boston's WGBH. The occasion was the only thing wanting to make it happen.

The seven weeks during which she and Simca had seen their book successfully launched had been both difficult and exhilarating, and Julia's first letter to Simca communicated the latter: ". . . how much we accomplished. I think it was a good thing, and thank heaven you came. Without you, I would have been quite useless as a promoter, and it would have been too bad. And thank heaven that final Friday evening turned out well! Frances Heard of *House Beautiful*, whom I talked to, said she thought it was the nicest party she had ever been to. Thank heaven! And we have made a good friend, and met a fine girl in Dione. And the fact that we are now accepted by the big food people is perfectly wonderful—we are now *quelqu'un*—Hooray." And in the same letter she reported that the house was entirely papered with fresh new wallpaper and the kitchen painted a beautiful blue, green, and white. They were still months away from being settled, but they were prepared to do it slowly now that they were in the place they most wanted to be.

After spending the preholiday days in Connecticut with Paul's niece and all the other Childs, Julia and Paul returned to Cambridge for their first Christmas on Irving Street. They planned a quiet one because Julia was scheduled for a hysterectomy on January 2. She wrote her first article for *House & Garden* before she left for the hospital and typically was more concerned about her *pauvre petit époux* alone in the house—"Who will cook for him, hold his hand, etc.?" But after little more than three weeks of convalescence, she was busy sorting out cookbook expenses, preparing income tax information, and helping Paul send out Valentines, a practice they had adopted years earlier as an alternative to Christmas cards. She was also engaged in correspondence with Simca about their recipes for *Cuisine et Vins*. When they were not occupied with planning dishes appropriate for the coming season, they were busy testing recipes for the magazine. And each was keeping a separate list of errors (which they thought excessive) in the first printing of their book and still present in the second printing. By mid-February 20,000 copies were in print with the third 10,000 on order. But Julia was impatient with the slow sales.

When Beatrice Braude, a friend they had known in Paris who was working at Boston's educational TV station at the time, suggested that Julia might be able to publicize *Mastering* on one of the station's book-review programs, she readily agreed to an interview, which aired in late February. Julia's account of the taping was a mere postscript in her letter of March 2, 1962, to Simca: "Last Monday I was asked by a local station here to appear on a ½ hour TV show, so we did. They wanted something demonstrated and had a hot plate! Knowing about hot plates, I not only brought omelette pans, but copper bowl, vegetables, and the works, just in case the hot plate didn't work. But it did work, so I made an omelette, then beat egg whites in the bowl, and fluted some mushrooms, and talked. The man interviewer was extremely nice, liked to cook, etc. Haven't heard a word of response and don't know anyone who saw the program except Avis, the Bob Kennedys, and our butcher. As usual, reviewing the thing afterwards, I could have said much much more about the book! 'Omelettes are illustrated in the book. Egg whites are illustrated in the book. Fluting mushrooms and cutting up veg, etc. etc. etc.' Dumb of me! Paul said I gasped less than usual, but talked too fast at times." On the other hand, WGBH received twenty-seven letters about the interview, expressing delight, asking for more. And as Russell Morash, a young producer-director at the station, put it, "Twenty-seven letters might not mean very much to a major network, but to a small, noncommercial station like WGBH it was impressive." He asked, "Would Mrs. Child be willing to consider doing a pilot program for a possible series of cooking shows?"

Julia was, and she did.

Bon Appétit

*This TV business has really become a whole life,
but it has crept up so slowly, I didn't get on to it.
I have always considered myself as a cookbook
[writer] and a teacher-vis-à-vis, and now find that
the TV is usurping these roles. Of course the TV
is selling the book, which is a great ego as well as
financial satisfaction, and the TV is a marvellous
teaching medium, but I am more at home in the
contemplative life of typewriter, files, and kitchen.*

JULIA CHILD

*T*he *French Chef* series, which debuted on Boston's public television station, WGBH, on February 11, 1963, was not only the validation of Julia's professional career, but also the beginning of a future of fun, friends, and fabulous good fortune. After almost fifteen years of "Care of U.S. State Department" postal addresses, Julia and Paul settled into the Cambridge scene and became part of Harvard's "02138 zip code set," distinguished by members of a cultural, academic, culinary, and politically active community who ranged easily from Boston to New York to Washington. And after more than ten years of a demanding apprenticeship in mastering the art of French cooking and successfully translating that cooking into an American idiom, Julia was at last beginning to move beyond what she would always call the solitude of cookery bookery to the great pleasure of "cooking for company in company."

Despite her first faltering steps in the showroom kitchen of the Boston Gas Company, where she made three pilot shows for WGBH in June of 1962, Julia's educational TV cooking programs captured the audience's attention in a more commanding way than those of any of her predecessors who had tried to use the visual-audio medium to teach cooking techniques. In 1946–47 James Beard's fifteen-minute segments on a commercial show, sponsored by Borden and called "Elsie Presents—James Beard in I Love to Eat," were primarily product oriented. In the 1950s, CBS's *Dione*

Lucas' Cooking School introduced Americans across the country to demonstrations by Gourmet Cooking School's Dione Lucas, who was billed in the heartland as television's "supreme European epicure." American audiences, however, were apparently not quite prepared for *poulet en demi-deuil* or *roulade Léontine*, or for the talented but somewhat quirky Dione Lucas. In 1962 Julia approached French cooking determined to take the "ooh-la-la" out of it rather than stress the complexities of a daunting recipe. Passionately believing that cooking is a "hands-on" experience, she patted plump chickens, minced garlic cloves with gusto, sampled the dish in progress, gingerly wiped her hands on the towel always at her waist, and beamed approval at the evolving dish with a "try it" smile.

With the Kennedys in residence in the White House in the early 1960s, French cuisine, especially official dinners prepared by their French chef, René Verdon, attracted attention. And with more Americans traveling abroad than ever, Julia was in the right place at the right time to introduce French cooking to the American public. But when she saw herself on television for the first time, she wondered why. After enjoying a steak dinner with a group of friends, the Childs took their newly acquired TV set out of an unused fireplace where it was kept out of sight and tuned in to the pilot show. Julia later described her reaction: "Here was this woman tossing French omelettes, splashing eggs about the place, brandishing big knives, panting heavily as she careened around the stove." To the true believers in the excellence of French cuisine, the program reinforced the appeal of *Mastering the Art of French Cooking*. To TV buffs, Julia was the embodiment of showmanship, a natural "ham," and, interested in cooking or not, they were enamored of her.

After the airing of the pilot shows, Robert Larsen, director of programming at WGBH, contracted for a series of twenty-six shows which went into production in January 1963. A fire in the studios of WGBH several months earlier necessitated taping the shows in an improvised location on the third floor of the Cambridge Electric Company, which boasted only a mobile unit parked in the lot next to the building for a power source and a fire escape and freight elevator for access. The early shows were all remotes, videotaped with two cameras linked by cable to the mobile unit. The nonprofit station financed the series, and the budget was so low that only one rehearsal was held before a taping and anyone who was interested in cooking could watch and learn firsthand by volunteering to wash dishes. To help cover expenses for the ingredients for the more elaborate shows, the prepared dishes were often auctioned off or enjoyed by the crew on special occasions. Julia and Paul did all the shopping and supplied utensils, serving dishes, and as much equipment as possible from their kitchen. On taping days they arrived at least an hour ahead of time to prep for the show or, if necessary, to shovel the snow from the fire escape.

Julia was soon part of a team dedicated to making the most ambitious TV cooking show to date succeed. Russell Morash was the producer-director of the show, but he also was responsible for other WGBH shows, so his assistant producer, Ruth Lockwood, became Julia's personal director. It was an ideal match, and from the days of the pilot shows, Ruth's instinctive camera sense helped Julia be herself at all costs. Julia enthusiastically described her to Simca: "There is a very nice girl, Ruth Lockwood, who is about my age. She and I work together all the time, and she rehearses with me. Is also very interested in cooking, and never moves without THE BOOK. She is just fine and devoted to the series. How lucky!" Together, Paul, Julia, and Ruth spent one day a week in the kitchen on Irving Street, drinking oceans of tea, planning the week's four programs, and working out provocative titles for the shows. Although there were no written scripts, time allotments and opening and closing lines were prepared ahead of time, as was the content of the program and the techniques to be developed.

The first thirteen shows were on simple subjects that used easy-to-get ingredients; the recipes became more complex as the series developed. But the idea of every show—from beef bourguignon to lobster à l'américaine—was "to take the bugaboo out of French cooking, to demonstrate that it is not merely good cooking but that it follows definite rules." What Julia had learned at the Cordon Bleu, practiced at L'Ecole des Trois Gourmandes, and expounded in Mastering the Art of French Cooking had become a culinary philosophy. More structured in her approach to cooking than James Beard (who once expressed the wish that he had written Mastering),

Julia had grasped the architectonic structure of French cuisine and demystified it for her American audiences. She not only knew the whys and wherefores of classic techniques but she also supplied the answers to basic questions about what to expect, what to do if something went wrong, how to substitute ingredients, and how much could be done ahead. She was analytic, and she communicated an enormous spirit of bonhomie. Asked if she was ever nervous about appearing in front of an audience, she simply said, "Think of the food, I always do." There was no such thing as a failure, she reminded her viewers, you are alone in the kitchen, nobody can see you, and cooking is meant to be fun.

The French Chef series proved it. Julia's old friends said the early black-and-white shows were the best—that in spite of the mishaps, or perhaps because of them, Julia was more herself than she would appear in the technically superior programs that followed. But Julia never regretted that the first thirteen shows of The French Chef were eventually lost because they were shown too often and there were no backup tapes. She felt that they were rushed and poorly conceived, that the pace of taping four shows a week had been too hectic, and that there were too many mistakes. She was chagrined when she raced through several steps only to have "time to kill" in the dining-room sequence. On the other hand, when an assistant forgot to take a pound of butter out of the refrigerator before a demonstration or a crêpe missed the pan, she seized the opportunity to show her audience how to cope with the common mistakes encountered in any kitchen. Behind the shrug and the smile of this telegenic home cook was a professional. And if audiences felt at ease and not awed in her TV kitchen, it was because she so unabashedly communicated the thrill of well-prepared food and didn't intimidate the novice cook.

Essentially an organized person, Julia devoted all her attention to the hundreds of details necessary for each show. "What a mess all mes affaires have been in during the last month, when I couldn't do a thing about anything but the TV," she wrote to Simca. "It is just so important to have plenty of rehearsal, and go through things exactly, and have a place for every knife, spoon, butter dish, flour jar, and fish piece. Our schedule has been: Saturday—plan and type up 4 scripts, Sunday—finish scripts and do laundry, Monday—9 to

6 rehearsal, Tuesday—10 o'clock hair done with Elizabeth Arden ($$$$$ but worth it!); PM—Do all pre-cooking, Wednesday— 8 AM to 6:30, TV tapings, Thursday—9 to 6 rehearsal, Friday— 8 AM to 6:30, TV tapings. OUF!" The hectic pace of two tapings a week continued from January until the end of March, with the taping schedule about five weeks ahead of the airing schedule.

When a pretaped show aired, Julia became aware of the interest the subject generated. After she demonstrated beef bourguignon, French onion soup, and chicken poêle, the station received more than 500 letters, amazing to read but time-consuming to answer. There were also letters requesting printed copies of the recipes. When the *Boston Globe* asked Julia to do a column, including the recipe, which would anticipate the next week's show, she readily agreed. The public had already caught something of her infectious enthusiasm and showmanship in the kitchen and wanted more of her. Paul had always said that with Julia there was "no fakery, no pretense, very free, natural, the same off screen as on." Viewers agreed.

And she was a quick study. Russell Morash called her "a real craftsman" because of the ease with which she learned to be aware of the camera's eye, the flash cards, the restrictions of her movements. Having been involved so extensively in recipe writing and teaching, she was inclined to be a bit too expository, and Ruth Lockwood kept reminding her that television was a visual medium and that points must be made visually. Although she had to remember to hold things longer for close-ups, and to move much more slowly from counter to oven so the camera could follow her, she soon was as comfortable in the "set" kitchen as she was in the kitchen on Irving Street. And, of course, her simple blouse, navy blue chef's apron, and ever ready hand towel visually reinforced the experience of cooking in a home rather than a professional kitchen.

From the beginning of *The French Chef* series, Julia made a practice of repeating the technical points involved in the preparation of a dish—"don't overcook" or "baste a lot," or "don't crowd the pan," and by demonstrating what she meant, she visually reinforced it. She also never made a mystery of the ingredients she used; she emphasized shopping at the supermarket. Depend on the integrity of the fishmonger and "hug" the butcher, she advised her viewers. Whenever possible, she anticipated last-minute pressures on the hostess and divided a recipe into steps that could be executed in advance with directions for the final preparation. In planning a menu, she cautioned, never have too many dishes that require too much time just before serving.

The last taping of the first twenty-six shows featured lobster à l'américaine and crêpes suzette. Paul brought bottles of chilled Riesling to the studio, and after Julia redid certain portions of the show because the microphone against her chest kept short-circuiting when she touched the cooktop, causing her to clutch her breast in panic, they had a splendid party. Because the next series of shows in *The French Chef* sequence was already "subscribed" by Safeway Stores and S & H Green Stamps, the party was not a farewell but the Childs' way of saying thank you to the crew before they were off to Pennsylvania, Washington, and New York for a working vacation.

By the time the Childs returned to Cambridge at the end of April, Julia was ready to tape twelve more programs and to try to keep ahead of the deadlines for her weekly *Boston Globe* column. But she had time for very little else. She had to abandon giving group lessons, and although the Cambridge house was settled, her recipe files were still in disarray from the time she had spent working on the book and moving from Norway. Fortunately, Ruth Lockwood's duties now included attending to all *The French Chef* mail that the studio received and acting as Julia's manager in matters relating to public appearances. Whether from a ten-year-old admirer or an octogenarian, fan mail was something Julia paid attention to, answering with a form letter whenever possible but patiently guiding a correspondent through the steps of a recipe whenever there was a problem that might need correction in the original recipe. Fellow Cantabrigian and old friend Avis DeVoto also offered to help whenever necessary, but it was becoming apparent that Julia would soon need a secretary.

Meanwhile letters went back and forth from Paris, or more often Plascassier, and Cambridge. Julia urged Simca to give lessons, continue her activities with the Gourmettes, and think about "our new book." Hoping to test recipes with Simca, Julia anticipated a two-and-a-half-month vacation in Europe when the current schedule of taping was over, the scripts for the next twenty-six shows were worked out, and the British edition of *Mastering* was edited. As Julia planned the trip, she and Paul would sail from New York on August 16, arrive in Norway for a ten-day visit, then fly to Nice to stay with Simca and her husband in Plascassier. They would then travel leisurely in France, cross the channel and spend some time in England, return to Le Havre, and sail back to the States on November 8.

As the date for their departure drew near, Julia finished proof-reading the British edition of *Mastering*, gave three demonstrations in and around Boston, prepared several advance articles for *The Globe*, and was busy planning a working session with Simca in Plascassier. Wanting to include recipes for croissants and brioche in their next book, she devised ways to pack enough American all-purpose and pastry flour to substitute for the soft wheat flour used in France. And because French ovens were often lacking in accurate thermostats, she planned to take along a good supply of thermometers for Simca.

With the same persistence that she had exhibited in the laborious years of preparing *Mastering* for publication, Julia now juggled her TV work, a weekly column, public appearances, and, on the back burner, her new book. But food—its availability, preparation, presentation, and enjoyment—always a passion, now became a way of life. And with the zeal of the newly converted and the focus of an entrepreneur, Julia also began to realize her unique position and to appreciate the fact that doors that had opened to her at the age of fifty could and would open to many others at a much earlier age because of her efforts.

Everybody was welcome in Julia's home, from students at the Culinary Institute of America, to James Beard swapping lobster recipes while he and Julia cooked together, to the Samuel Chamberlains, who were working on a revision of *Bouquet de France*. Irving Street became a stop on many cookbook promotion tours, and visiting chefs from France, especially, were invited to use Julia's kitchen and be interviewed in her dining room. "So far as the New England area is concerned, I am Mrs. Cook en chef!" she wrote to Simca. "Now, who would have dreamed of such a thing a year ago? No one. Just shows the power of the TV."

She also confided to Simca that it was a good thing that they had planned their trip to France so far in advance, because as the time approached she would simply have said that she couldn't do it, couldn't take so much work with her, couldn't leave their Cambridge house. But, as always, traveling in Europe, and especially visiting with Simca and her husband, Jean Fischbacher, were restorative. Julia loved the way that the Fischbachers had renovated the tumbledown old farmhouse, Le Mas Vieux, on the Bramafam property. With more rooms, more light, modern heating, and new bathrooms, it was the perfect place for Simca to write, teach, and entertain.

During the Childs' second visit there in 1963, after an idyllic luncheon of a special Dover sole soufflé accompanied by a bottle of chilled Meursault, Julia and Paul sat on the sunny terrace and decided to look at properties in the area. But for one reason or another, none of the available ones suited their needs. Jean Fischbacher then suggested that they build a house on the Bramafam property under an arrangement that would enable the Childs to lease the land during their lifetime and construct (at their own expense) a small house about fifty yards from Le Mas Vieux. Within a few months the building of La Pitchoune ("the little thing") began. When they returned to the States, their new home became another important topic of transatlantic correspondence. The number of windows in the back of the house vied with the newest version of *feuilletée au fromage* in importance.

And then in late November 1963, the Childs as well as many other Americans were caught up in a national tragedy that would make TV more of a communal experience than ever before. Reacting to the death of John F. Kennedy, Julia wrote, "Quelle douleur, as you can imagine, in this country over the assassination of our wonderful president. Nobody has felt like doing anything, except sit sorrowfully before the TV. Actually, the TV has been a solace, as one felt one knew what was going on, and that everyone else was right there too in spirit. It's unlikely we'll ever be so lucky in a president again—one so young, vigorous, intelligent, and handsome. What a wonderful gesture of friendship that President de Gaulle is coming to the funeral; that makes me feel a little better."

A born and raised Republican, Julia had become a "Stevenson"

Democrat after the war and her marriage to Paul. And along with many others during the early 1960s she associated the Kennedy presidency with a cosmopolitanism and vigor that she felt the former administration had lacked. The Peace Corps captured her imagination as did the civil rights movement. And as her personal influence grew, she unstintingly gave demonstrations and personally solicited funds for either political or educational causes that she supported. WGBH especially benefited from her dedication and generosity. For many years she accepted only a personal fee of fifty dollars plus expenses for each TV show. There was, however, another side of the coin. Julia was her own best salesperson, and the sale of her book was greatly enhanced by public appearances. The single most important factor in the soaring sales of Mastering was Julia's role as the French Chef.

Off the set and on it, she was attuned to her audience. They seem to like the bloopers best, she told Simca. And although she did not go out of her way to collapse a soufflé, crack a bowl, or drop an egg, she felt that any cook could and did encounter these mishaps. More difficult to explain are the dramatics that accompanied the various shows, like Julia donning a pith helmet and shooting a pop gun into the air to introduce the program "Small Roast Birds," or the giant saber she brought onto the set to carve her poulet sauté marengo. Perhaps these antics were a throwback to her tom-tom days; perhaps they were examples of what Julia called Ruth Lockwood's "talent for turning a recipe into a drama." But these attention getters were largely responsible for literally making "Julia" a cult figure in the confused and often polarized world of the sixties. If the medium was, indeed, the message, a more complex person than people realized was gradually becoming defined and, perhaps unfortunately, simplified by the instantly recognized persona named Julia.

Audiences couldn't get enough of her, JWs (Julia Watchers) appeared in the shops of Cambridge, Junior Leaguers volunteered to wash dishes and do prep work for her shows, and demands on her time continually increased. After the holiday season of 1963, Julia had nineteen more shows to tape, she continued to write her weekly column for The Globe, and she had agreed to teach a few classes for James Beard. On the eve of her departure for New York, she was exhausted from the latest schedule of TV tapings and still had two newspaper columns to write. That she had to make some changes in her life was becoming more and more obvious. "There was no fun in New York," she wrote to her newly acquired British friend the cookbook author Elizabeth David. "I finally blew, telephoned the editor [at *The Globe*], took a leave of absence [later made permanent]. . . . This TV business has really become a whole life, but it has crept up so slowly, I didn't get on to it. I have always considered myself as a cookbook [writer] and a teacher-vis-à-vis, and now find that the TV is usurping these roles. Of course the TV is selling the book, which is a great ego as well as financial satisfaction, and the TV is a marvellous teaching medium, but I am more at home in the contemplative life of typewriter, files, and kitchen. Well, I shall soon be so raddled and wrinkled that personal appearances will be disastrous." Her last observation, of course, seemed far from possible, because Julia was never unmindful of her appearance. She had given up smoking at the beginning of the new year, and she and Paul were very careful about getting their daily exercise and keeping calories to a minimum, dieting whenever the scale registered a gain of more than five pounds.

As for being more at home in the contemplative life of typewriter, files, and kitchen, Julia's words were more ambiguous. And during the summer of 1964, when sales of the book were averaging 8,000 copies every six months and Julia's royalty checks were literally building La Pitchoune, the complementary and often competing roles of cookbook writer and "French Chef" were becoming more evident. The success of *Mastering*, furthermore, had exceeded anything Knopf had anticipated, and William Koshland was interested in publishing a second volume as quickly as possible, but Julia's TV schedule prevented her from doing the kind of work on the book that she wanted to do. By midsummer, she had completed sixty-eight shows of *The French Chef* series and was under contract to do at least forty more by the spring of 1965. The material for the new book, of course, would have to be different, as would her role in the collaboration. As Simca liked to say, "I was the prime mover for Book I." For Book II, Julia had gained the confidence and the authority to shoulder the responsibility for both content and form.

Using the summer months of 1964 before the filming of the next

season's shows resumed, Julia worked on both croissants and brioche and tested some of the recipes that Simca had sent for the new
book. And she delegated most of her routine correspondence and
typing to her newly acquired secretary. She also freed more of her
time when she engaged the services of a cleaning woman and "for
the occasion" maids to help with entertaining, something she loved
to do but did not, in her opinion, do often enough except for
holidays. The house on Irving Street was also the scene of a gala
Bastille Day party when her visiting sister and her family mingled
with Julia's new TV family and they all celebrated with Champagne, *galantine de dinde, salade de riz,* and charlotte Malakoff,
subjects of the shows recently taped. But Julia was not content to
go over "old ground." What she most wanted to do was experiment with fondant frosting for petits fours and work on using
Wondra flour in the evolving brioche recipe.

No one was surprised, therefore, when she and Paul arrived in
Maine for their August vacation loaded down with not just her
usual armory of knives, spoons, blue denim aprons, whisks, and
skillets but a large array of bottles of peanut, olive, sesame, saf-
flower, corn, and cottonseed oils and also cake, all-purpose, rice,
and potato flours. All this stuff, she told Charles and Freddie Child,
was for a little something she was working on. As remembered by
Paul's brother, Julia spent days from sunup to sundown in the
kitchen experimenting. "After eight days of unremitting labor, she
finally made a batch [of brioche] that met with her approval. She
was overjoyed. I commented that she hadn't had much of a vacation working at the stove all the time. She only remarked that she'd
been having a glorious time, and she had." While Charles was busy
preparing an exhibition of his paintings and drawings, Paul spent
most of his time photographing, and Julia did what she loved to do
without the interruptions of phones ringing and deadlines looming.
All too soon, however, it was time to return to Cambridge and the
anticipated move into the new studios of WGBH.

The studio's new kitchen set was state-of-the-art "stupendous,"
complete with electric cooktops, two fine ovens, and a great work
counter in a beautiful, airy room with a French provincial ambience. But *The French Chef* crew was now in a large building rather
than on their own in an easily accessible loft, and Julia was con-

cerned that they might lose something of their "family spirit" with the move. Every show had to be taped within strict time limits. Everything had to be cleaned up in an hour, the set dismantled, and another moved into place. There were advantages, however, that outweighed the inconveniences. In addition to providing sophisticated sound and lighting, the move reduced Julia's taping schedule to one day a week. On Thursday afternoons she did two shows with only an hour and a half between.

For the most part, the 119 black and white shows in *The French Chef* series were adaptations of the classic *répertoire* with an emphasis on the cooking technique involved rather than the subtleties of prescribed garnishes and names. In a letter to Simca she described her anxieties and pleasure in doing the show "Soufflé au Chocolat": "I did the soufflé in a 7 cup oven-glass mold 3 1/2 inches high, with a 2 inch aluminum foil collar, making a mold 6 inches high. We found it took just 55 minutes to bake at 375°. So our nice young director got everything all set—found if we put it in at 4:08, and the show started at 4:38, it could come out around 'minute 26' in the show. And by gum, when I went to that oven and took out the soufflé, it was the most beautifully risen thing I ever saw in my life, and the collar came off perfectly, and there she stood. I managed not to look at all surprised, or unusually pleased, and took it into the dining room, showed how to serve it, and ate it—delicious it was, too. But I'm so glad that one is over!"

By late fall of 1964, *The French Chef* aired in more than fifty cities from New York to Los Angeles, *Mastering* was in its eighth printing, and Julia was tentatively scheduled for five days of cooking demonstrations in San Francisco for the last week of March 1965.

Toward the end of that winter, and before the grueling week of public appearances, the Childs spent most of February and the first week of March in France. Julia was guest of honor at some of the classes at L'Ecole des Trois Gourmandes on the avenue Victor Hugo, an event which a former student remembered as a frantic attempt by both Simca and Louisette to impress Julia. The Childs then drove to the south of France to view the progress in the construction of La Pitchoune and to make final decisions regarding its interior and furnishings. Under the Fischbachers' vigilance, it was rapidly nearing completion, and they looked forward to spending time there and offering it to their relatives and friends to use as a base for exploring the Alpes-Maritimes.

From France they traveled to San Francisco. Julia had resolved to make her public appearances more manageable. In this, as in every phase of her TV work, Paul was indispensable, arranging for lighting and water, acting as liaison with the women in charge, chopping whatever needed chopping, and being *"un homme d'affaires*, public relations, and commis—and wonderful as always."* Ruth Lockwood also accompanied the Childs, making many of the arrangements, doing the setups, assisting Julia on stage by unobtrusively moving things out of her way and discreetly holding up cue cards so she could move easily from one step to another. In San Francisco, Julia was also assisted by Rosemary Manell, a friend from Paris days and a talented cook. She did much of the prep work, and for the week's roster of recipes peeled tons of asparagus, made thirty quiche shells, and prepared lunch for the crew. As the week progressed, the key players in Julia's entourage and their roles became more clearly defined, and Julia became more confident that she could simply delegate much of the work entailed in these events. Unlike her TV shows, the demonstrations proceeded at a leisurely pace. She could comment on equipment used, answer questions, and feel more like a teacher, and she enjoyed it. Her usual fee was $500 plus expenses. Half went to WGBH, and the amount collected from tickets minus her fee went to the sponsor— Smith College Club, the Planned Parenthood organization, a local charity, or some other designated cause.

When they returned to Cambridge in early April, the busy schedule of TV work resumed, and Julia was caught up in filming a color "test" for viewing by the members of National Educational Television, who were in Boston for their annual meeting. She prepared a "Dinner in Ten Minutes" consisting of a *salade Niçoise, blanquette de veau,* and *tarte aux fraises* and was delighted with the difference color made. Every shade of the salad, the creamy colors of the blanquette, and the beautiful red of the strawberries gave a wonderful visual dimension to the food and seemed to open possibilities for a new kind of series. Because Julia had received the George Foster Peabody Award for distinguished achievement in educational television in the spring of 1965, there was no doubt that she would continue at WGBH. The only question was, would her shows be broadcast in living color?

During the last half of 1965, "You won't be hearing much from me" began to echo in her letters. Working out the scripts for the rest of the TV series occupied much of her time, as did the actual tapings. She longed to be in Plascassier, where Simca and Jean Fischbacher were completing and landscaping La Pitchoune. But it was not to be. And she realized that even her social life was drastically curtailed. Accustomed to catching a movie and then returning home for a late supper or attending a concert, she and Paul now had to put Julia's schedule first. There was also the nagging fear of simply getting stale.

Inviting Paul's brother and sister-in-law to join them, the Childs impulsively decided to spend the holidays and welcome in 1966 at La Pitchoune. After sailing from New York and traveling by train from Paris to Nice, they arrived at their new home two days before Christmas. Simca and Jean were there to greet them, the lights of the rambling one-storied villa were blazing, and there was a great *potée normande* on the stove. Although moving into La Pitchoune accompanied by five other people was difficult in the midst of the holiday season, Simca had the heat and hot water in working order and had made the house beautifully livable with carefully chosen curtains, comfortable chairs in the living room, and bedrooms furnished to the last detail. Paul and his brother hung the pots, pans, and utensils in the familiar "Child" arrangement in the kitchen. And a week later, the Fischbachers, Childs, and their guests enjoyed a wonderful New Year's evening with Dom Pérignon, foie gras, and oysters.

During the three months of their settling into La Pitchoune, the Childs worked out arrangements to frame their terrace with olive trees and mimosa, and they partially renovated the old tile-covered *cabanon* next to the house so it could be used as a spare bedroom and a studio for Paul. Because Simca had classes to teach, the Fischbachers returned to Paris shortly after the first of the year. But by phone (now so convenient) and by letter, Julia shared her ideas and experiments with her friend to file away for the time when they would be working together. Now that La Pitchoune was a reality, the Childs planned to use it during the holidays and for as many months as possible when Julia was not involved in TV work.

Even though she had intended to limit her activities after she returned from France in the spring of 1966, Julia agreed to be a "consultant" for the first book in the Time-Life series on Foods of the World, believing that it would not cut too deeply into her working time. She told Simca, "I will have nothing to do with recipe writing or anything like that, only yes or no. . . . They have an enormous staff, recipe finder people, an overall good writer, and all sorts of test kitchens and money $$$$$$, and of course the Time-Life staff to draw from. They want typical, authentic recipes in the book, yet ones which can be done by the average US housewife. Will be interesting to see what happens."

Although at the moment there was nothing on booksellers' shelves, including Elizabeth David's *French Country Cooking* and the newly translated *L'Art Culinaire Moderne* by Pellaprat, that in any way overshadowed *Mastering*, Julia thought it was better to be on the "inside" of the first book in the series, especially because it was on French cuisine bourgeoise. The enticement of the consulting arrangement was, furthermore, an opportunity for her "to get out and see more people," to meet M. F. K. Fisher, the designated author of *The Cooking of Provincial France*, and Michael Field, the book's editor.

In the summer of 1966, Julia also won an Emmy for the first show on educational TV that was ever so honored by the industry. She made little of the "banquet type of thing" with 1,500 people in attendance, even the award itself ("a sort of TV Oscar"), choosing to tell Simca about the WGBH auction, an annual event that she and Paul contributed to by appearing at the station and soliciting donations for everything from a Volkswagen to crates of dog food to copies of *Mastering*. What she didn't tell Simca was the sort of end-of-the-line treatment that public television's cooking show received or the fact that the award was presented to her at her table after the ceremonies were over. She chose not to regard it as a slight, but there were many critics who were not as unforgiving of the arrangements committee. Julia was simply breaking new ground again, and awards to public television shows became more frequent in subsequent years.

Because she had an agreement with WGBH that she would not

begin a new series of TV shows until Volume II of *Mastering* was written, the station planned to schedule reruns of *The French Chef* series in cities that had previously carried the program and extend the series to approximately 104 stations that had not subscribed to it in the past. When the new stations requested recipes for publicity purposes, Julia was dismayed to find that so many of them that had been station handouts or printed in newspapers were poorly written, incomplete, and not acceptable. Fearing that they might reflect unfavorably on her reputation, she began the arduous task of rewriting them and on James Beard's advice approached Knopf about publishing them in a simple paperback edition. But evidently William Koshland considered the sequel to *Mastering* to be more important, and the project was not pursued.

No one realized more than Julia that the audience for Volume II would be very different from the one she had addressed in 1961. Everywhere there was evidence that cooking at home was the "in" thing to do. And the success of *The French Chef* reinforced the idea that Americans were beginning to turn away from convenience foods, especially when entertaining. In a decade known for protests, there was also a reaction to the mediocrity and anonymity of processed food. Basic cooking techniques were emphasized as cookbooks proliferated in ever greater numbers. And kitchens were seemingly reinvented by architects and decorators as they opened into family rooms or, in the spirit of "country," became the heart of the house, the gathering place. If artichokes and snail butter were exotic foodstuffs to the readers of Volume I, they, along with beef Wellington and quiche Lorraine, were familiar menu items to the potential purchasers of Volume II.

Beginning with a series of what not to dos, Julia was determined not to create the impression that the second volume outdated the first. She was also convinced that the second book should not repeat recipes found in the first but should refer the reader back to the master recipes in Volume I. With a narrower focus, the new book would be a continuation and expansion of the first, with two strikingly new chapters, "Baking" and "Charcuterie." By mid-November 1966, Julia wrote to Simca detailing exactly those recipes that would be most crucial for them to work on together when they were both at Bramafam.

But as the recipes and format of the new book developed and plans for an extended stay in Plascassier became more definite, Julia found herself in the middle of interviews for a projected *Time* magazine cover story on the renaissance of cooking sweeping America. "I have heard from Avis [DeVoto] that Knopf has ordered 40,000 copies for its next printing, rather than the usual 10,000," Julia wrote to Simca, "so it [*Time* article] should have some happy effects for us. I find I am shamelessly avid for sales of our book. I can't say I would do anything at all, of course, but I will certainly expose myself (or you!) to any number of things which would have appalled me some years ago, when good breeding meant never having one's name in print!" Not only was Julia's name writ large as the most influential factor in America's culinary coming of age but Boris Chaliapin's portrait of her also distinguished the cover of the Thanksgiving issue of *Time*, which appeared the week of November 20, 1966. Although the editors featured "everyone else as well," Julia wrote to Simca, "they just bring us in as being the most influential."

The article caused more than a little excitement at the Child family's Thanksgiving dinner in Lumberville, Pennsylvania, and Julia thought it a fine story, but she was sorry that the picture of Simca teaching a class at L'Ecole des Trois Gourmandes had not appeared. Knopf reported that 3,500 books were sold the first five days after the *Time* article was published. The many benefits, both financial and personal, that the article had generated were only beginning.

With the need to get the new book into print more compelling than ever, Julia and Paul launched into a vigorous working period at La Pitchoune from mid-December until the first week in May 1967. Used to perfecting recipes for TV, Julia seemed more critical of the information Simca sent from Paris, and she was often distressed by Simca's stubborn persistence on some minor point. Working with well-known techniques, she felt that it was necessary to experiment with all the methods of making something like *pâté-en-croûte*, taking notes on every one that differed from hers. She explained to her collaborator, "I am sure this drives you crazy, but it is the only way I can work—I want to know everything, and why, and what's no good and why, so that when our master recipe is done there are no unsolved questions." But by the time of her departure from Plascassier in May, she realized that she probably would have to ask Simca to accept her "façons de faire" although they might differ somewhat from the instructions Simca worked out for specific recipes. One reason was Julia's reluctance to reinvest more time than the many hours already spent on each one, and another, perhaps more important, reason was the fact that Julia was "on the spot," the one who got blamed if the recipes didn't work. "If my method turns out to be wrong," she did not hesitate to add, "or if your method turns out to be better, it will naturally be changed so that the final result will be correct." But the final decision, she felt, was hers.

There were also other matters that had to be addressed in the joint venture. A series of meetings arranged by Julia's lawyer, Brooks Beck from Hill and Barlow, with both a legal representative from WGBH and William Koshland from Knopf took place to get publication rights defined, to know "who owns what and when in the way of TV recipes based on any of our book or books." Julia also wanted to change the rather informal arrangement whereby she acted as an agent for the other two collaborators so that royalties would be paid directly to each one by Knopf. What concerned her most, however, was to provide for the control of the book in the event of her untimely death. Citing the fact that she felt *The Fannie Farmer Cookbook* and *The Joy of Cooking* had been "ruined" by commercialism and heirs who were not cooks, she felt that the final control of *Mastering* should be in responsible hands.

The resolution of all these matters was time·consuming, and it inevitably focused on the collaborative arrangement and the delicate issue of Louisette Bertholle, now Comtesse Henri de Nalèche, who had contributed little more than the original idea for a book on French cuisine for an American audience. Although she had agreed to only 10 percent of the royalties, she had received over $20,000 during the five years since *Mastering* was published and an additional $10,000 as a result of the sales generated by the *Time* article. Whether to use her name on Volume II or effect a suitable "buyout" settlement with her became a pressing question. Further complicating the issues was Julia's renewed interest in publishing an edition of the recipes from *The French Chef* TV series, "to keep things going a bit until the new book is finally out." She had already expressed a desire to share the royalties with WGBH; the question of remuneration for Simca and Louisette was thornier. About one-third of the recipes were from Volume I; the rest were developed by Julia, although ideas and suggestions for them had been exchanged between Julia and Simca. On the other hand, Julia had really been an unpaid publicist for *Mastering* for over five years, and her TV show had virtually guaranteed its continuing sales. Her lawyer thought that the most desirable arrangement was to name her sole author of the TV book and to copyright all the recipes in Julia's name vis-à-vis her collaborators, and this was ultimately done in the contract for *The French Chef Cookbook*. Knopf also agreed to disperse royalties for Volume II directly to Julia and to Simca when a buyout settlement between the two authors and Louisette was amicably reached. Julia, however, retained the copyright for all the recipes.

During the fall of 1967, the resolution of these legal entanglements and a projected "Julia" tour of the White House kitchen with Chef Henry Haller were juxtaposed with Julia's determination to produce a perfect loaf of French bread with American flour in an American home oven. In Paris, Professor Calvel had offered his help with the French bread recipe, and Julia and Simca spent some time with him, but the recipe that would become the centerpiece of the new book had taken much more time than Julia anticipated. There was simply no way to complete the manuscript by December of 1967, as their publisher had hoped.

Although no TV shows were in her schedule, Julia was responsible for writing an introduction for *The French Chef Cookbook*, approving the page proofs of the Time-Life book on French provincial cooking, and recording the audio for the White House special—this had to be done in Washington in early February and necessitated a quick trip back to the States. Before they could return to France, however, a more serious problem arose that prevented Julia from resuming her work with Simca until late April. A routine physical examination disclosed a small tumor in her left breast, and an operation that was expected to be a routine biopsy became a mastectomy. After more than ten days in the hospital, Julia returned home, but her recovery was slow. She felt lucky, indeed, that neither radiation treatments nor skin grafts were necessary, but her left arm was weak and the muscles had to gain strength before she could return to France. Once there she continued to experience a pattern of postoperative "ups and downs" that would plague her for months.

From April until July, Simca spent as much time in Plascassier as her teaching schedule permitted, and she and Julia tested as many recipes as possible. But as had happened with Volume I, there were simply too many recipes to consider, adjust, and refine. So Julia returned to the States with a major job of editing and writing to do. At the end of August she wrote to Simca from Maine, "I am closeted with this tiresome Vol. II, and have been for all the time we have been here. This is the last book I shall have anything to do with, I think—too damned much work and no let-up at all."

She also began to realize that moving back and forth from Cambridge to Plascassier, while enjoyable, worked against the concentrated effort needed to complete the book. Although the Childs had decided not to spend the winter holidays in France, they relented and booked a round-trip flight from December 18 to January 8, 1969. It was agreed that James Beard would join them around December 30, and Julia thought it would be a wonderful vacation despite the fact that there were "comments on comments" that needed resolution, especially in the cake recipes. To no one's surprise, however, there were more guests waiting in the wings, and more distractions. The *Time* article had made Julia's recipes, advice, and lifestyle the most sought after copy on the magazine circuit. Not content to feature holiday meals served in the dining room of her Cambridge home, photographers and journalists wanted to follow her to Provence to re-create La Cuisine de Pitchoune for their readers. So it was not unexpected when Julia announced that people from *Vogue* would visit on December 28: "We must have much in preparation for that day and a magnificent lunch for them to eat. That should be fun, and will give them plenty to photograph."

The months following the Childs' return to the States in January 1969 were filled with a never-ending series of letters, experiments, first, second, and final drafts of recipes, and suggestions. Not really comprehending the amount of time and work that each of her recipes and suggestions required of Julia, Simca sent more and more material across the Atlantic with abandon or perhaps with the hope that her ideas would prevail. "Ne te décourages pas, chérie," Julia replied in her familiar franglais, "I am just being *extremely* difficile, which we both must be." And she hoped that Simca would not be too upset because only a small number of the "milliers de recettes" that she had sent to Julia were actually being used in the book: "That is why it so much distresses me that you are not writing on your own, so that your own things will be done the way *you* want them."

Julia walked the fine line between friendship and professional correctness, at times seeking to direct Simca's recipes elsewhere. For example, when James Beard indicated that *Gourmet* was definitely interested in an article to be called "A Cocktail Party Française," Julia told Simca that it would be a wonderful opportunity for her and might lead to a regular column. Julia also urged her collaborator to establish a culinary niche to display her talents as she herself had done in American television. If the French culinary scene was limited, American magazines and culinary schools, Julia thought, could certainly provide her with many opportunities to write and teach. But when Simca simply suggested that she save all of the extra recipes for a possible Volume III, Julia offered no encouragement: "Volume III? I have no desire to get into another big book like Volume II for a long time to come, if ever. Too much work. I can do nothing else, and I am really anxious to get back again into TV teaching, and out of this little room with the type-writer."

Getting Volume II into print had been a seemingly endless chore. For one thing, there was much more editorial involvement in the evolving manuscript than had been the case in Volume I, with Judith Jones occasionally flying to Cambridge to spend two or three days from eight in the morning until late in the evening going over the copy editor's corrections with Julia. The illustrations were also more elaborate and copious than those in the first volume. The same procedure of furnishing Volume I illustrator Sidonie Coryn with photographs taken by Paul was followed; however, Paul also did a series of technical drawings of shellfish, meat cuts, and utensils. The text had to be completely in sync with the illustrations and drawings, and Julia tailored her explanations and instructions accordingly. With firm deadlines looming for the completion of the remaining chapters, the Childs spent Christmas in Cambridge and welcomed in the new year not with the customary foie gras and Champagne they savored at La Pitchoune but with a toast to Volume II slated for publication in November 1970.

For over a year, work on the color series of *The French Chef* had been postponed because of Julia's total involvement in her book. But in May 1970, with only an introduction still to be written, the Childs were in Plascassier again. And Julia was part of a team from WGBH recording on color film French food markets, restaurants, kitchens, fishmongers, confectioners, bakeries, and, of course, people. To give *The French Chef* a slightly different format, the producers planned to insert the scenes into at least twenty-three of the thirty-nine programs of the new series, scheduled to begin in October. As resident photographer, Paul Child kept an accurate journal of the six weeks of shooting in France, detailing the "hundreds of large bowls full of tangerines, citrons, pears, sliced pineapples, and kumquats" that they saw being prepared at Maiffret, the best shop for fruit confit in Cannes. And while filming in Nice, he described the crew and Julia "all linked by electric wires as they move in concert from potatoes, to fish, to onions, to olives, to herbs, followed by mouth-gaping marketers in old Nice." From there, the itinerary included boulangeries, *pissaladière* shops, hilltop restaurants, and fish markets in Provence; Dehillerin's cookware store and Les Halles in Paris; and Camembert cheese makers at work in Normandy. Paul was in his element: "I was taking stills, Willie, huddling over his recorder, sat on the floor right by Julia's feet, his rear end covered with sawdust. He was taping questions and answers. . . . Julia and the little chef continuously shared a bottle of Vichy water to keep their throats from drying up." Julia wrote to Mary Frances Fisher, "How much more fun TV is than writing a book is."

Returning to the States in late August, Julia and Paul were soon into their TV schedule. On Monday they and Ruth Lockwood planned the two shows of the week. A rehearsal for the first one, including a complete cook-through, took place on Tuesday, and the second show was rehearsed the same way on Wednesday. Both shows were filmed in the afternoon and evening on Thursday before a live audience of one hundred who paid a seven-dollar admission charge for each. Like the earlier black and white shows, the color series required a staff of twenty-two technicians, including aides to help with the prep work and volunteer dish washers. Thanks to a handsome grant from Polaroid Corporation, there was, in addition to the special segments shot in France, a new kitchen, new set decor, and, of course, color, which had several pluses as well as a few minuses. Certain foods like mashed potatoes were so glaringly white they had to be toned down by mixing in egg yolks.

"Bouillabaisse à la Marseillaise" was the first of the color shows of *The French Chef* that debuted in October 1970, and over 200 public television stations carried images of Julia in the middle of Marseille's noisy fish auction, the Criée aux Poissons, as well as Julia simmering onions, leeks, and garlic as the first step in making the soup. The same month *McCall's* magazine, whose editors had negotiated the serial rights to publish a collection of recipes from *Mastering II*, began the series with a major article on Julia. Both were timed to anticipate the publication date of the book in November. Knopf highlighted the occasion with a much ballyhooed event that differed markedly from the "do-it-yourself" publicity campaign that Julia and Simca had devised for their first volume. "Knopf now laid on a big party in New York at a mansion on the Upper East Side, an impressive exercise in the grand style," Simca wrote, and she described a majestic staircase to an upper balcony and about 250 members of *le tout New York* (cuisine branch) circulating to taste the Champagne and the elaborate buffet. Somewhat restricted by her TV schedule, Julia nevertheless joined Simca in a publicity tour for the book, going from New York to Los Angeles.

With at least one of her books on the *New York Times* best-seller list often for several weeks running, Julia was as popular in print as she was on TV, and there was every reason to anticipate brisk sales of Volume II, especially since the reviews were, for the most part, glowing. The only discordant note was sounded by Nika Hazelton in *The New York Times Book Review* when she observed that the elaborate step-by-step recipes would appeal to the kind of people "who learn to drive a car by having the workings of the internal combustion explained to them in full detail. To those who, like myself, are overwhelmed and confused by the book's many details and many words . . . I recommend my method of preparing the luscious Child and Beck food. Take the recipe and write it out in conventional form."

And, indeed, there were others who took exception to the lengthy recipes, especially if they did not consider the book as primarily a teaching manual. Between *The French Chef Cookbook* and *Mastering II*, the recipe for Roast Suckling Pig swelled from three pages to five and a half, including four illustrations. The French Bread recipe (Julia was elected a member of the Confrérie de Cérès for this) required sixteen pages, and the comprehensive treatment of *Pâte Feuilletée* was developed in thirty-two pages. For many readers, however, these two recipes "launched *Mastering II* into the gastronomical stratosphere," and left Volume I behind "in a shower of spun sugar," making that "honorable world of trout mousse and cassoulet as naive as Spam."

While many of the black-and-white TV shows had referred to Volume I, many more anticipated Volume II. The recipe for half-boned chicken in the show "Operation Chicken" became *Poularde en Croûte* in the second volume and served as one variation of the *en croûte* theme that Julia was able to develop by referring her readers to the extensive baking chapter. Electing not to repeat the chapter headings of the first volume permitted Julia to focus more effectively and elaborately upon those techniques that were common to various recipes. Although the ingredients and timing were different in *Filet de Boeuf en Croûte, Gigot Farci en Croûte,* and *Jambon Farci en Croûte,* the "master" *Brioche* recipe was the same, and the procedure of encasing meat, fish, or pâté in dough had been established by repeated testing.

Whenever possible, Julia also demonstrated the use of modern mechanical aids rather than "the holy and Victorian feeling about the virtues of sweat and elbow grease" that marked the difference between France in the 1950s and the dawning of the age of the Cuisinart. Worth noting as well was the fact that Julia's TV experience with the visual presentation of recipes prompted her literally to double the number of illustrations and drawings in the second volume.

Because many have thought of *Mastering II* as simply a continuation of the first volume, it has not always been evaluated on its own merits, which are considerable. Undoubtedly, it is the book that Julia agonized over more than any other, not because it might not be accepted for publication but because it was being published by the most prestigious publisher in the business (she dedicated it to Alfred Knopf) and because she had to protect her reputation for conducting the most widely attended cooking course ever given in America. The book had to be good, and it was.

After the accolades were conferred upon *Mastering*, not only did Julia continue to prepare and tape the remaining programs of *The French Chef* (now playfully titled *The French Chef Faces Life* by Julia) through 1972 but her collaborators also seemed to find their stride. Collecting sketchy recipes from many of France's Michelin-starred restaurants and rewriting them, Louisette Bertholle published a handsome book called *Les Recettes Secrètes des Meilleurs de France*. And she planned to follow that publication with a book for beginners. Simca, with the aid of Patricia Simon, who wrote "The Making of a Masterpiece" for *McCall's* in 1969, published a book of "menus of the kind that I serve to my family and friends in France," incorporating dishes from the three provinces that formed the basis of her cooking repertoire. *Simca's Cuisine* not only enhanced her reputation in France but also opened doors in the States. From 1971 on, she occasionally taught at James Beard's Cooking School and gave demonstrations throughout the country. And then in 1974 she built La Campanette on the Bramafam property to accommodate the furniture that she had inherited from her mother. By design if not intent, the rambling, functional *mas* soon became a cooking school that attracted many students from the States.

Julia involved herself more in TV work and in doing demonstrations that would promote the shows and *The French Chef Cookbook*, which Bantam brought out in paperback in late 1971 with an unprecedented first printing of 540,000. But because the hardcover of that book three years earlier had also been so successful, Knopf now urged her to consider a book of the recipes from the current color series of *The French Chef*. In April 1972 Julia wrote to James Beard, "As for bookery from us, Son of the French Chef is *mijote-ing* on the back burner, and fortunately all the recipes are written and fully tested—but we don't know when we shall stop adding them. This will be a joint one by Paul and me, fully illustrated with photos."

With only the TV schedule limiting their time during the first half of the 1970s, Julia and Paul spent some of the most ambient years of their marriage enjoying the rewards of their efforts. Shuttling between Cambridge and Plascassier enabled them to experience the best of both worlds, and Julia's celebrity status opened doors from the White House to Le Moulin de Mougins. Limos waited for her; restaurateurs sent special dishes to her table. From San Francisco to the Gritti Palace in Venice, she was invited to give lessons and demonstrations. But there was also time, especially at La Pitchoune, for Paul to get his studio in order and paint and for Julia to enjoy Bramafam's resident *poussiequette*, read on the terrace, and savor simple lunches of French bread and wine with Paul under the mulberry tree. There were few telephone calls in what she lovingly referred to as Mimosa Land and few temptations except gastronomic ones. After a particularly joyous holiday ushering in 1973, Julia confided to James Beard, "I should be doing French Chef Book #2, but I'm really not ready to—will spend May and June here, and get it finished. Judith [Jones] says I should be more personal, but I don't know. I don't really like being personal in a book. Just because everyone else is being personal, why do I have to follow suit? NO."

Departing from the format of *The French Chef Cookbook*, which was a show-by-show compilation of recipes without further comment, Julia found that in assembling the seventy-two color shows of *The French Chef* that she wanted to spend more time on the recipes. To pull the strands of her past twenty-five years in the kitchen together, she works through the evolution and variations of certain recipes and shares experiences and anecdotes from the past. In doing so, she tells some interesting stories and presents a book that resonates with her own voice. She also takes a stand vis-à-vis the American exponents of nouvelle cuisine, reworking the sauce introduction of the book to mention the new reduction

French sauces while still recommending roux-thickened sauces as fundamental to French home cooking. As a result of rearranging the recipes into chapters, everything from soups to desserts has a context, a point, a reason to be, and Julia transports her readers into "a private cooking school."

The title, *From Julia Child's Kitchen*, set the tone of warmth and informality. She felt free to include Apples Rosie, Mrs. Child's Famous Sticky Fruitcake, New England Fish Chowder, and Cole Slaw along with French Croissants and Tripes à la Mode. The recipes are, after all, from her kitchen, and the photograph on the title page takes the reader into one of her more memorable kitchens, overlooking the Vieux Port of Marseille. That photograph, along with all the others, was taken by Paul. Missing is the caricature of Julia with the big spoon and garlic braid (also designed by Paul) that had introduced the French chef of the earlier book of TV recipes. In its place is a reflective Julia photographed in profile with only a table, a casserole, a wine bottle, and some fruit in the foreground. The handsome photographs that illustrate the book are a striking tribute to the country where it all began, the France that had enticed Julia with its cuisine and its seriousness about that cuisine.

With Nika Hazelton's criticism of Volume II in mind ("It hurts, dammit"), Julia addresses her "Fellow Cook" in the introduction and develops a strategy of full explanation, "to take up whatever hows, whys, whats, and wheres that I believe we should all know about." She also suggests that the cook's experience, dexterity, and sense of taste along with the ability to skip through the full explanations if not needed will ensure that all the important techniques will be mastered. But she makes it very clear that "cookery bookery" writers have a problem. Not wishing to insult the reader's intelligence, she chooses to err on the side of generosity by telling all. And structurally, the chapters progress from basic techniques to the application of those techniques in dishes that are derivations from and variations on the master recipes. From sausage making to French pâtés, from boiled beef to tenderloin in truffle sauce, from French brioche to American doughnuts and coffeecakes, the individual TV shows are regrouped into a thematic scheme.

Unlike her former books, this cookbook introduces the reader

to an unusual cast of characters—Caesar Cardini, Chef Max Bugnard, Colette, James Beard, Rosemary Manell, Ruth Lockwood,
and a host of past and present cookbook writers—and Julia tells
interesting stories about them within the text. Colette's special
interest in the Consommé George Sand that was served to Julia in
the dining room of the Hôtel de Paris in Monte Carlo in the early
1950s adds drama to the soup chapter. And Chef Bugnard's insistence that Madame Child make an omelette over and over again
does more than prove a point about practice in the kitchen. The
reader comes to know the teller of these tales as more than a
cookbook author as the narratives weave in and out of the recipes.

To think of *From Julia Child's Kitchen* as only a "how-to-do-it"
for those who missed a recipe on the TV show is to miss meeting
Julia the college girl who wanted to write novels and Julia the
accomplished cook who wanted to do it *her* way. "My own favorite
book is *[From] Julia Child's Kitchen*, which is entirely my own,
written the way I wanted to do it," Julia wrote years after its
publication. And in the context of the work that had preceded it
and the books that would follow, it is a celebration of French food
and American taste, and a triumph of the longer allegiance between
Paul and Julia, for which she gives "sincere thanks": "Those romantic photographic spreads at the beginning of each chapter,
those pictures that so much capture the atmosphere of La Belle
France, the lovely land that has made this book possible—they also
are Paul's, a handful collected from his years of observing France
with his fond artist-photographer's eye."

This tribute was especially poignant because it was written immediately before Paul's double bypass operation in October 1974.
From that time on, their lives as well as their sunny days in the
south of France would never be quite the same. Although Paul did
gradually and almost completely recover from the operation during
the early months of 1975, he was diagnosed with aphasia, which
caused some impairment in his facility to use and understand spoken and written language. For a man who had spoken foreign
languages easily and written letters with grace and style, the diagnosis was a source of considerable despondency.

While nursing Paul back to a semblance of their daily routine,
Julia completed the manuscript of *From Julia Child's Kitchen* by the

end of January 1975. And after a vacation in Bermuda in late spring, she and Paul spent a leisurely summer in Cambridge and Maine. Publication of Julia's new book in early fall, however, meant decisions about the advisability of more travel for Paul. Like troupers with an imperative for the show to go on, Julia and Paul agreed to go on a publicity tour in September 1975, promoting *From Julia Child's Kitchen* from New York City to San Francisco. Of necessity, they returned to Cambridge as often as possible so Paul could rest briefly between trips to major cities. To further ease the situation for him, Julia was assisted by Elizabeth Bishop in New York and by Rosemary Manell on the rest of the tour.

As they traveled around the country, Paul seemed to be in better spirits, although his mental processing difficulties were very slow to improve. What he heard did not always register, and his considerable linguistic ability was hampered when he could not recall or remember foreign equivalents for ordinary words. He still enjoyed painting, continued to write letters, and, of course, was always in the middle of the first row when Julia did a demonstration. If the dish she was working on was not centered exactly in the reflecting mirror, he motioned the direction toward which it should be moved. If time was running out, he signaled Julia. They were a team.

Whether preparing recipes from the book for department store shoppers or conducting more formal demonstrations, Julia enjoyed playing to a live audience. It was not as confining as TV work, and the informality gave her a chance to pitch the presentation to the interest of her audience. "Don't clap yet," she would warn when she finished a spun sugar cage for a charlotte Malakoff. And with good reason. Once when she accidentally dropped it, she shrugged and laughed. "We'll just have to do it all over again." And she made another one to thunderous applause. She was in her kitchen, and there might be 800 people there with her. "I know what it is about her," a member of a San Francisco audience said during an intermission. "She's just like a child playing. Anybody who has that much fun just has to be irresistible." James Beard often spoke of her "all-embracing quality," sweeping everyone up and carrying them away to the land of "can do."

The immediacy of demonstration work was only part of her

decision to give up *The French Chef* series in 1974. "We simply decided," she wrote to Judith Jones, "we didn't want to set aside 3–4 months of time to do 13 [or] 26 more shows. It's just too confining, and we are really prisoners, unable to do anything else. . . . We are not stuck with public TV, of course, but the only way one can get prime showing time is on those stations, otherwise all is for housewives in the daytime and that's not our audience."

Yet when an idea for a joint James Beard and Julia Child series dedicated to American Revolution-era cooking in anticipation of the bicentennial surfaced, the two worked out a pilot show in Boston at the end of February 1975. And indeed the series had possibilities. Having shared the kitchen at La Pitchoune and in Cambridge many times in the past, the friends worked well together, and they were assured that there would be a staff of researchers to do the basic work. But by the end of the year, Julia began to have serious doubts about making a commitment to the project, and Beard did not want to do it alone. Julia appreciated his decision: "If we all were 20 years younger, or even 10 years younger, it is fun to do. But it is a total life, 12 hours a day, 7 days a week, and nobody can tell you different. . . . That's why we pulled out of it—I just couldn't see submitting Paul to any more of that kind of life. And that's also why, really, I said NO to any cooking commitment with you. I just don't want to tie us up like that."

Considering Paul's condition and more than a little aware that in August she had celebrated her sixty-fourth birthday, she announced that 1976 was going to be a sabbatical year, devoted to traveling back and forth between Cambridge and Plascassier with perhaps only a demonstration or two. Furthermore, the Cambridge house needed some sprucing up, which meant spending an extended period of time there emptying cabinets and disassembling the kitchen for the painters.

Julia was also interested in promoting her friend Anne Willan's newly established Parisian cooking school, La Varenne. Months earlier the Childs had purchased shares in La Varenne, and Julia helped to plan and attended a gala cocktail party in New York to publicize the school and attract American students to it. Everywhere there was evidence that women were moving into the culinary profession, and Julia, by example and support, was in the vanguard.

Awards acknowledging her role in developing America's understanding of French cuisine came her way with increasing frequency—an honorary doctorate in humane letters from Boston
University in May 1976, and the French Ordre du Mérite Na-
tionale on December 15, 1976—and Les Dames d'Escoffier offered
Julia an honorary membership in February 1977. Department
stores like Macy's promoted "model" rooms decorated for famous
individuals; Julia's kitchen was one. *Architectural Digest* featured
the house on Irving Street; Horst photographed La Pitchoune for
House & Garden.

Because Julia sought to influence as many audiences as possible,
she accepted *McCall's* offer of a monthly column in 1977. And in
March of that year, she wrote to Simca about several planning
sessions for a new TV series: "Only 1 a week this time, and we will
stop at various places, rather than go right through non-stop a
whole half hour. We shall try to give the impression of a whole
meal, but show only 1 major and 1 or 2 minor dishes—as far as we
can tell now." Two months later, when the Childs were relaxing in
Plascassier, Julia pursued the project further, telling Mary Frances
Fisher that she was "getting down to the gritty of our TV show
planning." With her second *"sacquepee"* successfully performed in
Cambridge when they returned in August, she was ready to begin
taping the new series in October 1978.

Julia was convinced that the level of cooking in the States had
improved tremendously and that the public was well informed in
culinary matters. The new series, therefore, would have to address
a more sophisticated audience. With over 125 cooking schools in
the Los Angeles area alone, a show on "basics" was ruled out as
repetitive, and she felt that limiting herself to French recipes would
be too close to the format of *The French Chef.* Getting out of what
she called "the French straight jacket," she wanted to use techniques and recipes from everywhere, as she said, "do what I want
like Boston baked beans and a chocolate-chip rum cake!" And the
studio provided her with a fully equipped kitchen designed by Fran
Mahard to do it in. No more movable sets, and no more disman-
tling the kitchen from show to show. Also worth noting was the
greatly expanded staff whose skills she could draw upon.

Because the producers of the new series thought that the shows
would be greatly enhanced if the audience could follow the demon-

strations with a book in hand, Knopf agreed to publish a companion volume. With recipes to write and test, Julia obviously did not have time to write the book as well. So Peggy Yntema was hired to create the narrative sequences and write the text from tapes and by observing rehearsals. For this particular series much more cooking was necessary, not only for the display in the dining room adjacent to the kitchen (always the final scene of a show) but also for the photographs needed for the book. Julia was, therefore, assisted by Elizabeth Bishop and Rosemary Manell plus a number of volunteer associate cooks. Under Ruth Lockwood's direction, half the shows were taped before the holidays, and the rest were scheduled for the first three months of 1978.

In April the Childs left Boston for an extended vacation in Europe, visiting friends in England, touring Spain for the first time, and resting at La Pitchoune before the demanding business of publicizing the new TV series. They returned to the States in September and began a schedule of appearances in New York and various cities along the West Coast to promote *Julia Child & Company* and to attend the Emmy Awards dinner (her second nomination) while in Los Angeles. Even before the first *Company* series debuted in October 1978, however, a sequel of thirteen more shows, billed as *Julia Child & More Company*, was contemplated, with taping tentatively scheduled to begin in January 1979.

The series *Julia Child & Company* and *Julia Child & More Company* were both markedly different from the 200 *French Chef* programs. Using occasions like birthday dinners, potluck suppers, cocktail parties, barbecues, and dinners for the boss, Julia planned entire meals that made "gastronomic sense," exemplifying the principles of contrast, balance, beauty, savor, and style. She also expanded the idea of menus to include shopping lists and tips, variations because of season or availability, remarks about specific ingredients, use of leftovers, hints, and postscripts, as well as the actual preparation, cooking, and presentation of a recipe. The way that Julia herself, either formally or informally, entertained in her own kitchen was dramatized for audiences and readers across the land.

In an immediate and dramatic way, the series projected Julia Child's *cuisine personnelle*. Some of her signature recipes were recast into prevailing food styles, but many of the old familiars were simply enhanced. Bouillabaisse made with chicken became the centerpiece of a low-cal dinner. Making paella in an electric wok accompanied an essay on rice. Dishes as diverse as New England chowder and coulibiac were featured in different menus for different occasions. The *Company* shows and the books that accompanied them were warm, personal invitations, summoning guests via TV to have fun in the kitchen as well as the dining room. Part of the persuasion, of course, was Julia making it all look so easy in the stylish green, blue, and white kitchen dominated by a double oven, professional cooktop, roomy refrigerator, and heavily used food processor. And if her audiences did not quite relate to veal Prince Orloff in 1964, they could certainly savor eggs Benedict in 1978.

Both of the *Company* books also have something for everyone. The large format and profusion of handsome photographs certainly owe something to the "spare no expense" multivolume series on international and national cuisines published by Time-Life and to the ever-growing artistry of food photography exhibited so lavishly in French and American culinary magazines. But Julia also insisted that the "how-to-do-it" photos be taken over her shoulder, just as the illustrations in the *Mastering* books had been focused from the cook's and not the observer's point of view. If the photograph did not show the relationship of the cook to the food she was chopping, boning, sautéing, and assembling in front of her, no matter how appealing the dish looked, Julia believed it was useless as a teaching device. And both books were conceived with a simple premise in mind, namely that words, whether spoken or written, are not enough to make a recipe comprehensible. Visual aids— either the TV screen or photographs—are necessary to illustrate the ingredients, techniques, and final appearance of a dish, especially if there are unknowns.

Although both of the *Company* TV series and the accompanying books are similar in concept, there are some subtle and not so subtle differences between *Julia Child & Company* and *Julia Child & More Company*. For one thing, the occasions in the second book are more generic. "Country Dinner," "Soup for Supper," "A Vegetarian Caper," and "Rack of Lamb for a Very Special Occasion" focus attention on specific ingredients and the techniques of their preparation rather than on a defined party. And perhaps mindful of Mimi Sheraton's comments about "some unnecessarily gimmicky recipes that smack of ladies' magazine cookery," and "too many references to Mrs. Child's other books, an annoying feature when referring to a process needed to complete a dish in this one," Julia added a question-and-answer culinary gazetteer in *More Company* instead of the cross-referenced "Menu Alternatives" she used in the first book, and she promoted the tried-and-trues like cassoulet, *moules farcies*, and French onion soup gratinée.

Undoubtedly the addition of director Russell Morash's wife, Marian, an accomplished chef from Nantucket's Straight Wharf Restaurant, and Sara Moulton, an innovative chef from Cybele's restaurant in Boston's Quincy Market, to the *More Company* team sparked an already enthusiastic and accomplished ensemble. And their presence gave Julia much more time to experiment. Consequently, the recipes as well as the actual text of the second book are less dependent in an obvious way upon Julia's former books and current *McCall's* articles. And Peggy Yntema's prose more accurately capture the rhythms and verbal patterns of Julia's voice than the first book did. As Mary Frances Fisher said, "The language is better. The subtitles have caught the way JC talks."

Not everyone agreed. A prominent reviewer labeled the book "too chummy," with an overuse of *I*, and others complained that the book "patronized" the French. "What I like about it this time," Julia told Mary Frances, "is that it really is a 'joint' effort by a most devoted and enthusiastic team, and we had a rewarding number of months together." She did, though, think that there were too many pictures of her—an objection that was overruled by her team. In January 1979, the New England chapter of the National Academy of Television Arts and Sciences had named Julia Woman of the Year, and the *Company* team thought that she deserved every picture included in *Julia Child & More Company*.

The thirteen programs of the *More Company* series were completed in June 1979, and in August of that year Marian Morash invited Julia to spend a week prepping and working the "line" at the Straight Wharf Restaurant. It was her first experience in a professional kitchen serving from 80 to 90 luncheons and 125 dinners a day, and she thoroughly enjoyed every minute of it.

"How I'd love to do that kind of work more often, especially with people who are such fun to work with—a real team," she wrote to Simca, describing the *feuilletées* with lobster and white butter sauce and other seafood entrées that she prepared on the line while the two other stations turned out salads and desserts.

By September the *More Company* manuscript was proofread and the index, which Julia insisted on doing herself, was finished. Plascassier beckoned, and the Childs left the States to spend the holidays at La Pitchoune with a crew from *Bon Appétit*, who were commissioned to photograph a magnificent Christmas dinner à la Provence. What some of her colleagues might have considered an intrusion, Julia welcomed, and there was no part of cooking—shopping, prepping, sautéing or roasting, plating up, serving, and even the cleanup—that she did not enjoy. The phenomenon of journalists and photographers enjoying themselves at her table was all very "familial."

The new year began less auspiciously, with a quiet Reveillon shared with the Fischbachers at Le Mas Vieux. Not only the new year but also the 1980s would bring many changes to the four people who toasted it so happily. Simca and her husband traveled much less after the publication of her second book in 1979, and ultimately Jean Fischbacher's declining health confined them both to Domaine Bramafam. Julia and Paul still maintained a vigorous tour and demonstration schedule, but Paul became more sensitive to noise and confusion, tired easily, and found the harsh New England winters more difficult. Julia looked to the future, vowing not to be "old Mrs. Non-compos in a big Cantabrigian mansion in that c-o-l-d c-o-l-d climate."

Since childhood, California had been a kind of "paradise" to her, and it was easier to reach than the south of France. So the Childs decided to rent a place there for at least two months during the winter of 1981 and explore the area in and around Santa Barbara. While there, they purchased a condominium in Montecito Shores, which Julia enthusiastically described to Avis DeVoto as large enough with two bedrooms, two baths, an enclosed balcony for Paul to use as a studio, and a dining area that could double as Julia's office: "I am peering over my green meadow to the ocean waves . . . not too far away. I have my binoculars at my elbow too in case any interesting events occur, like fishing boats, surfers, walkers, or pussycats. . . . Soon we shall trot out to our swimming pool. . . . This apartment was a good move, I must say."

With the California residence a reality, many of Julia's personal affinities and professional activities slowly shifted to the West Coast. Strong family ties were already in place, but now in addition to Julia's sister, cousins, nephews, and nieces, Paul's widowed twin brother was staying with his daughter and her family in Pasadena. Visiting them and friends like Rosemary Manell, Mary Frances Fisher, and James Beard, who frequently taught in the Portland and San Francisco areas, kept Julia and Paul in the mainstream of West Coast culinary events. California also offered a splendid array of scenes for Paul to paint, the ocean and pool for swimming year round, a dazzling selection of fruits, vegetables, and wines for cooking, and small, excellent restaurants for dining. Proximity to the major studios in Pasadena also had its advantages.

On July 14, 1980, Julia ventured into commercial TV for the first time when she signed a contract with ABC to tape a series of short segments for the *Good Morning America* show. She posed only three conditions: "It has to be interesting, fun to make and useful, it has to be something I'd like to do. And it must be something we can prepare in the facilities we have." Under the able direction of ABC's Sonya Selby-Wright and with the assistance of longtime TV, book tour, and demonstration associates Elizabeth Bishop, Nancy Barr, and Sara Moulton, Julia made everything from apple clafoutis to watercress soup comprehensible in three-and-a-half-minute segments. The shows were so successful that her contract was extended into 1986, with the provision that segments be filmed in France, Italy, and California, literally wherever Julia happened to be engaged in some culinary adventure, whether it was the Escoffier Museum in Villeneuve-Loubet or a winery in the Napa Valley.

The approach of her seventieth birthday notwithstanding, in December 1981 Julia exchanged one monthly writing commitment for another when she gave up her *McCall's* column to become food editor for the weekly Hearst magazine *Parade*, with its 40 million readers. In her introductory article she wrote about why she was "glad" to be with *Parade*, citing "freedom to develop interesting subjects, [and] the opportunity to do some really fine photography with photographers I like to work with—Jim Scherer who did the pictures for our two Company books, and on the west coast, Brian Leatart whose work in Bon Appétit many of you may know. He's good, he knows food, and he works fast." The arrangement was ideal because Julia planned to spend extended periods of time in California and because she could also engage the assistance of Rosemary Manell as a recipe developer and food designer. From February 1982 until April 1986, they produced some of the finest culinary articles then appearing in American newspapers. Mary Frances Fisher collected the monthly articles with interest and was more than generous in her praise of them: "I always find something very good and very Julia."

During the early 1980s, Julia also gave a considerable amount of support to professionalizing the culinary community by actively participating in the newly established International Association of Cooking Professionals, even to the point of joining the ranks and taking the certification examination. She cofounded the American Institute of Wine and Food with the California vintners Robert Mondavi and Richard Graff; and an ongoing concern for culinary education was apparent in her continuing interest in La Varenne; her support of the culinary collection at the Schlesinger Library at Radcliffe College in Cambridge, Massachusetts; and her frequent appearances at culinary schools.

To keep the Julia banner waving was, however, her main priority. The comfortable but not ostentatious Child lifestyle necessitated it, and, as Paul's health continued to decline, Julia found in the culinary community the largesse of spirit and the commonality of purpose that made being one of that group, albeit an extremely successful one, very satisfying. When William Cross at Mondavi Vineyard wrote to Julia inviting her to spend some time with them because they were interested in developing a special week called A Private Week with Julia Child, she happily accepted. "The Mondavi Vineyard cooking 'do' was tremendous fun, tremendous work, and extremely rewarding to Rosie [Rosemary Manell], our nice friend Maggie Mah who helped us, and me (PC took photos of all the doings)," she wrote to Avis DeVoto after completing the cooking classes in Napa Valley in the spring of 1981. In the company of twenty or more cooks and waiters, "enthusiastic young people in the kitchen," she taught recipes that the participants dined on for lunch and dinner. Their meals were accompanied, of course, by the best Mondavi wines, "and we had to do as much prep as possible not only for our lesson but for the meal following it. Very much like working for our TV shows—intense work, but intense pleasure connected with it." Repeated at least three more times during the early 1980s, Julia's classes were extremely successful and good publicity for the vineyard.

In addition to the heightened interest in California's wines, a phenomenon labeled California cuisine began to shift attention away from the eastern culinary establishment, focusing attention on a new breed of restaurateurs and on the various ingredients produced on the West Coast. Olympia oysters, chèvre, Pacific salmon, sourdough bread, artichokes, and designer pizzas acquired a certain cachet. And just as Julia had read the culinary mood of the country by presenting chicken stew rather than coq au vin to the audiences of the *Company* series, she now began to put together a mélange of product information, wine savvy, and cooking techniques in a projected series called *Dinner at Julia's*.

Unlike all her other TV shows, controversy plagued the series from the very beginning. Hill and Barlow lawyer Robert H. Johnson, who had represented Julia since the death of Brooks Beck, and WGBH producer-director Russell Morash could not agree on either the budget or the format of the show, and Julia refused to take sides—"I'm a package that comes attached to Bob, who is our lawyer and friend, financial advisor, and literary, TV, and general agent. I just would not think of entering into any kind of business relationship without his advice and help." With a million-dollar grant from Polaroid to support a projected budget of $843,215, however, some of the financial difficulties regarding the project were at least partially eased. And when the decision was made to have Julia Child Productions, Inc., coproduce the series with WGBH Boston, the planning began.

Apparently striving to achieve an upscale "California" ambience, the series was filmed in a Santa Barbara seaside estate with guests arriving in Rolls-Royces and enjoying cocktails before they were ushered into the dining room for dinner. Julia's preparation of a main dish was still the centerpiece, but the program also included the "gathering" of an ingredient central to the menu, a dish made by a guest chef, and a wine selection and tasting before the actual dinner was served. While a pianist evoked the fleeting memories of the Tin Pan Alley tune "These Foolish Things," Julia appeared in a hostess ensemble appropriate to the guest list and occasion. Shots of guests sampling hors d'oeuvres and drinking aperitifs were cut with scenes of Julia in muddy boots foraging for chanterelles in the hills above Santa Barbara, or Julia in a yellow rain slicker fishing for salmon aboard *High Hopes*, or Julia aloft in a cherry picker gathering dates in Indio, California.

From the smokehouse or vineyard, it was a quick shift to a chef's dream kitchen, with beamed ceilings, hardwood floors, a brick fireplace, two large islands for food preparation, a professional chef's range set into a bricked arch, double ovens, and a separate wine cellar, where the wine sequences were taped. On cue Julia, now dressed in her familiar apron, demonstrated preparing boneless chicken breasts, grilled jumbo shrimp, Alaskan salmon steamed in white wine, braised sweetbreads in puff shells, and designer duck.

A parade of guest chefs from former White House chef René Verdon to Wolfgang Puck then met Julia in the garden or at the stove to prepare either a trendy first course—salmon soufflé with zucchini, Maine lobster in shallot butter sauce, duck breast *aiguillettes buissonnière*—or a delectable dessert, such as tulipe Marie Louise. And then to gild the lily a bit more, the scene shifted to a sampling of wines for the evening's meal—Robert Mondavi recommending a Fumé Blanc for the grilled shrimp, Louis Martini deciding upon a vintage Pinot Noir for the roast saddle of veal, and Richard Graff selecting a Chardonnay for the Winged Victory chicken breast, while Julia tasted the wine and asked all the right questions. If the audience didn't know that a botrytised Sémillon was appropriate for the orange soufflé, or that caviar and Champagne were a match made in heaven, the obvious delight of the guests at the dinner table and Julia's enthusiastic invitation to join them all again next week made the point with panache.

Julia thoroughly enjoyed taping the series and invited many of her friends and acquaintances to join the weekly party. In a card urging Mary Frances Fisher and her sister Norah to participate in the show, she wrote, "All going well with our programs, and we're mightily pleased with our format, which fits right in with whatever we're doing. We're expecting the Davies [Schramsberg Vineyards] and their champers [Champagne] this week, and shall give them Olympia oysters, sweetbreads, and maple mousse (the latter prepared by a young American chef [Bradley Ogden] from The American Restaurant in Kansas City—good to have some red-blooded Americans doing things)." But the logistics of time and transportation prevented Mary Frances and Norah from making a cameo appearance on the show, although James Beard, Judith Jones, and other friends did. With Marian Morash as executive chef, Rosemary Manell assisting Julia as food designer, an assistant cook, a food and beverage manager, two cleanup people, and three waiters, a thoroughly competent staff produced the series in style.

Certainly the most complicated and ambitious of Julia's TV programs, the *Dinner* series was also the most controversial. It displeased many loyal viewers, dismayed some members of her former team, and disconcerted many of her friends when it premiered in the fall of 1983. Audiences of WGBH in Boston, always somewhat protective of their celebrities, thought the Santa Barbara production did a disservice to Julia's homespun image. A devoted viewer tagged the new series an "embarrassment," suggesting that the level of menu planning seemed more inspired by Sheraton or Hilton hotels than by Julia Child's kitchen and that the program reflected a number of tawdry underwriting deals. James Beard missed the Julia of earlier programs; Mary Frances Fisher found the hostess of the *Dinner* shows "not at all the Julia Child I know and love," and Anne Willan simply thought her friend "ill-advised." If Julia had doubts about the series, Paul was her only confidant, and her only oblique reference to the criticism the show generated was the observation that if she ever did another TV series, it would be less "campy" and more informative than the *Dinner at Julia's* programs.

A spin-off of the *Dinner* series was, however, explored by Russell Morash and Knopf. Videocassettes by other cookbook authors were already on the market, and Knopf was interested in debuting their VideoBooks with a series that would capture the audiences of "America's most celebrated cooking teacher" in a culinary course of instruction for home use. During the taping of the *Dinner* series, Morash had taped additional "poultry" preparations as a pilot. And Julia was "all for an encyclopedia of cooking," especially if most of the *Dinner* team would do it and it could be done in Santa Barbara. It was not long before a plan for six one-hour full-color videotapes of cooking instruction took shape. Covering the basic areas of the cooking repertoire, the intent was to include poultry, meat, soups, vegetables, eggs, and fish.

In November 1984, Julia wrote to Mary Frances Fisher from Cambridge, saying that it was about time to leave for Santa Barbara, where she and Paul would spend the winter months and tape some video teaching cassettes: "I'm working on the scripts now, finding it difficult indeed to get, for instance, SOUPS, SALADS, BREAD, and PASTA into one comfortable hour. It is a question of elimination, and the retention of what really is basic, so that the viewer will feel he/she has gotten a good and satisfactory value. We'll have many of our same team, including, of course, Rosemary as valued colleague and food designer. Marian Morash will be executive chef, and Russ our Producer-Director. We'll not need an elaborate set-up, just a barn or a loft that we can fit with the prep kitchen and TV stove-sink-oven–work counter. Will be fun and fraught with interest."

Renting enough space for a prep kitchen, demonstration kitchen, and dining area at 40 Lospatos Way in Santa Barbara, Julia worked out the recipes with Judith Jones; then in fifteen-minute segments she and the crew taped the six one-hour cassettes that her devoted followers would welcome as "Julia's return." In *The Way to Cook* there were no more guest chefs, wine mavens, and candlelit dinner parties, just Julia in a denim shirt and chef's apron, her high-pitched voice cracking as she wondered if the Bavarian would ever slide out of the mold. What distinguished this set of culinary VideoBooks from others produced before or even after 1985 was, of course, Julia's TV reputation and her detailed explanation of the various techniques that she taught. The tapes worked because Julia knew her medium and her crew knew how to handle a TV camera.

A minor problem associated with the set of VideoBooks was that the accompanying pamphlets containing the recipes that Julia demonstrated were not designed to withstand the wear and tear of

the kitchen. But by the time *The Way to Cook* cassettes were dis-
tributed in the fall of 1985, Knopf announced that a new cookbook
with the same title would be forthcoming in 1986, and many of the
cassette recipes would be in it. "I have no intention of ever retir-
ing" became more than a statement in a publicity kit; Julia was
determined to go on "till I drop."

Although Julia enthusiastically became computer literate in the
mid 1980s, "the miraculous improvement of getting ideas down on
paper" with a word processor could not offset the serious interruptions in her work schedule that slowed progress on the new book.
Paul, who was still somewhat grief-stricken over the death of his
twin brother in 1983, seemed to tire more easily and was often
impatient with himself because his memory did not serve him well.
Julia tailored her plans to his moods and needs, traveling whenever
it was good for him, declining engagements if they proved too
strenuous. Seeing Jean Fischbacher steadily decline while they were
in Plascassier in November 1984, then receiving the news that their
friend James Beard had died on January 23, 1985, deeply saddened
both Paul and Julia. And Beard's death only seemed to reinforce
the sense of time's relentless passing. During the ensuing months
they were more than a little unsettled by the void created in their
lives by his departure. But for Julia there was, as she told Mary
Frances Fisher, the never-ending refuge of her work.

By mid-July 1985, after a ten-city tour for *The Way to Cook*
VideoBooks, Julia and Paul returned to Cambridge and to all of the
mail that had accumulated during their months in Santa Barbara.
They returned also to a schedule of preparing, photographing, and
writing a sequence of *Parade* articles, which were usually done in
two sessions with four issues per session.

"All this work lately has given rise to one of those career and life
decisions," an exhausted Julia wrote to Mary Frances Fisher. "I
shall not participate in the actual photo sessions this next time. I am
turning that over to our wonderfully capable Rosemary and to
Nancy Barr. It will not be done here (I'm still cleaning up after the
last session two weeks ago!), but from now on all will be done sans
moi, at our photographer's studio. I have loved the photo work
and love working with our team, but it takes too much time, and
time is not what I have much of."

Removing herself from the photographing sessions, however, was but a prelude to the more important decision to resign from the food editorship of *Parade*, which she decided to do in November 1985. With a major book to write, she just could not justify giving four months of the year to the magazine. In the April 27, 1986, issue, she introduced the new food editors with the words, "I'm delighted to be succeeded by such vibrant and talented young women as Julee [Rosso] and Sheila [Lukins]." The "good times girls" fresh from the success of their second book, *The Silver Palate Good Times Cookbook*, pulled out all the stops with the "in" foods of the eighties—pesto, chèvre, arugula, and ginger. And Julia was happy to be "out of it."

Determined to get *The Way to Cook* into print by the fall of 1986, Julia thought that during the winter months a good secretary in Santa Barbara could put on disk the recipes that she had culled from the *Parade* articles, the *Dinner at Julia's* series, and the teaching cassettes that were not in a format appropriate for the book. Her ambitious schedule, however, was forcibly interrupted when she underwent microsurgery on her knee in February. And two months later Paul was hospitalized for a second prostate operation. Writing to Simca, Julia commiserated with her friend over Jean's bedridden state: "You must be bien fatiguée, ma pauvre, with all the physical work involved, and the anguish. . . . Paul seems a bit better . . . he is cheerful, enjoys his food and wine, works a bit on his painting, takes many cat-naps which he is not aware of, spends a great deal of the day reading. I just hope he can continue." As California was conducive to recovery, the Childs extended their winter residency there until the end of August, with a week in May devoted to another cooking session at the Mondavi Winery in Napa.

The chapters on poultry and vegetables were completed before Julia and Paul returned to Cambridge and some of the festivities celebrating Harvard's 350th anniversary. But further work on the book and their New England Indian summer days were interrupted by one-day trips to New York to tape a number of *Good Morning America* spots, "3 1/2 minutes of deathless and breathless cooking per episode," as Julia described them. And then they planned a "no work" trip to Alsace, Venice, and Plascassier, where Simca was still in mourning for her husband, who had died on the first of June.

Julia and Paul's presence at Domaine Bramafam was salutary. They gradually coaxed Simca to join them for dinners at their favorite restaurant, Roger Vergé's Moulin de Mougins, and they encouraged her to record the story of her life, along with her memories of good food shared, for all of the readers and students who knew her through her classes and cookbooks. But Jean's death had cast a pall on their days in Plascassier, and although they could not know it when they departed at the end of October, Paul would not be able to return to their home in that sunny corner of Provence again.

Back in Cambridge, Julia hosted an American Institute of Wine and Food reception and book-signing party for Roger Vergé at the Meridien Hotel, and she joined the Women's Culinary Guild in sponsoring an evening with Marcella Hazan, who was promoting her latest book. The Childs also took an active role in raising funds to purchase James Beard's New York townhouse in order to establish a culinary center aptly called the James Beard Foundation there. Although the deadline for her new book, probably unrealistic, was long past, Julia resolved to plunge once more into cookery-bookery in Santa Barbara after the holidays were over.

"I am plowing along in my mammoth book, now more than halfway through Fish," she wrote to Mary Frances Fisher in February 1987, "but that is only Chapter 3. Luckily we love our work!" She also confided that Paul was really beginning to feel his eighty-five years, and it was advisable to stay close to home. And in a similar vein, she told Simca that Paul had deteriorated considerably since they had been together in Plascassier in October: "He is suddenly now un vieillard . . . unsteady on his feet." She said that he had slipped from her grip and fallen down a flight of wooden steps and sustained injuries to his ribs and wrist in mid-February—a painful accident that only highlighted his steady decline. "Fortunately I am in excellent health, and my knees are OK! And thank heaven I have plenty of work to do. . . . There is no possibility of our coming over to France this year, and I wonder if we shall even get back to Cambridge."

More or less confined to Santa Barbara, she missed working with her team and found writing her cookbook more solitary than ever.

By the middle of April, when she was midway through the meat chapter, she told Mary Frances Fisher, "[I] never feel I know enough, and have to keep going out looking at chops, cooking them, etc. A book is so final, even though I keep saying 'in my experience,' etc., to show that I am not stating eternal truths as I see them." What had begun as a compilation of recipes from *Parade*, *Dinner at Julia's*, the *Good Morning America* segments, and *The Way to Cook* cassettes was becoming a magnum opus of sorts. Mary Frances encouraged her friend to write a book that would be pure Julia, to do a dictionary from asparagus to zucchini, a whole book on cabbage, two volumes on meat from *agneau* to *veau*: "Why should you send off all those really good words to New York and have them cut you and cut you . . . down into the corporate wastebaskets." But Julia's confidence in Judith Jones was unshakable, and, as planned, she organized the recipes into chapters that closely paralleled the topical arrangement of the VideoBook cassettes. In spite of Paul's steady decline and a broken hip, which she sustained in the spring of 1988, Julia completed the manuscript of *The Way to Cook* by the end of that year.

In the December 1988 issue of the *Radcliffe Quarterly*, Julia wrote about cookbook writing in the eighties and expressed more of her doubts and concerns than would appear in the introduction to her book. Beginning with the title, "presumptuous, I know, but it was picked for me," she stated her preference for "Cooking My Way," which she felt the book really was. And she spoke candidly about the difficulty of writing for a 1988 audience: "Are they interested in real cooking anymore, or is it all pasta salads? I personally love the pure mechanics of the art, including the chopping, the shredding, the sautéing, the butchering, even the clean up. And I am fascinated by the basic principles, and what you can do with them once mastered."

But between 1960 and 1988, two-career families and single parents necessitated changes in many traditional domestic patterns, and the thrust of the food industry was to provide products and equipment that would produce meals quickly, conveniently, and economically. Add to this the concept of restaurant dining as high drama and the host of superstar chefs whose establishments benefited from the conspicuous spending of the eighties, and the corol-

lary decline in home cooking was in evidence everywhere. Cookbooks were often paeans of praise to the newest restaurant or chef,
or ersatz travelogues, or lifestyle "I wish" books, until a national
obsession with health spurred a whole new single-subject category
with fiber heading the list. Was there anyone who shared Julia's
impatience with "the nervous nutritional nellies" and the "food-as-
medicine approach"? Would a book that only mentions the microwave oven in passing, puts salt in the soup, and finds diet beef
"mushy" find its way out of the bookstore and into the kitchen?

The Way to Cook did. As Elizabeth David had been quick to point
out in her reading of Mastering more than twenty-five years earlier,
"As her predecessors [Eliza Acton, Madame Saint-Ange] had this
quality of quiet persistence, so has Mrs. Child, and it seems to me,
in an enviable degree. She has style, too, and heart. She keeps vigil
over every stage of the creation of a dish, from the choice of
cooking pot, mixing bowl, stirring spoon, knife, and egg whisk to
the moment when it is time to check that your serving dish and
sauce boat are heated. . . . It could be exasperating to find somebody constantly at your elbow with a reminder and a word of
advice. Julia Child's presence by your side is a comforting one,
kindly and reasonable. She is shedding light, not holding a stick.
She has been out shopping with you, leading you away from the
chicken that tastes like the stuffing inside a teddy bear, telling you
on the way what can and what cannot be prepared ahead of time."

Julia was a friend as well as a teacher, a surrogate mother in an
ideal kitchen, and most of her readers wished they had both. The
Way to Cook, like Julia's other six books, had a captive audience—
the JWs of The French Chef, students from culinary schools all over
the country who were inspired by her to don toques and whisk up
a perfect beurre blanc, the Cambridge residents who nostalgically
remembered the large wooden spoon Julia used to tie on her back
bumper in order to find her car in the supermarket parking lot, and
the multitudes who simply said, "Julia taught me how to cook."

The Way to Cook was described by Judith Jones as Julia's "masterpiece," a book that blended the basic French techniques that Julia
had interpreted and popularized in the States for more than a
quarter of a century with the new flair and inventiveness that
characterized American cooking in the eighties, and Knopf pub-

lished the book in kind. Designed in a handsome, oversize format with three columns per page, Caslon-style type, and more than 600 color photographs reproduced from Julia's original *Parade* articles, the book reflected attention and care in every aspect. Despite its fifty-dollar price tag, it was chosen by the Book-of-the-Month Club as the main selection in October 1989, the first cookbook ever chosen in its top slot. With a 75,000 first printing, Julia promoted the book from coast to coast, concentrating on people who took food seriously, autographing copies at the American Institute of Wine and Food annual convention in Chicago, and giving interviews with largesse.

But the culmination of four years of hard work was bittersweet. A series of strokes and almost total memory loss necessitated greater care for Paul than she could provide, and in the fall of 1989 he was moved to a nursing home near Cambridge. As *New York Times* columnist Molly O'Neill concluded after an interview during that stressful time, "Even so, something fundamental in the matter-of-fact world according to Julia never changes. She referred to herself as 'we.' And even though she has earned more than $1 million on her cookbooks, she maintained that 'marrying a nice man and cooking nice food' were the most important things a woman could do." Julia meant every word of it, and no one will know the personal cost to her of pursuing her career without her partner, closest friend, and adviser at her side.

When she was away from Cambridge, Julia called Paul twice a day; when she was home, she visited him every day, sometimes with no recognition on his part. And that continued until his death on May 12, 1994. It was a loss she was prepared for, yet one deeply felt all the more because it resonated with other deaths of those close to her—Simca, Elizabeth Bishop, Elizabeth David, and Mary Frances Fisher, who had all passed away in the early 1990s. Her sister and brother and their families became her mainstays, celebrating birthdays and holidays with her, and the cabin in Maine continued to be a family refuge. And there was always the blessing of work.

While in many ways the Julia everyone feels free to call by her first name and to talk to whenever they meet her in Cambridge is a very private person, she has a public agenda, which she works

tirelessly to promote, offering an alternative to encroaching technology and either the indifference to or the fanatical fears of too
many people regarding "the pleasures of the table." One of her
goals is to increase the membership roster of the American Institute of Wine and Food. Another and more far-reaching effort is to
gain academic recognition and validation for the culinary arts. And
who could serve this cause more effectively than Julia? Now in its
thirty-fourth printing, with over 2 million copies sold, the revised
Mastering the Art of French Cooking, volumes I and II, is a classic.
And as the culinary counterpart to Camelot, *The French Chef* series
remains a watershed in the history of TV's approach to food and
cooking, the high ground separating the commercialized, less successful culinary programs of James Beard, Dione Lucas, and the
galloping Graham Kerr from the dubious frenetic machinations of
Keith Floyd and the "Methodist minister [Jeff Smith] whose bully
pulpit," Barbara Grizzuti Harrison notes, "is the kitchen range." In
contrast, Grizzuti Harrison defines Julia as organized, passionate,
sophisticated, humorous, and homey: "Julia cooked. Julia ate. Julia
felt no obligation to fill our minds with pure and lofty thoughts
while we were filling our stomachs with sauce velouté. Julia, bless
her soul, was old-fashioned."

Perhaps that was the reason Julia wanted to slip into her octogenarian years quietly, with only a modest family celebration on
August 15, 1992. But her friends and associates would not acqui-
esce. Boston's WGBH producers and staff, AIWF chapters in cities
around the country, and various culinary groups sponsored over
thirty public celebrations of Julia's eightieth birthday during 1992,
culminating in "Merci, Julia," in Los Angeles. Described as a
"love-in" featuring nine multistarred chefs from France and another sixty American chefs who specialize in French food, the event
raised about $35,000 dollars for the AIWF's Educational Founda-
tion and kept the Julia banner waving.

It was all about food and friends, Julia said. And that particular
combination was probably a hint of an explanation of why Julia
signed on to do another sixteen-show TV series in 1993. When
approached by Maryland Public Television and A La Carte Com-
munications to host a series highlighting American "master chefs,"
Julia jumped at the chance to play "Mrs. Alistair Cooke" and

"Alistair Cookie," although she no doubt realized that filming on location would take her to New York, New Orleans, San Francisco, Los Angeles, Washington, D.C., Connecticut, Houston, and Hawaii. Hers also would be the responsibility of editing the recipes of the virtuoso chefs for the home cook in the planned companion volume, *Cooking with Master Chefs*.

Throughout her career, Julia had always entertained the idea of working with professional chefs, but, for one reason or another, a series with that format did not evolve. In this series she introduces Jacques Pépin, André Soltner, Charles Palmer, Patrick Clark, Emeril Lagasse, Robert Del Grande, Nancy Silverton, Mary Sue Milliken and Susan Feniger, Michel Richard, Jeremiah Tower, Lidia Bastianich, Jean-Louis Palladin, Jan Birnbaum, Amy Ferguson-Ota, and Alice Waters. At times Julia's role is simply to introduce the chef and comment on ingredients used; at other times she samples a Louisiana boil or a risotto with the chef and his or her family. She joins Jacques Pépin in the preparation of "Lobster Soufflé à l'Américaine," questions Jan Birnbaum about smoking salmon, and discusses the merits of different kinds of oranges with Alice Waters. There is enough variety in the chefs' personalities, in the dishes they demonstrate, and in Julia's interactions with them to prevent predictability. There is only one constant: they are as dedicated to their chosen profession and as passionate about cooking as is their host.

There is little indication of a feeling that the torch has been passed to another generation. Julia's enthusiasm about learning something new every day is infectious—whether it's a tip for beating egg whites or rubbing a garlic clove over the tines of a fork. "The art of cooking is indeed a noble hobby, and a fully satisfying profession," Julia writes in her introduction to *Cooking with Master Chefs*. "I've never run into a serious cook or chef of any age who didn't say: 'Every day I learn something new!' That point of view turns home cooking and the pleasures of the table into a wonderful adventure."

Merci, Julia, indeed.

CHAPTER SIX

Seasoned in Provence

There was still something native to the European way of life that attracted me, and that was cooking from the market. This basic attraction towards the very freshest ingredients was our most prominent inspiration.

ALICE WATERS

From the day the front door of Chez Panisse opened to the public on August 28, 1971, no single phenomenon has characterized Berkeley's "new sensibility" or signaled the shift in culinary attention from the East Coast to the West more than the demand for dinner reservations at Alice Waters' restaurant. In the 1970s alone, James Beard, Craig Claiborne, Julia Child, and M. F. K. Fisher dined in the flower-filled and bread-scented ambience of the Chez Panisse dining room, where a different menu was offered every evening and diners came to expect the finest ingredients California had to offer. Prepared and presented in Waters' freewheeling kitchen, each course was a curious blend of Mediterranean flavors, Provençal simplicity, and studied déjà vu.

So dramatic was her success as a chef-patron, and so continued are her attempts to realize a wish that she had been born in the sunny Midi world of Marcel Pagnol's characters with their honest pleasures and passions, that it is difficult to appreciate just how ordinary Alice's childhood in Chatham, New Jersey, was. Moreover, very little seemed to distinguish the early years of the second daughter of accountant Pat Waters and social worker Margaret Waters except Alice's love of skies filled with falling apple blossoms, and the taste of fresh tomatoes and other vegetables growing in the Waterses' victory garden. Born on April 28, 1944, into a world of wartime shortages and rationing, Alice said her earliest memories were of food, of sitting in the middle of a strawberry patch and picking the ripest berries to eat, of walking through her mother's kitchen and smelling applesauce cooking on the stove. And when she grew a little older and the war ended, she remembered summer vacations with her parents and three sisters on the lake in New Hampshire that later served as the location of the film *On Golden Pond*. There were blueberries, clambakes, freshly picked corn on the cob, tomatoes still warm from the sun, and oysters on the grill, tastes that years later would make her nostalgic for New England, even in the midst of California's bounty.

Birthdays in the Waters family were also memorable, with the celebrant given the choice of a favorite dinner and a trip to the Museum of Natural History in New York City. Alice loved rare steak and fresh green beans, "done just a certain way . . . and served on a plate just right." And even more impressive than the Museum of Natural History was the trip to a Horn & Hardart Automat. Not only was the lemon meringue pie the best she ever tasted but she also discovered that behind all that stainless steel and glass there were actually people at work baking hundreds of pies and then slicing, plating, and distributing them, poised to instantly replace her slice of pie as soon as she removed it from its slot.

There were also difficult childhood experiences. As the second child she often fell heir to the criticism of her sister Ellen, who was four years older. Alice protested especially when Ellen made fun of the way she set the dinner table. Having difficulty in knowing her right hand from her left, she couldn't get the utensils in the right place. When her father taught her to use the Mickey Mouse watch on her left arm as a guide for the placement of the fork, her problems were solved. And she soon distinguished herself as the official table setter and flower arranger whenever the Waterses entertained.

Perhaps the most significant memory Alice associated with her childhood involved a costume party held in a neighborhood park. Ellen went as a newspaper; Alice wanted to go as a vegetable. "I must have been four or five," Alice reminisced as she described the costume. "Radish bracelets, an asparagus skirt, peppers around my ankles, and a crown of strawberries." Worn over a swimsuit, the fruit and vegetable ensemble was not only original but emblematic. The Waterses' second daughter had a way with food, second only to her talent for making things happen. Petite, always smiling, she loved to socialize and party. And although the family moved to northern Indiana when she was fourteen years old and then three years later relocated in Van Nuys, California, she never wanted for friends and allegedly wore four boys' rings during her last year in high school.

Enrolled at the University of California campus at Santa Barbara the next year, she and three roommates pledged Alphi Phi. Friends' memories of Alice during those early college years for the most part center on her "pre-Raphaelite angelic" good looks and her preference for Wonder Bread, an indulgence never allowed at home, where her mother's main concerns were nutrition and health. Soon, however, the freedom associated with living away from home, the sun-and-surf orientation of the Santa Barbara campus, and the party atmosphere of the sorority house began to seem irrelevant in the emerging political consciousness Alice and her friends experienced. "We were not political radicals," Eleanor Bertino, Alice's roommate and one of her best friends, said. "We just felt we could get more out of college at Cal [the University of Calilfornia at Berkeley]. We transferred in spring '64. . . . Fall of '64, the Free Speech Movement happened."

Between spring and fall of 1964, Alice joined a group of students on a credit-earning tour of Europe that began in France. It was there that Wonder Bread gave way to *pain de campagne* and eating took on more importance than Alice could ever have imagined: "I experienced a major realization. I hadn't eaten anything, comparatively speaking, and I wanted to taste everything." Her days were filled with choices about where to eat breakfast, lunch, and dinner. She and her friends would read the posted menus outside restaurants, cafés, and country inns, then either reject and move on or enter and enjoy. With eyes and taste buds open, they traveled in Brittany, stopping at a small *auberge* where a single experience would shape the future of the diminutive bon vivant who seemed never at a loss for words: "I've remembered this dinner a thousand times. C'est fantastique! The chef, a woman, announced the menu: cured ham and melon, trout with almonds, and raspberry tart. The trout had just come from the stream and the raspberries from the garden. It was this immediacy that made those dishes so special." At the end of the meal, everyone stood up and applauded the chef. Not lost on Alice was the fact that in France food was a serious consideration and a sure way to please other people. Midway through the trip, Alice realized that France was providing a tremendous learning experience. As the other students moved on through Europe, she chose to remain there and celebrated her twentieth birthday in Paris.

In the fall when she returned to Berkeley, an interesting scenario began to play out, and the early days of the Free Speech Movement engaged the energies of Alice and her friends in a more immediate way than classes did. Free speech and advocacy became the central issues that riveted the campus. When the police arrested a highly visible activist, thousands of students protested by immobilizing the squad car. The event instantly made Berkeley the epicenter of student rebellion and radicalized campuses across the country. As the drama of sit-ins, barricades, and activism played out, the sense of outrage and utopian hopes collided head-on in violence. Still, in the fever-pitch years of initial protest, there was a generational solidarity, frequently called a sense of community, and an implicit trust within that community that a new world was dawning. Alice remarked that it was not even necessary to lock her bike. She also remembered the wonderful feeling that "you were best friends with the person next to you." But privately she wondered why her fellow protesters existed on Campbell's tomato soup and peanut-butter-and-jelly sandwiches when even the striking Communists in France were discriminating in matters of food and wine.

After the participants in the Free Speech Movement achieved their agenda in the early months of 1965 and student activists refocused their attention on civil rights and the escalating Vietnam War, Alice chose to work for political change. In 1966 she participated in the congressional campaign of Robert Scheer, who challenged the incumbent Democrat in the June primary election, running for the seat as a radical Democrat. More than 1,000 people worked on the campaign; 500 walked from house to house, knocked on doors, and talked with voters; campaign workers registered more than 10,000 new voters. As the "Scheer for Congress" liaison, Alice delivered copy and photos to the Berkeley Free Press, assisted in production, and returned the printed material to campaign headquarters. It was a heady time of getting things done with the maximum of human effort, and, for Alice personally, Scheer's defeat after all that hard work was disaffecting. Somehow in the midst of all of this activity, Alice completed her French culture major and the requirements of a Bachelor of Arts degree.

To her parents' chagrin she did not bother to attend graduation on March 18, 1967, nor did she plan to return to Van Nuys. Shortly after she had met David Goines at the Berkeley Free Press during the Scheer campaign, he wooed her with Monnet Anniversaire Cognac, and invited her to share his apartment. By this time Goines's days of organizing mill-ins and sit-ins outside the university's Sproul Hall were over. He had decided to make his suspension from the university permanent and to work at the Berkeley Free Press as an apprentice pressman.

In June 1967 he had the balance of a court-imposed Free Speech Movement sentence to serve in the Santa Rita jail because he had refused to pay the fine in solidarity with other FSM offenders. Alice dutifully visited him on the four Sundays of his month's imprisonment, and when he returned to Berkeley, their apartment functioned as a well-known gathering place again.

Alice's friend Eleanor Bertino recalled those days: "Although we were all very traditional, we all did eventually move in with men just after college; it was like the first marriage—the women did all the cooking." And Alice, especially, began to cook seriously. Elizabeth David's French Country Cooking was her favorite book because the recipes in it were rather imprecise and "derived from French regional and peasant cookery, which, at its best, is the most delicious in the world; cookery which uses raw materials to the greatest advantage without going to the absurd lengths of the complicated and so-called Haute Cuisine." Elizabeth David, however, taught Alice more than just food preparation. The British author's great sense of the bounty of the seasons and her conviction that life centers on the pleasures of the table were especially congenial to Alice's notion of bringing food and politics together.

"The Left in Berkeley dressed in dingy T-shirts. You weren't supposed to enjoy things," Eleanor said. But Alice felt it didn't have to be that way. So she tried to "seduce" her fellow communards to develop a more discerning palate. "She'd cook a cassoulet—an inexpensive bean dish back then. But she'd insist on getting the best sausage, the best duck, the best white beans. It had to be perfect." Dinner parties distinguished the Waters–Goines apartment. Whether a planned event or a last-minute invitation, Alice stretched the chicken or daube to provide for their guests in the dining room, which in the spirit of the times was informally dubbed Alice's Restaurant.

Eventually Goines acquired the Berkeley Free Press, renamed it the St. Heironymous Press, and expanded his production by designing and printing books, wedding announcements, and posters, doing all his own presswork. By 1968 Goines, Alice, and many of their friends were involved in the fledgling weekly called *The San Francisco Express Times*. Amid the cartoons and drawings depicting the latest activities of the Stop the Draft Movement, the Black Panthers, and politically polarized rock, mime, and counterculture groups, a recipe appeared every week and stood out dramatically in the fifteen-cent tabloid. The calligraphy for the recipes was always distinctive, as was the design. Under the title "Alice's Restaurant," more than thirty-five recipes appeared from February 8 to October 9, 1968. They were contributed by Alice Waters; David's mother, Mrs. W. C. Goines; graduate students and friends Lindsey and Charles Shere; and Sara Flanders, and some were even provided by cookware shops like The Kitchen in Berkeley. Goines ultimately gathered most of the recipes into a looseleaf portfolio cookbook called *30 Recipes Suitable for Framing*. This early collection of recipes—including Poppyseed Stuffing for Lamb, Paella Valenciana, and Stuffed Grape Leaves—was only a prelude to another collection, undreamed of at the time, that would showcase the collaborative efforts of Alice Waters and David Goines after both had outgrown the constraints of their modest dining room and moved into their respective careers. But there was something rather amazing about the *Express* recipes because they linked a more sophisticated approach to food with the counterculture.

By intent, however, *The San Francisco Express Times* was less an artistic and gastronomic vehicle than it was a statement that the times were volatile. The Free Speech Movement had established the fact that activist students could under certain conditions win victories against large bureaucracies like the university, city hall, and the draft system. But there were also victories denied. Goines got tired of "radical causes, being tossed in the clink, and eating cold beans out of a can," and Alice felt that everyone had a serious readjustment to make in the late 1960s, when the movement deteriorated into waves of flower children along Telegraph Avenue, and hippies dealing drugs, and the real hope for change became impossible. Alice and Goines went their separate ways. Intrigued by its hands-on, explore-the-sensory-world philosophy, Alice flew to London to study at the Montessori School and to "hang around" Elizabeth David's cookware shop.

When she returned to Berkeley in 1969, she began to teach, and she resumed an active social life with many former acquaintances and friends who, like her, were part of the Berkeley scene. Films were the rage, and there were select showings of vintage U.S. and French movies at the Pacific Film Archive on Durant Avenue. Alice met and fell in love with film archivist Tom Luddy and eventually moved into his Berkeley cottage, where Marcel Pagnol's films and the familiar combination of politics and food distinguished Alice's second domestic venture. Mutual friends of the couple as well as Alice's circle of men and women admirers, including David Goines, dined together regularly. But now the meals were followed by the screening of old films or poker, which Alice loved to play. The evenings usually ended with dessert. They were happy times fondly recalled: "At the earliest dinners you had to learn flexibility. It was always two more and you would never say no to anyone for dropping by. . . . You just improvised—figured out how to serve two more with half a chicken. It was a great feeling to be able to make so many people happy."

Her ideas about community, her dream of returning to a simpler lifestyle, and her idealized perception of life as it was lived in the south of France all came together in Pagnol's trilogy—Marius, Fanny, and César—in which the same actors played the same characters as the stories of their trials and tribulations unfolded. "Panisse [an old sail maker in the films] was Alice's dream of a Provençal man," observed Tom Luddy, "not in the romantic sense but a warm fatherly man with humor and wisdom. She had these romantic fantasies about France—the food, the men, the life. Whenever she'd see the films, she would cry buckets." The spirit of another time was compelling, and she became convinced that teaching was not quite fulfilling enough for her. The prospect of nurturing an extended family within this community of her peers began to grow in her imagination.

Alice left her teaching position at the Montessori school, and because her home kitchen was not big enough to accommodate her friends and acquaintances, she thought of extending it into a café or restaurant. At first she toyed with the idea of opening a creperie, where her friends could sit around all day, sipping apple cider and eating crepes made to order. A business-minded friend, however, advised her that she would have to sell about 5,000 crepes a day just to pay the rent. Alice went back to her original idea of a restaurant, and when she learned that a house on North Shattuck Avenue was for sale, she persuaded friends and likely partners to help her purchase it. Estimating that they needed $10,000 to launch a restaurant, her associates pooled their cash and arranged for a few small loans.

From the beginning, the restaurant that came to be known as Chez Panisse was a group effort. Enlisting the help of her many artisan friends, Alice planned to use the existing living and dining rooms of the house as the main dining room of the restaurant and to reserve one of the larger bedrooms upstairs for private parties while using the room at the head of the stairs as a sort of informal coffee and croissant café known as Le Matin. The kitchen would serve as the restaurant's kitchen, and a small cottage behind the house became the pastry kitchen. During this transformation the house underwent plumbing, electrical, and interior renovations with her friends wielding hammers, wrenches, and paintbrushes. Alice's French friend Martine Labro remembered joining Alice in canvassing secondhand shops in a search for chairs, old china, and linens.

Alice envisioned a sort of *steak-frites* bistro with flower-filled Perrier bottles on red-and-white-checked tablecloths, a place where the ambience was friendly and the conversation relaxed and opinionated. Berkeley graduate student Victoria Wise had become enamored of charcuterie while she was in France in 1967, and she left her studies to become the first chef of the restaurant. Former student and Berkeley resident Lindsey Shere offered to serve as pastry chef, and Alice pitched in wherever needed. The three women formed the nucleus of the staff.

Chez Panisse began as a true neighborhood café, serving coffee and croissants in the morning and dinner every evening. Martine designed the original poster that was placed in front of the restaurant the day before it opened. During the night someone stole the poster, but, notwithstanding, the first dinner was a great success, featuring pâté en croûte, duck with olives, salad, and fresh fruit. Victoria Wise, assisted by Leslie Land and Paul Aratow, prepared it with ducks from San Francisco's Chinatown and with other ingredients from two local supermarkets, the Japanese produce concession at U-Save on Grove Street, and the Co-op across the street from Chez Panisse. The cooks were basically home cooks unaware that there were specialized restaurant suppliers, and, in retrospect, Alice thinks that their ignorance was "an important, if unwitting, factor in allowing Chez Panisse to become what it is." Alice had worked as a carhop one summer and as a waitress in a pub during the months she was in England, so she had charge of the dining room.

From the beginning Alice and her associates wanted to try many kinds of new dishes made from the freshest seasonal foods they could find. Another thing the original group of staff, volunteers, and friends tried to do was keep the restaurant a dynamic place, with a new menu every day. But by December 1971 an à la carte steak was added to the menu for diners who might prefer it to the offering of the day. Alice believed that they really had to experiment because as amateurs they weren't expert enough to restrict themselves to a few masterpieces flawlessly turned out meal after meal. Establishing an authentic relationship with diners fascinated and motivated Alice: "I want people to share the excitement of good things, beautiful foodstuffs, little lettuces from our garden, herbs in bloom, a gnarly local pippin from somebody's old tree— and if I can see that people are receptive then something wonderful happens: time stops—you're a child again, but still an adult, and not just a satisfied, pleasure-seeking hedonist either, but a participant in something shared: And you know, it may not matter whether or not the soufflé turned out perfect."

At any given time in those first months, there were many more people than needed, voluntary or paid, involved in the restaurant. At least two staff members were assigned just to wash the lettuce, discarding most of it, then washing and drying the rest by hand. Being novices, the staff relied on the local Berkeley-Oakland marketplace, but they soon began to forage for quality foodstuffs, establishing a network of small suppliers and growers that would distinguish Berkeley's rapidly developing "gourmet ghetto." With shops like the Cheeseboard and the Monterey Market already in place, the staff gathered watercress from nearby streams, picked nasturtiums and fennel from roadsides, and gathered blackberries from the Santa Fe tracks in Berkeley. Friends planted fresh herbs. The mother of one of the cooks grew fraises des bois in Petaluma. Still, in the early days of the restaurant, the sources for foodstuffs of the quality that Alice wanted were unpredictable. And she admitted that "with the exception of Chinese and Japanese markets that even in the early seventies emphasized flavor and quality, we really had nowhere to turn but to sympathetic gardeners who either already grew what we needed or would undertake to grow it for us."

Victoria Wise's early departure to establish her own charcuterie across the street from Chez Panisse and the parade of cooks who entered and left the kitchen eventually necessitated Alice's move to the back of the house. With only her reputation for cooking great meals in her own kitchen and the necessity of serving the patrons who were crowding into her restaurant as prerequisites, Alice conquered her terror of taking over the back of the house. When Chez Panisse was closed, she visited other restaurants to find out what they were doing. One thing she learned from these forays was that being able to lean back and enjoy oneself was going to be a high priority in her own restaurant; any trace of superciliousness in her staff would have to be avoided.

Alice was also convinced that professional training was not a prerequisite for a position in Chez Panisse's kitchen. The cook's spirit was always more important than credentials; the excitement of being connected to food's source, to nature, was more desirable. Cooking taught "hands on" with as little regimentation and as much communication as possible was her idea of a cooking school.

In those early days, she found it in Josephine Araldo's home in

San Francisco when she attended classes there a short time after Chez Panisse opened. Again, the French experience was translated into a personal idiom for Alice as this seventy-year-old Breton woman who had lived in San Francisco since 1924 passed on to her students the art of "cooking from the garden" that she had learned from her grandmother as well as the techniques that she had learned from Henri-Paul Pellaprat at the Cordon Bleu. Alice described the classes, which were held in Josephine's kitchen: "Sometimes she'll interrupt herself to rush out to the garden to pick something to demonstrate a point—and food is constantly being handled, smelled, and tasted. . . . There's nothing regimented or dry or sterile about it. She's passing on a great tradition—the cuisine of honest, frugal Frenchwomen—but she's doing so with love and a light heart."

Alice's immediate inspiration, however, came from Elizabeth David and Richard Olney. Neither author espoused detailed recipe formulas, and both brought a sense of freedom, relaxation, knowledge, and imagination to their personal interpretations of simple French cooking. Alice and her fellow cooks would meet in the early afternoon, begin with a recipe, then improvise in terms of the ingredients available. If the dish was not exactly perfect at the first seating, if the flavors didn't marry, or the color was wrong, they made the necessary changes for the second seating.

Working in the kitchen soon became its own reward, because even though Alice and her friends had decided to limit the restaurant's service to dinner, it did not generate enough income to balance the books. In the "hangout" atmosphere of Chez Panisse, friends and staff members opened bottles of wine without much thought about inventories when they gathered at the end of the dinner service. Various methods of checking out were devised, but Alice's sense of hospitality, which was handsomely carried out by maître d' Tom Guernsey, often sabotaged all efforts at cost control, and Alice wanted to keep menu prices affordable. David Goines's "birthday" poster for August 28, 1973, advertised a cassoulet, half liter of wine, and salad, accompanied by a Marcel Pagnol film for the modest sum of $5.25. And the celebration the following year featured hors d'oeuvres variés, Panisses [miniature pizzas], salade verte, glace de fruits, and a demi-carafe of wine for $5.00 compris.

The restaurant that had started on a $10,000 shoestring had ac-cumulated $40,000 in debt by the time some investors came to Alice's rescue.

It became apparent, especially to Tom Luddy, that Alice worked herself to the point of exhaustion every day the restaurant was open. After she had put in an eighteen- or twenty-hour day, he'd pick her up and she'd faint from total fatigue when they reached the front door of his cottage. Or he'd find her sitting on an overturned stockpot in the kitchen at Chez Panisse with her head in her apron waiting for her eyesight to come back. Her lack of business acu-men, probably most evident in a policy of hiring only friends and children of friends, who at times took advantage of her, along with her total involvement in the restaurant eventually caused more problems than either Alice or Luddy could resolve. Alice moved out and into an apartment in a Victorian house on Oxford Street, only a few blocks from the restaurant.

In the carefree climate of Berkeley habitués, Alice had a few more affairs and then precipitously married a French filmmaker, Jean-Pierre Gorin, Jean-Luc Godard's collaborator in a series of political films in the late 1960s and '70s. It was not exactly a match made in heaven in the opinion of her friends, who believed that Alice was merely living out a fantasy of being married to both a Frenchman and a Marxist. Because they were seldom seen together, it soon became apparent that this was not a conventional marriage. Gorin left Berkeley within a few years, but Alice did not file for divorce until about ten years later.

Second only to its opening, the addition of Jeremiah Tower to the staff in late 1972 contributed immensely to the reputation of Chez Panisse as a serious dining mecca, and it also initiated a period of flamboyant innovation in the kitchen. Although Tower was an amateur cook, he had spent his youth in England, pursued graduate work at Harvard, and had his defining culinary experiences in the Washington, D.C. home of his aunt and Russian uncle, all of which, along with his degree in architecture, contributed greatly to his inventive style of cooking. "I hired him because he had such an *air*," said Alice. "He taught me that you can really spoil food for people if you seem apologetic, that you have to appear confident even if you don't feel it."

In the creative and often frenetic atmosphere of Chez Panisse's kitchen, Tower and Alice ranged from Escoffier and *La Cuisine du Comte de Nice* to Michel Guérard's *cuisine minceur* with abandon, cooking their way right through nouvelle cuisine, perfecting their skills in the honing process of trial and error. At the end of Tower's first year at the restaurant, he went to Yelapa near Puerto Vallarta, Mexico, for "some severe recuperation," which consisted of lying in his hammock watching the day boat arrive and leave while he consumed about six margaritas. Given to neither understatement nor self-effacement, Tower played impresario to Alice's genius and popularized her efforts with panache. "He was not hesitant," Alice said. "His cooking is more elaborate than mine, more flamboyant and richer. I'm more garlic and olive oil—he's more cream and butter. But initially I was fascinated by his combinations, things I wouldn't have thought of."

Together Alice and Tower planned and executed a series of memorable menus for the yearly celebrations of the restaurant's anniversary, Bastille Day, the famed Garlic Festival (a week of completely different garlic dishes on the menu), and the arrival of Joseph Phelps Zinfandel Nouveau. In the fall of 1973 Tower also introduced the idea of regional dinners celebrating the food of the various provinces of France as well as distinctive dinners in honor of artists and writers like Gertrude Stein, Baudelaire, and Salvador Dalí, and menus prepared for favorite patrons, wine makers, and world-class chefs. These dinners generated attention and provided occasions for the exhibition of that curious blend of creativity and showcasing that marked the kitchen of Chez Panisse. In addition to various film luminaries like Werner Herzog, Jean-Luc Godard, Federico Fellini, Roberto Rossellini, François Truffaut, and Francis Ford Coppola, who were usually escorted to Chez Panisse by Tom Luddy of the Pacific Film Archive or by Gorin, there were the movers and shakers of the culinary world—James Beard, Craig Claiborne, Marion Cunningham, and others—who sought out the dining room that was heralded as a culinary adventure.

It was inevitable that the restaurant's cuisine would defy any label. After dining at Chez Panisse for the first time in 1973, James Beard wrote, "What Alice has done from the beginning is to create a style entirely hers that broke away from the formal French restaurant. She's established the Garlic Festival each year, and has had her own vegetables grown. These things declare her individuality. You can't call it *nouvelle cuisine*. I think it's Alice Waters' cuisine." From the beginning days of Chez Panisse, Alice incorporated all of her food experiences into the restaurant's menus, but the subtle nuances of both the ingredients used and the flavors favored were redolent of the south of France. Furthermore, the distinctive tastes of Provence captured in the *mesclun* and goat cheese signature salad frequently served at the restaurant, the presence of virtually unknown Provençal wines on the wine list, and a menu written in French certainly suggested a French country restaurant.

In 1975, however, with one regional dinner featuring the bounty of Northern California, Jeremiah Tower precipitated the turning point in the restaurant's evolution and, in his words, "changed the face of American dining." The courses that Alice and her guests as well as the other diners enjoyed that memorable evening began with Tomales Bay bluepoint oysters and progressed to cream of corn soup Mendocino style, Big Sur smoked trout steamed over California bay leaves, Monterey Bay prawns, California-grown geese from Sebastopol, Vela Monterey Jack cheese from Sonoma, and fresh caramelized figs—all accompanied by California wines. The possibilities seemed endless, and, indeed, they were.

After that evening both Tower and Alice decided to abandon menus in French and use English, specifying wherever possible the origin of the ingredient used. Wines from California also merited a prominent place on the wine list. In a concerted effort, the kitchen strove to prepare California's foodstuffs from a French country perspective. It wasn't long before "a flood of New York journalists" were writing about the new California cuisine. And, as an article in *Rolling Stone* stated, "Neither Tower nor Waters was particularly interested in sharing the limelight, and their vaunted collaboration began to collapse." Tower admitted that everything started to change when the flashbulbs began popping.

Other changes also subtly affected the restaurant's kitchen. In 1976 Alice and Tower hired French-born and -trained chef Jean-Pierre Moullé. With his demanding culinary apprenticeship and back-of-the-house experience at Sans Souci, he, as co-chef Mark Miller later said, taught the Chez Panisse chefs "how a kitchen should really run." "We all (including Tower) learned from him," Miller added. "And Jean-Pierre has certainly been one of the undervalued contributors to the prestige of the restaurant." Somewhat self-effacing, Moullé became a member of a team that "let Tower be Tower," and he remained a constant during the years that further established Chez Panisse as a "larger than Berkeley" success.

Whatever the cost, letting people do their own thing was an important part of Alice Waters' policy. "This restaurant," she said, "takes on the feeling of whoever is cooking. We've had various chefs pass through our kitchen, myself included, and each of us has put our own stamp on the food." But the underlying aesthetic of the restaurant was and continued to be Alice's own. While she was delighted with Tower's accomplishments in the kitchen and with the restaurant's move toward a regional feeling celebrating California's produce, a growing sense of the philosophical differences between his vision of dining as drama, as mise-en-scène, and her own sense of home-style communion made Tower's departure in 1977 an inevitability. "My improvisational cooking evolved after he left," Alice said, but her zeal to please and to educate with food remained a constant.

During Jeremiah Tower's tenure, Alice had incorporated the restaurant under the name Pagnol et Cie., distributing stock so that each of the friends who worked with her had the same number of shares that she did. Tom Guernsey, who headed up the front of the house, had been and remained president. Other partners were Jerry Budrick, an outrageous mimic who had, among other things, convinced Alice that he was an Austrian waiter; Gene Opton, owner of The Kitchen Store; Jeremiah Tower; and Lindsey Shere. As always, the lines of authority were somewhat murky, in part because there were sixteen shareholders, four of them working, voting members, and an overseeing board of seven with Alice as chairman, and in part because personnel was always shifting. Within two years of the forming of the corporation, Jeremiah Tower had decided to leave Chez Panisse to consult and eventually open his own restaurant. Because he demanded cash for his stock, Alice had no choice but to raise $50,000 to buy him out and then redistribute his stock to other employees.

Tower's departure created a seismic division in allegiances. Some patrons were resentful about what they considered Alice's dismissal of Tower. Others were so loyal to Alice that they vowed never to patronize the Balboa Cafe and the Fourth Street Grill, where Tower worked as a consultant and chef, or Stars, the restaurant he later owned. In small and not very well disguised ways the two principals were alternately cool and politically correct, but Tower's description of Alice as a "limo-commie" and the conspicuous display of one of Alice's love letters, framed, at Stars were needling reminders of their years together at Chez Panisse.

At a time when Alice and Jean-Pierre Gorin were leading separate lives and her partner and sometime lover Jerry Budrick was urging her to open a café with a wood-fired brick oven upstairs to promote more cash flow, Alice concentrated on the kitchen. She also continued to expend more effort on developing a network of suppliers. On a tip from Gorin, who had gone on to a teaching career in the Visual Arts Department at the University of California in San Diego, Alice was introduced to the Chino family, a group of Japanese truck farmers who owned a fifty-six-acre farm and farm stand called the Vegetable Shop twenty-one miles north of San Diego and five miles from the Pacific.

In retrospect, discovering their produce was perhaps Alice's greatest inspiration to concentrate not only on the seasonal but also on the finest and freshest ingredients available for the dining room at Chez Panisse. "I was absolutely dazzled the first time I saw the Chinos' vegetables," she recently told Mark Singer of *The New Yorker*. "It was the most beautiful produce I had ever seen. Now after years of knowing—or trying to know—this remarkable family, I see that the beauty of those vegetables comes from a commitment to tradition and integrity that is very rare and precious. Their vegetables are [an] endless source of inspiration, and their standards and approach have changed the way cooks regard vegetables." Initially, arranged like jewels in their various protective boxes, unfamiliar varieties of dazzlingly fresh peppers, white eggplants, striped tomatoes, and various scented basils began to arrive at the restaurant every Wednesday via Greyhound bus. Fear of a Cavaillon melon rushing to forced ripeness in the cargo bay of the bus, however, soon precipitated a shift to air freight. Thursdays, when the menus for the following week were decided by Alice and the other chefs, the vegetables and fruits received from the Chino farm the day before were incorporated into their dishes.

While the Chinos' farm was an important source for many fruits and vegetables, other ingredients were not as easily obtained. So the search went on. Stories abound about people knocking at the back door willing to barter their homegrown potatoes or other fruits and vegetables for a dinner at Chez Panisse. Jean-Pierre Moullé actually planted a small garden in a patron's yard to supply the kitchen with certain vegetables and herbs. For her part, Alice paid little or no attention to cost in her efforts to approximate the perfect taste of remembrance.

She also refused to be limited by the budget her partners tried to impose upon her. She paid handsomely for the original floral pieces that Carrie Wright arranged for the restaurant twice a week. She commissioned David Goines to design the yearly birthday posters and his assistant, Patricia Curtan, and calligrapher Wesley Tanner to design special menus. She continued to enlist the creative efforts of all the artisans she knew to contribute to the restaurant's success. She was also extravagant in sharing her passion for certain foods with Chez Panisse's clientele. If white truffles from Alba were $550 a pound, the experience of introducing them to her patrons was well worth the cost, and guests remember her walking through the restaurant with a basket of truffles, shaving slices of the pungent fungi over their gratins and salads. As her friends and associates said, with Alice it was always "spending money like Waters."

Alice has been variously described as a "seductress," a revolutionary, a person with a constant need to prove herself, and a loyal friend, but perhaps her greatest asset was to push people to do what she saw they could do even if *they* could not see it, as her French friend Nathalie Waag explained it. But her relationships were never one-sided. In 1977 Nathalie had sought Alice out because Martine Labro told her that an American woman in Berkeley had a restaurant that served the same kind of meals that Nathalie had served in her restaurant, called Le Hasard, in Vence. Accompanying her husband on a business trip to California, Nathalie met her American counterpart on the steps of Chez Panisse. Alice immediately asked Nathalie to accompany her to the fish market, and later in the day she invited her to attend the special "Sauternes Dinner" that evening and enjoy Tower's brilliant pairing of Château d'Yquem with entrecôte of beef as the main course in a series of courses served with Sauternes from Barzac and Sauternes. That inspired first meeting eventually paved the way for both of Nathalie's sons to join the kitchen staff at Chez Panisse, and for Alice's extended stay in Nathalie's farmhouse near Bonnieux during September and October 1978.

At that time and during the succeeding years, Alice's friendships increasingly extended into various wine and food communities. In France, especially, the tightly knit circle that included Richard Olney, wine makers Lucien and Lulu Peyraud of Domaine Tempier in Bandol, Nathalie Waag, and expatriate cookbook author Martha Schulman also included Berkeley wine importer Kermit Lynch and Alice Waters in their number. Not only did Alice serve Domaine Tempier's wines in her restaurant, but Lulu Peynaud's legendary bouillabaisse, which Alice had sampled during the vendange at Domaine Tempier, was also one of the favorite fish stews that she served to the patrons at Chez Panisse. And Lynch supplied many of the imported wines on the restaurant's list.

Richard Olney's influence was perhaps the most critical when Alice tried to formulate and translate French country cooking into the "California" idiom that characterized Chez Panisse. During her visits to the south of France, she experienced his way of life first-hand, and, of course, his cookbooks reinforced the experience. Like Alice, Olney was an American with an ongoing love affair with France. Early in the 1970s, Alice had visited him at his home in Provence and enjoyed a meal that he had created out of the abundance of his garden and various other provisions from the open markets in nearby Toulon. The first course was a salad of just-picked green beans, nasturtiums, hyssop, and rocket flowers, all tossed with olive oil and homemade vinegar. It was followed by rack of lamb grilled in his stone fireplace, garnished with pureed white vegetables. The various courses were all served with a succession of Chambertins from young to old.

"For me he is a cook's cook," Alice wrote, and not only did his French Menu Cookbook and Simple French Food influence the way she cooked at Chez Panisse, but these two books also helped her to formulate the basic philosophy that her first cookbook would communicate to readers. Olney's concept of simple food was one neither of elementary nourishment nor of ease of preparation. Rather it involved a broader aesthetic principle, namely the artist's injunction to "Respect your medium," applied to food. Since 1962 Olney had lived in a little village where the narrow streets were regularly blocked by the shepherd and his sheep. Cultivating a garden that served as a dining room as well as an extension of his kitchen, and gathering foodstuffs in local out-of-door morning markets, he discovered the subtext that formed the basis for his cookbooks. And although World War II had brought about enormous changes in most French households, he mastered the dishes that in an earlier and sunnier time had belonged to every Provençal housewife's repertoire.

Although Alice learned *la vraie cuisine de bonne femme* by traveling in the south of France, by visiting and living for short periods of time in Provence, and by reading about food and wine through the filter of Elizabeth David's postwar years of habitation there, Olney's appreciation of French food and wine was analogous to her own. Mixed with a disdain for the alienation promoted between grower and consumer in America and a fondness for the hand-scribbled notices that informed customers at the open market that the vegetables were "untreated" and the chickens, whose eggs were laid that morning, were grain fed, was a conviction that, at least in the 1960s and '70s, the French valued fresh garden produce and traditional recipes more than their American counterparts did. Olney broke with his past and chose to live as an American in Provence. Alice realized, she later said, "that in order to experience food as good as [she] had had in France, [she] had to cook and serve it [herself]." Olney had found the perfect place to paint, cook, teach, and write. Alice opened Chez Panisse and embarked on a mission to do "the very best we could do with French recipes and California ingredients."

Alice also reached out to members of the culinary community on this side of the Atlantic. One of her earliest friends was Marion Cunningham, who found in Alice an important advocate for the time-honored tradition of home cooking and enjoyment of the pleasures of the table instead of turning the ritual of dining over to some unseen manufacturer who was simply interested in profit. That there was never a frozen vegetable, a dish zapped in the microwave, or purchased pasta served in the dining room at Chez Panisse impressed James Beard's pupil, and Marion Cunningham brought not only Beard, but also scores of her friends to the restaurant, where Alice greeted one and all as guests in her own dining room.

Beard was also involved in Alice's celebrated dinner in honor of M. F. K. Fisher's seventieth birthday on July 3, 1978. Using the titles of some of Fisher's books, the meal consisted of a first course composed of a selection of oysters in remembrance of *Consider the Oyster*. Four more courses were dishes redolent of Marseille—snails sauced with Pernod, tomatoes, and garlic; charcoal-grilled rockfish with wild herbs and anchovies; spit-roasted pheasant; bitter lettuce salad with goat cheese croutons; and three plum sherbets in orange-rind boats—all inspired by *A Considerable Town*. The dinner concluded with a Muscat de Beaumes-de-Venise suggested by *A Cordiall Water*. Alice liked to say that "a special occasion is any occasion you wish to be special," and she had a flare for creating one.

She also had a unique gift for bringing people with similar interests together. Friends in common like Chuck Williams, James Beard, and Marion Cunningham were links between Mary Frances and Alice. After the acknowledgment of the dinner and an invitation to Mary Frances's home on the Bouverie Ranch, friendship between the two women developed slowly, with an uncharacteristic reserve on Mary Frances's part. "I'm touched that she [Alice Waters] has any affection for me," she told a *New York Times* interviewer. "I certainly do for her in a strange way that is mixed up with my innate suspicion that she is a phenomenon. I have only met two or three of these in my life, and am both bedazzled and scared of them, I think. What really frightens me is that they are quite helpless . . . they cannot possibly understand or even accept the unwritten conditions for being as they are. In this present case, I feel that things are fairly well under control . . . but who knows why or how."

From the beginning, however, the very fact that Alice was a

"phenomenon" attracted creative young people to service, paid or unpaid, in the kitchen of Chez Panisse. Most of them had no previous culinary training, and several came from fields totally unrelated, but all of them discovered that Alice Waters had a wonderful sense of how to eat and an understanding of food that was second to none. La Varenne–trained chef Jonathan Waxman spent about nine months at the restaurant in the late 1970s. Even after an apprenticeship in the kitchen of Ferdinand Chambrette in France and then experience as day chef at the Domaine Chandon restaurant in Napa Valley, he felt somewhat unprepared for the Chez Panisse experience: "Every night at Chez Panisse the menu changed, and every night I was scared. There is an air of excellence and everyone is entitled to criticize. I learned that you don't serve a dish unless it's perfect." And Waxman discovered that it was more important to taste things and not merely look at them. He went on to open Jams, a California-style grill in New York City.

With ever greater insistence, the search for people who thought the way that Alice thought went on. The operating principle in hiring help for the restaurant continued to be Alice's need for an extended family. "I know it's a definite prejudice I have," she admitted, "but I will always take the bet on a friend or a friend's child and hire that person over a stranger. If you're not able to sit down and dine with the people you want to cook for, at least you can work with them. There's a little bond made when there's a tie. I need that."

Ironically, she seemed to need it more as the number of "strangers" entering her restaurant increased, and the cost of producing "perfect food" necessitated a steady rise in the cost of a fixed-price dinner in the dining room. In 1980 Alice finally decided to take Jerry Budrick's advice and transform the space upstairs into a lower-priced informal café serving both lunch and dinner. In a major remodeling of the building, in which the downstairs dining room and kitchen were redesigned, Alice extended the second floor to accommodate the café and installed an oak-burning brick oven for pizzas in the open kitchen situated between two light and airy dining areas. The handsome white rooms with hand-crafted redwood and metal lights were inviting, as were the floral arrangements on the bar. The menu was à la carte, featuring salads, pasta, and pizza, and it appealed to patrons who wanted the quality of the restaurant's set menus without the cost of a fixed-price dinner. After an initial slow start under Carolyn Dille, Joyce Goldstein tightened production in the kitchen and increased the number of lunches served from 50 to 150. With the café's à la carte menu and no-reservation policy drawing patrons in increasing numbers and Jerry Budrick as combination maître d' and impresario deftly managing the crowds who appeared for lunch and dinner, the reputation of Chez Panisse soared. Alice was urged to write a cookbook that would record many of Chez Panisse's menus and introduce readers to recipes associated with the restaurant.

She signed on with M. F. K. Fisher's agent, Lescher and Lescher. Because James Beard, Marion Cunningham, and M. F. K. Fisher were already in Judith Jones's stable at Knopf, they encouraged Alice to place her book there. But Judith Jones, who was already on record as "not interested" in restaurant or chefs' books, was not sent the proposal. Jason Epstein at Random House read it and was so enthusiastic that Alice's agent, Susan Lescher, urged her to sign on with Random House. With a contract in hand, Alice soon relegated the book to the back burner. The kitchen was a more compelling place to spend her time, and Alice lived on the excitement of being the person in charge of the restaurant that M. F. K. Fisher described in a letter to Eleanor Friede as "quite an experience." "You must get there, by hook or crook, when next you are near San Francisco. It's a small restaurant run by my young friend Alice . . . in its tenth year by now, and very famous. Really, the food is the best I have ever eaten in America . . . in a public place, I mean."

Since the opening of Chez Panisse, Alice had not kept a master recipe file. And she reaffirmed her intention not to stray from her idea of experimentation: "To sit on my chocolate mousse, as it were, isn't my cup of tea. When it is no longer interesting, we will not do it. As hard as it is to create a new menu each week, I wouldn't have it any other way." But now with a book under contract, recipes inspired by the memory of the most satisfying taste of a kind of dish became the starting point for the reinvention of that dish. New dishes were created the same way. The unusual combination of buckwheat pasta, goat cheese, and rocket went through several tastings. The first time it was served, the pasta was a bit heavy. The second time the pasta was lighter, but the goat cheese was too sharp and the rocket leaves not quite right. After lightening the cheese with reduced cream and adding some *haricots verts*, the texture, color, taste, and aroma came together in balance. It was always cook and taste, and with a cookbook to write, Alice's faultless palate, and Jean-Pierre Moullé's culinary expertise, recipes began to evolve.

Without doubt, her personal library also contributed to the kind of cookbook Alice wanted to write. Passionate about cooking, she was drawn to cookbooks that made her hungry and eager to taste the food that was described and formulated therein. Food grown in its native soil, food picked and rushed to market, food prepared to enhance its freshness, and food served as a part of the day's rhythm, these were the recurring themes she expected to find reading between the recipes. What she saw, felt, remembered, loved was as important as the specific directions, perhaps more important, because the sight, the smell, the taste, even the touch of ingredients contributed to the inherent enjoyment of "good food on the board, and good wine in the pitcher" and the special kind of pleasure M. F. K. Fisher described as sitting for hours over a meal of soup and wine and cheese as well as a dinner of twenty fabulous courses.

Alice Waters selected her cookbooks with more than a sense of déjà vu; she selected them with the same passion that she brought to her cooking. As a novice cook, she had espoused Elizabeth David. As an aspiring cookbook author, she found other and more amazing qualities to admire in Britain's laureate of the "literature of cookery." The first was, of course, Elizabeth David's keen palate, developed by years of tasting foodstuffs from the open-air markets of France and Italy. And then there was her obvious enjoyment of picnics where freshly made cheeses, *saucisson*, *pain de campagne*, and wine were taken at leisure from a bountiful basket, making out-of-doors dining a soul-satisfying experience. Appealing also was Elizabeth David's preference for *mesclun* salads dressed lightly with olive oil, and her appreciation of meals prepared with fish fresh out of the water and eggs gathered that day in the barnyard. Hers was an overwhelming conviction that a good dish gained by being served on its own, without fussy garniture.

Moreover, when Elizabeth David wrote about food, her articles and books were always about more than food. They were about eating, subtle preparation, pleasure, and the conundrums of living well while the world, too often unmindful of good food, lived poorly. "Her aesthetic is about simplicity and a kind of fragrance," Alice said. "She had a great sense of the seasons and always about life around the table—the setting, the conversation. It was always more than just the food because the recipes were not very specific. . . . I remember being frustrated, but it made you think." Alice also knew that her British mentor was saying something profound about the recipe process. There are no inflexible rules because food changes continually. Traditions, climate, location, and the soil all make a difference. Dishes like bouillabaisse or cassoulet exemplified regional cooking and utilized the ingredients native to a district, but even they were constantly evolving as newer equipment, faster transport, and improved agricultural methods made change inevitable. Resourceful housewives and creative chefs continued to use the ingredients at hand and by doing so preserved the local flavors of a specific region, but it became more and more obvious that recipes were at best approximations. Elizabeth David never lost sight of that fact, neatly balancing a carefree and at times lyrical touch with technical knowledge and the "constant practice of the difficult and complicated profession of cookery."

During 1980 the scenario of producing a manuscript began to evolve. With a team consisting of Carolyn Dille, who extracted and codified the recipes; Jean-Pierre Moullé, who had the responsibility of preparing the meals for the dining room and testing most of the recipes; Patricia Curtan, who brought professional design and printing expertise as well as cooking credentials to the project; and David Goines, who designed and illustrated it, Alice also had the enthusiasm of a handpicked staff, who shared her dedication to life on the cutting edge. Still, as her deadline loomed, she confessed to Mary Frances Fisher that writing did not have the immediacy, the involvement, or the satisfaction that cooking had for her, and she was doubtful that she could finish the book. Mary Frances, who took a dim view of advances and contracts signed only on proposals, offered encouragement along with the advice simply to do it.

Other friends had more practical suggestions for translating her compelling verbal skills into print, and Alice talked most of the introductory material into a tape recorder. Linda Guenzel literally transcribed and edited the material as the unheralded collaborator of the book.

In 1982 Alice was thirty-eight years old, a professional success, and still the emotionally freewheeling interpreter of the heady Age of Aquarius. Dotting the last *i*'s and crossing the last *t*'s in the manuscript of her cookbook had brought a sense of satisfaction. Champagne in hand, she toasted the new year as she always did, unmindful that during the months to come both disaster and wide-spread fame as well as a new personal commitment would intro-duce many changes into her life. Mary Frances replied to Alice's holiday card, "One part of my delayed celebration will be seeing you again. Please let me know whenever there's a chance of your coming up here. It would be fun to see Kermit [Lynch] and anyone else on your list, truffles or not! The main thing, though, is to take a good look at you."

Affection and generosity toward friends had always been an important facet of the largesse that characterized Alice. Friends received baskets of flowers arranged by Carrie Wright, or Alice arrived on their doorstep with comestibles from Chez Panisse—loaves of bread baked by Steve Sullivan, a Lindsey Shere dessert, a basket of the Chinos' peppers, or a simple daube from the kitchen. When the restaurant was closed, she often invited a fellow chef to an impromptu lunch at Greens or the Mandarin restaurant. And frequently she would ask Marion Cunningham, Diana Kennedy, or other members of the food community to drive to Glen Ellen with her to visit with Mary Frances. But it was in the restaurant especially that her generosity coexisted with her innate skill as a hostess. Sending a complimentary glass of Champagne or wine to the table of a visiting friend, journalist, or celebrity made her hospitality noteworthy and created the ambience that has al-ways been associated with Chez Panisse. It also made the disaster that destroyed a large area of the first floor of the restaurant more sympathetic to its patrons.

In the early hours of Sunday, March 7, 1982, a smoldering log, inadvertently returned to the outside woodpile next to the kitchen after the dinner service, had ignited a fire that was eventually seen by the workers in the laundry across the street. They immediately called the Berkeley fire department and Alice, who rushed to the restaurant only to weep in disbelief as she saw flames engulfing the first floor while the firemen removed expensive bottles of wine, table linens, and even the marble bartop before they were forced to break through the kitchen and dining room walls.

News of the fire spread almost as fast as the fire itself. Cards and notes of sympathy arrived immediately, as did offers of help from her former employees and other restaurateurs. Mary Frances wrote, "My dear little Alice, I just heard (radio) about the fire—I am *so* sad for all of you! All I can do is send my love." And Julia Child, with whom Alice had recently talked about her cookbook, sent condolences about the "dreadful business," adding, "but at least your book manuscript didn't go up too—that's a great book, very you, and now we wait to see it formally presented. Our fond thoughts to you, and best of luck in re-establishing." In the days after the fire, many more of Alice's friends rallied. Old customers sent wine from their own cellars, former Berkeley students sent checks from all over the country, even the local police force and firemen helped in the restoration.

Although damage was estimated at $200,000 and the dining room was in need of major repair, the second-floor café was back in business within a few weeks. In a characteristic gesture, Alice sent her thanks to the firemen for saving as many items as they could accompanied by a huge bouquet of flowers and an invitation to all of them to have dinner with her in the café. The entire experience made her realize how important the restaurant had become to people in the community. And the heightened awareness that Berkeley's residents celebrated special occasions like birthdays and anniversaries there gave rise to small but important changes in the restaurant. As preferences in food were made known to Alice, she incorporated them into the various menus.

Those closest to Alice believe that after the fire the restaurant "grew up" and became more closely bound to the Berkeley community. Just as Alice had envisioned her original role to be bringing food and politics together, she now became more involved in civic causes, contributing dinners and foodstuffs to auctions benefiting public television or to any needy project that would benefit the city of Berkeley. Chez Panisse would not be "just friends cooking together anymore."

Burdened with all the details of insurance and refinancing, and also involved in the decisions of rebuilding, Alice realized that she had an opportunity to make those changes in the restaurant that she had long felt were necessary. One of the priorities she worked through with builder Kip Mesirow was to eliminate the wall between the kitchen and the dining room as the first step in removing the barrier between the chefs and the people for whom they were cooking. Because of the change, the dining room seemed to flow naturally from the open kitchen. Seeing the chefs working, Alice believed, added to the sensory pleasure of the meal. And the beautiful displays of produce on a table jutting out into the dining room exhibited the sensory appeal of the food that was being prepared.

Shortly after the remodeled dining room opened in May 1982, a major article on Alice Waters, written by a young journalist who worked one day a week at Chez Panisse, appeared in *Savvy*. Among other things, the article detailed her current relationship with Todd Koons, a handsome young chef who divided his time between the kitchen at Chez Panisse and France. It also stressed the continuing importance of Alice's ex-lover friends—Goines, Luddy, and Budrick—in her life. When pressed by the interviewer about the possibility of a family of her own, however, Alice was forthright about her decision against one: "I can't imagine being with one person—can't stand the exclusiveness. I think it puts a terrible demand on somebody to expect all from one source. So many of us here aren't married or don't have kids. We singles are an extended family. Love affairs don't last. Friendships do."

When *The Chez Panisse Menu Cookbook* was published in late July 1982, it was a testimony to those friendships and to her deep-seated need for community. Handsomely designed and illustrated by David Goines, the book also acknowledges Alice's indebtedness to the extended family who had supported her both emotionally and professionally since the restaurant opened in 1971. Between the lines of the cookbook there is also an enthusiastic appropriation of ideas from Elizabeth David and Richard Olney, along with a special appreciation of *cuisine de femmes* as presented in Madeleine Kamman's *When French Women Cook* and Josephine Araldo's *Cooking with Josephine* and *Sounds from Josephine's Kitchen.*

Certainly in "What I Believe About Cooking" (not the usual beginning to many American cookbooks) much that is characteristic of Elizabeth David's work—namely, the feeling for the villages and towns of the Mediterranean, a sense of the exquisiteness of the simple, and an invitation to be creative in the kitchen—translates itself into Alice's words. To call attention to the alienation that existed between America's growers and cooks and between cooks and patrons in the standardized, mechanized, sterilized technology of modern food production, Alice wants to stand in supermarket aisles and say to shoppers, "Please . . . look at what you are buying! Food should be experienced through the senses and I am sad for those who cannot see a lovely, unblemished apple just picked from the tree as voluptuous, or a beautifully perfect pear as sensuous, or see that a brown-spotted two-foot-high lettuce, its edges curling and wilted, is ugly and offensive. It is a fundamental fact that no cook, however creative and capable, can produce a dish of a quality any higher than that of the raw ingredients."

Alice takes the concept farther. In a kitchen that has always been known as labor intensive, she places a high priority on the time and effort expended by the cook, not on highly garnished plates or on Elizabeth David's disavowed "Technicolor cooking" but on hand-work—picking over each raspberry, using a mortar and pestle, hand-rolling pasta, involving all the senses in the cooking process. Editor Jason Epstein describes Alice's genius as the gift of capturing the essence of a quail or an oyster, a sack of flour or a bottle of oil: "In some mysterious way, Alice's ingredients speak to her so that her cooking is like a dialogue with them, from which heretofore unsuspected meanings surprisingly emerge."

If a reader concentrates on the text rather than selecting certain recipes from the pages of *The Chez Panisse Menu Cookbook*, it soon becomes clear that its author is focusing her attention on meals in their entirety, following closely Olney's advice "That for a menu to emerge as a single statement, a coherent entity, it must be made up of single statements, each of which relates to the others creating larger single (or simple—or harmonious) effects within the whole. The courses of a meal relate to each other as well as each to its accompanying wine, and each wine is chosen not only in terms of perfect fusion with a course, forming one statement, but as a harmonious prelude to the wine that follows it, forming another." Olney's ideas validate what Alice has emphasized since the opening of Chez Panisse. The decision to offer a different multicourse meal each night is a continuing creative and refining process. Because an ever-changing menu is the hallmark of her restaurant, Alice makes menus the leitmotiv of her cookbook.

Unlike Olney, however, she is more specific and less theoretical when she discusses composing a menu, carefully stressing the words *seasonal* and *harmonious*. And she considers the interplay of weather, temperature, patrons, and what the cook in the kitchen feels about what to cook and eat on a particular day. Rather than the usual instructions not to repeat similar sauces, ingredients, preparations, colors, and textures from one course to another, Alice cautions balance and warns that bread or soup (unless it is the main course in a one-course dinner) can overpower a meal rather than be a part of it.

She believes that a first course should awaken and entice the palate. An entrée should be of equal weight and importance with the other courses of a meal and not a dominant dish of meat or fish, potatoes, and vegetables. If a first course also includes saladlike ingredients, it need not interfere with serving a salad after the entrée, depending upon the menu. And although it is her preference to conclude the meal with a cheese course followed by a piece of fruit, toasted nuts, and perhaps a dessert wine, she also feels that a meal should have a definite ending, which can be an appropriately light dessert to satisfy and not overwhelm the diner.

Recipes are to be guidelines—not infallible formulas. While she acknowledges that bread and pastry making require attention to basic techniques and procedures to achieve the desired product, Alice clearly states that precision and elaborate details are not her goals to ensure the success of other recipes. She wants to *suggest* the expected taste, the appearance of the completed dish, the combination of ingredients, and the overall harmony of a meal. "I would like these recipes," she says, "to be understood by someone who doesn't know how to cook at all. The absence of technical knowledge need not prevent a person from understanding the inspiration of rubbing the bread with garlic!"

There are flags on every page signaling that this is not a "how-to-do-it" book. Readers in search of techniques for making a perfect *beurre blanc* or a *demi-glace* are referred to procedure-oriented cookbooks. Recipes are not given for every dish in every menu. Equipment and utensils are not specified. The focus is always on the food itself and the effectiveness of using fingers, hands, and all the senses because knowledge comes through the senses. Taste and taste again is the most important instruction. Above all, a cook should never be so comfortable with a tried-and-true recipe that re-creating it in another form inspired by new ideas, other cookbooks, or a restaurant experience is abandoned.

Organized idiosyncratically, menus inspired and adapted from Elizabeth David's fondness for picnics, James Beard's food fancies, Jeremiah Tower's family traditions, and Richard Olney's wine pairings demonstrate the "patchwork" of influences that had helped Alice arrive at the meaning of gastronomic enjoyment. These are followed by four seasonal menus and menus for special occasions like Bastille Day, the arrival of fresh white truffles, the Garlic Festival, and the chef's birthday. Because open hearth and fireplace cooking is so much a part of the tradition of food preparation, Alice is instinctively drawn to grilling, and she includes a section on grilling menus to stress the wonderful aromas that can engage diners when they smell garlic baking in the coals and inhale marinades dripping from the meat and fish into the blazing fire.

There are also "Uncomplicated Menus," featuring California's bounty of fresh lettuces, goat cheese, grilled chicken, and pristine seafood. These are followed by "Themes and Variations," which reflect the influence of memorable restaurant meals that had inspired Alice to adopt Japanese, Zen, Chinese, and various Mediterranean dishes into the menus at Chez Panisse. In a series of three menus, she demonstrates how to use lobster, artichokes, and lamb in a variety of dishes that reflect cross-cultural culinary influences. Included also are recipes for the breads baked and served at Chez Panisse.

The last set of menus is formally labeled "Memorable," and it concentrates on the special dinners served at the restaurant from 1971 to 1981. With no accompanying recipes, the menus chronicle the history of Chez Panisse during the decade that secured its international reputation. And because many of them were devised by Jeremiah Tower, their inclusion is also a thank-you note signed by Alice.

If the content of the book was unlike many of the cookbooks published the same year (*The Silver Palate Cookbook, Everyday Cooking with Jacques Pépin, The Victory Garden Cookbook, Cooking with Lydie Marshall*, to name a few), the format further broke with tradition. There are no illustrations, no drawings of technical processes, no glossy colored photographs. The menu opposite the title page and the cover are the work of David Goines, who was assisted by Patricia Curtan in the book's design.

Craig Claiborne credited Alice Waters with "revolutionizing American cooking in the 70s and 80s" and put *The Chez Panisse Menu Cookbook* on his "essential cookbook list." Not only did the book make the clearest statement to date about what had come to be known as California cuisine, but it also created a style and provided a philosophy and insight into the direction contemporary cuisine was taking. Hailed as a major statement on food in America, *The Chez Panisse Menu Cookbook* soon had 90,000 copies in print. From New York to California, slick culinary magazines and metropolitan newspaper food sections featured the book and its photogenic author. In a world increasingly insistent on what was "In," "In Again," and "So In, We Could Die," Alice Waters belonged to the latter group. Hers was the only cookbook selected to appear in the chic I. Magnin Christmas catalog. Seasoned advice was, Put this tempting, delicious book on the top of your Christmas list.

Alice went on the usual book tour promoting *The Chez Panisse Menu Cookbook*, gave interviews, and planned an elaborate celebration in late August to honor the eleventh birthday of Chez Panisse. With a Cajun band playing nonstop in the brick-edged courtyard in front of the restaurant, guests exchanged vouchers for oysters, spit-roasted lamb, and a host of other dishes as they ranged from kitchen to dining room and café, eventually ending their revels on Shattuck Avenue.

Compared with Craig Claiborne's birthday and publication party for *A Feast Made for Laughter*, which occurred on Long Island a week later, the Berkeley celebration was understated. Beginning in early June, Claiborne had invited Alice as well as thirty-five other world-renowned chefs to prepare a special dish for the 400 guests he intended to assemble for the East Hampton weekend. "The whole affair will be unique in the history of cooking in this country—great international food, Indian, Indonesian, Chinese, French, Spanish, Mexican, Creole, soul food and so on—and it won't be the same without you," Claiborne wrote to Alice, along with the news that a documentary movie, a cookbook, and extensive TV, magazine, and newspaper coverage would probably result. Alice flew to Long Island with a basket of red, orange, green, brown, and yellow peppers from the Chinos' farm in hand. The morning of the party, she prepared them in the home of her host and editor, Jason Epstein, who described the huge platter of roasted peppers streaked with silvery California anchovies as "an edible autumn landscape." Having declined an invitation to attend the gathering of the food famous, Mary Frances confided to Alice, "By now, I think you are firmly imbedded in all of the excitement of Craig's tiny private secret personal bash for only one thousand close friends in East Hampton. . . . Yes, I'd have loved to be at the party."

Keenly aware that her friend was seldom able to travel, Alice planned small Provençal fêtes for Mary Frances in Glen Ellen. On September 20, she, along with Tom Luddy and Kermit Lynch, arrived at Last House with a Pagnol film, a daube, bottles of Domaine Tempier 1971 Bandol, cheeses, and a flamboyant basket of roses. Mary Frances scored it as the second of the "nicest, most heart-warming, happiest" parties of her life, the first being the dinner in her honor at Chez Panisse. She acknowledged it in a letter and elaborated on Alice's generosity: "That is what the excellent Profile in Savvy told about, in a necessarily journalistic way . . . a hint, not much more, but still very aware of what you have and what you are doing about it." She concluded by saying, "I seldom wish that I could live any longer than I shall, but I would really like to watch you and know you through the next decades."

Mary Frances was not the only friend who recognized the demands that Alice faced daily and the heightened expectations, but she may well have been one of the few who also realized that Alice couldn't say no. To play "bad guy" to her "good," Alice asked her father to act as consultant on the restaurant's board of directors, and he implemented some of the difficult decisions Alice could not or would not make. For the first time in her life, Alice became a homeowner. Using royalties from the book as the down payment, she purchased a small, unpretentious cottage about a mile from the restaurant. *The Chez Panisse Menu Cookbook* had also contributed to her already high visibility, and the restaurant finally began to turn a modest profit. From coast to coast, Alice Waters was reputed to "have it all." The only question was what she would do next.

Required Reading

> How can you convey, in words and
> pictures in a cookbook, what it is to
> pick something at its peak of
> ripeness from your own garden, and
> cook it and eat it, and how different
> that is from cooking and eating
> something processed and packaged
> from the supermarket? How can you
> get across that sense of
> immediacy?

> ALICE WATERS

239

Row after row of *The Chez Panisse Menu Cookbook* in one of Cody's display windows in September 1982 emphasized the changes that more than a decade had brought about. Reviewing the book in *The Nation*, David Sundelson referred to Chez Panisse as a "new privatism" turned inward rather than outward on public issues and commitments. And he wrote that "the counterculture has become a Counter Culture—the counter at the gourmet butcher, the pastry shop, the charcuterie . . . the [*Chez Panisse Menu*] *Cookbook* shows how we have changed. 'Aesthetics' is the ruling term in its vocabulary; life must be pretty. 'Understanding,' 'philosophy,' and 'ideology' now apply only to the kitchen." And he volleyed the charge that Berkeley had always been serious, "but in a braver time, that seriousness was applied to the Vietnam War and not to an apricot soufflé."

There was no denying that Shattuck Avenue in North Berkeley had become what some called a "gourmet ghetto," with Chez Panisse as a focal point and the Co-op, Pig by the Tail, Piet's Coffee, the Cheeseboard, Cocolat, and the Monterey Fish Market as satellites. It was a known fact, however, that for anything really to happen in Berkeley, it had to have a complex intellectual underpinning. And when Chez Panisse had opened in 1971, the rationale for its existence was already in place and a momentum to effect change was in motion. Protesting against the problems of a degraded food supply, produce ripened artificially by gas, and genetically altered foodstuffs, a group of American-born Zen Buddhists farmed the land on a retreat by the sea, scores of nouveau utopians formed communes in California's valleys and foothills, and the vegetarian movement had already scattered fragments of an ideology that simply needed cohesion. Inducing the university's department of agriculture to put taste back into tomatoes and lobbying agribusiness to reexamine the use of pesticides and the abuses of mass production was one step; offering alternatives to the supermarket was another. An advocate of both, Alice carried on her own personal crusade at the restaurant and within ten years formulated her political manifesto in the opening pages of *The Chez Panisse Menu Cookbook*.

While devotees of the restaurant (and there have always been patrons who dine there more than once a week) applauded Alice's efforts to capture the excitement of cooking and dining at Chez Panisse in the pages of her book, reviewers and critics lined up on opposite sides. One group predictably echoed the academic dismissal of food and the way it can be emblematic of culture and society as an ephemeral field. Unlike studies of art, politics, literature, and music, the idea of "cookbook as statement" or art form was summarily dismissed. And Alice's occasional unbridled enthusiasm for fictional heroes like Dodin-Bouffant met with raised eyebrows from those who espoused an "eat to live" philosophy.

On the other hand, the food establishment hailed the book as "a *new* type of cookbook" and "a reading experience rather than a cooking guide." They praised the author for "reminding us that our hands can work very well, often better than time-saving machines, and allow us the simple sensuous luxury of being a participant in the food preparation process." For many readers Alice Waters articulated the new California lifestyle of informality, of dining in small, unpretentious, but no less distinctive restaurants, and of engagement in the serious pairing of wine and food.

After the publication of *The Chez Panisse Menu Cookbook*, the elite circles of film royalty, chefs, wine experts, and food writers orbited around Chez Panisse with more insistence than ever. Patrons made reservations a month in advance and would have made them for more distant dates if possible. Working in the kitchen of Chez Panisse became the sine qua non for aspiring chefs, culinary credibility, and, yes, that unspoken word, fame. And many of those chefs who had worked with Alice in the early days of Chez Panisse followed her lead and wrote their own cookbooks, adding to the definition of California style.

More than most restaurateurs, however, Alice knew that she could not rely on the success of the moment. During the fall of 1982, she developed a growing fascination with Italian food and decided to change some of the personnel in the kitchen. She encouraged the newly-married Jean-Pierre Moullé to move on to greater challenges and planned to replace him with a chef who, she hoped, would introduce some of the flavors of Italy into the restaurant's menu. Alice had refused to hire Paul Bertolli two years earlier because he was too generous with nasturtiums, and, more to the point, he cooked asparagus *in an aluminum pot* when he prepared his presentation dinner, a prerequisite for obtaining a position at Chez Panisse. After working in two other Bay Area restaurants and cooking in Florence for a year, however, ex–music student Bertolli prepared another meal for Alice. As she remembers it, "He came back very inspired and started doing things like making his own olive oil and vinegar. He's got the gutsy taste I like—olive oil, vinegar, anchovies, and garlic. He makes everything taste good!" Lamb carpaccio with artichokes and mint, risotto with smoked pigeon, grilled swordfish, and an herb salad got him the job, and his presence in the kitchen introduced an Italian flavor to the menu at Chez Panisse.

It was not long before Paul Bertolli, relief cook Shelley Handler, Lindsey Shere, and Alice were planning a series of Italian regional dinners, featuring tortelli filled with pumpkin squash, Chianti sherbet, and fonduto with white truffles. The menus were inspired and foreshadowed changes to come. Because Alice believed that Italian cooking had "a lot of connection with what was going on in California" in the early 1980s and Bertolli had a palate for strong flavors, the food became somewhat more rustic, but certainly no less complex, than the dishes that the patrons of Chez Panisse had come to expect.

During the last months of what had been a year of great change, Alice met an aspiring artist who had come to Berkeley after studying painting at the Art Institute of Chicago. When Stephen Singer and Alice were introduced, one of her friends remembered saying, "He'll be good for you, but we don't know if you'll be any good for him." And there were others who thought that Singer's aloofness and Alice's gregariousness could never be compatible. But Singer was soon under her spell, and they were seen everywhere together.

After her life history of "difficult relationships," Alice's affair with Singer proved different. By the end of the year, she was expecting their child. "Don't think about it, just do it. You can't possibly plan it, just do it," she told a younger chef five years later, and the advice echoed the spontaneity of her own decision to become a mother as did the ticking of her biological clock. For legal as well as other reasons, she finalized her separation from Jean-Pierre Gorin in a divorce early in 1983. At the time, although she and Singer were living together and looking forward to parenthood, Alice was not even considering remarrying.

Toward the end of March, Alice joined a group of chefs for a three-week trip to China. As she confessed later, the political repression and squalor that she saw left her distressed and somewhat depressed, although she welcomed the opportunity to learn firsthand how certain ingredients like ginger were used in local cuisines. Returning to Berkeley, she helped Steve Sullivan launch the Acme Bread Company because the kitchen and pastry department's schedule at the restaurant could no longer easily accommodate bread production. She also encouraged and partially funded the Farm Restaurant Project, initiated by former salad chef Sibella Kraus to establish a bridge between small specialized farmers who were producing the best seasonal produce and restaurants frustrated by the inadequacies of the existing marketing and food distribution system.

As always her own time was divided between involvement in the restaurant and projects that found a larger audience for her ideas. An offhand remark to Jason Epstein at a Random House party raised the possibility of a pasta cookbook. Alice also began collaborating with Therese Shere, Lindsey's daughter and a Sonoma-based market gardener of flowers and vegetables, on a monthly column in Cook's magazine early in 1983. Whether the subject was basil, garlic, sweet peppers, or strawberries, the "Kitchen Garden" articles considered the varieties, growing characteristics, and soil and light requirements of the subject along with mail-order sources. Included as well was an appropriate recipe.

Always very specific when talking about food, Alice developed a formidable vocabulary to express her preferences in precise terms. Qualifying adjectives as in Meyer lemons, green garlic, pink fir potatoes, and white eggplant differentiated these items from their generic counterparts. Specificity, however, was only a part of the process. Seed companies willing to adapt to American soil seeds that were theretofore available only in Europe also played an important part in the search for varieties of produce. The Heirloom Seed Company in Boise, Idaho, and Le Marché Seed Company in Dixon, California, became part of the network that Alice was trying to forge.

By mid-May of 1983, Alice's pregnancy was widely known and a matter of some concern to her friends. Mary Frances urged her to be "sensible about not working too hard for too long." But Alice was busy planning an "Alliaceous Dinner for James Beard" to be held on May 26, and, although his health was far from robust, the eighty-one-year-old culinary pioneer attended. The hand-painted menu she presented to Beard when he and many of his friends dined at Chez Panisse that evening was among the 638 items the William Doyle Galleries listed in its auction catalog for the Beard estate two years later.

Since Beard's first visit to Chez Panisse in the early 1970s, Alice had made a point of reserving the adjective *great* to describe his culinary contribution, convinced that when journalists referred to her and to other women chefs as "the greatest women chefs in America," they were confusing success with greatness. "Great means James Beard–level, people who have spent their whole lives cooking," she insisted. "Great for someone thirty or forty is too strong. It doesn't apply to us." Theirs was a mutual respect, and the high regard Beard had for Alice was evident to the many friends who knew both of them. When Alice visited Beard in New York that summer and admired a small oil painting of a brioche in a very ornate frame, he took it off the wall and instantly presented it to her. "She [Alice] will be an interesting mother," he wrote to Mary Frances a few weeks later. "I think she might have been created by

James M. Barrie. She's so whimsey at one point and so practical at another. She's a bit of Maggie Wiley and a bit of Mary Rose."

Shortly after Alice's return to Berkeley, her child was delivered by cesarean section on August 15, 1983, and named Fanny. Eleven months later mother and daughter posed for pictures in a small stand-up café tucked between the Acme Bread Company and Kermit Lynch's Wine Shop. Café Fanny was more than a first birthday gift, it was a mother-to-daughter legacy, as were the illustrious honorary godmothers Alice selected to watch over her child. Nathalie Waag was one of them. Having been encouraged by Alice to introduce the markets and cuisine of Provence's hill towns to American food lovers by offering a week of touring, shopping, and cooking to small groups, she was the perfect choice to give Alice's daughter "a French sensibility." Another "honorary" godmother was M. F. K. Fisher. "Don't worry! That side of me will always stay invisible," she told Alice five weeks after Fanny's birth, adding, "When can I inspect my new god-daughter?"

During the fall and early winter, Alice took a "leave" from active duty at the restaurant, dividing her time between caring for Fanny and working on a cookbook featuring pasta, pizza, and calzone. From the beginning, Alice enlisted her French friend Martine Labro and Berkeley friend Patricia Curtan to collaborate on a book which she wanted to be totally different in subject and format from her first.

Her challenge was to answer the question Does the world really need another pasta cookbook? She was ready with an emphatic yes. Selecting the themes of seasonal and fresh from *The Chez Panisse Menu Cookbook*, she focuses on unusual and interesting ingredients—more specifically, on vegetables and herbs from the garden or farmer's market. And she presents recipes for pasta and pizza—those most basic of comfort foods—as mediums for the creative cook's expression. More personal than the name-dropping, eye-blinking menus of the first book, these dishes, which could be accompanied by a salad and a glass of simple wine, followed by fruit or berries in season, are redolent of Provençal meals gathered from a *potager* and of the meals which Alice prepares in her own kitchen, "because," as she says, "I cook so much pasta for myself. When I'm too tired to come up with something imaginative—I pull out the pasta, go out in the garden and grab some lettuce, and have dinner."

Would her readers make green pasta with the leaves of thyme, rocket, hyssop, marjoram, basil, sage, parsley, chervil, or sorrel? Was the U.S.A. really ready for herb flower pasta, floral and perfumy? More to the point, would others believe, as she did, that a kitchen without onion confit was unthinkable? Supported by conviction and success, she told an interviewer, "It seemed the right time for a book like this, because although there *is* a lot of interest in pasta just now most of the recipes are still pretty traditional. There are some variations on the classics, of course, but nobody has made a real *big* breakthrough with unusual and interesting ingredients based on a seasonal approach." This book provided the opportunity to make her point with panache.

The table of contents indicates how different *Chez Panisse Pasta, Pizza & Calzone* is from the number of pasta books already on the market. Only a year earlier, James Beard had published *Beard on Pasta*, in which he stressed "the good times to have with pasta." But with the exception of perhaps a few recipes like "Basil Lasagna," which appear in Alice's book in a lighter version minus the ricotta and mozzarella cheeses as "Pesto Lasagne," there is very little repetition or even similarity in their respective recipes. Beard was a teacher, and he provided background, presented a thoroughgoing discussion of the various methods of making pasta, and covered Asian as well as other ethnic noodle possibilities. His recipes were usually introduced with a personal observation, a list of ingredients, clear steps to follow, and variations.

As a restaurateur, Alice is intent on making the ordinary extraordinary by the pairing of unusual ingredients with traditional pastas. Pappardelle with Barolo duck gizzard sauce; tagliarini with mussels, radicchio, and anchovy cream; thyme blossoms, oysters, and green fettuccine; and crawfish bisque sauce and linguine are light-years away from Beard's spaghetti carbonara, chicken tetrazzini, and pasta primavera. In a generous concession to spaghetti and meatballs, Alice adds a prosciutto bone, sprigs of oregano with flowers, and fresh basil sauce to the traditional dish. But in her culinary lexicon, there is never a reference to using dried herbs, opening a can of plum tomatoes or tuna fish, or unsealing a package of frozen spinach or artichoke hearts. Only one-fourth of the thirty-six pizza recipes that Alice includes in her book list tomatoes (whether roasted, sun-dried, sliced, chopped, or puréed) as an ingredient.

Although Alice maintains that she wants *Chez Panisse Pasta, Pizza & Calzone* to be "lighter and more whimsical" than *The Chez Panisse Menu Cookbook*, which she considers "more of a philosophical statement about the restaurant," she says she has tried "as [she] did in the first book to pick out things for their shocking effect—to give readers some surprises and to get them involved." Deliberately or not, she is making a statement. By repeatedly encouraging improvisation, she discourages the tyranny of listed ingredients and step-by-step instructions found in the usual collections of recipes. Once the techniques of making pasta and pizza dough are mastered, an unlimited number of dishes are possible if the cook simply goes into the garden or to the seasonal outdoor market, selects whatever is fresh and appealing, and then lets the ingredients inspire the meal.

Seasonally organized, the four sections, which include eighty-seven pasta recipes, are each introduced by an evocative watercolor illustration and a culinary ode to the season. In spring, the cook's fancy lightly turns to thoughts of young fava beans, sweet peas, asparagus, baby lamb, and salmon. The summer garden is "a cornucopia of pasta possibilities," with tomatoes, peppers, and summer squash ripening on the vine. Wild mushrooms, pristine shellfish, and the bounty of the harvest contribute to a heartier pasta meal in fall. And the preserved foodstuffs of winter team up with pasta for an array of appetizing first courses that could be followed by roasted fowl or simmering stews.

In design, format, and content, *Chez Panisse Pasta, Pizza & Calzone* makes the kind of innovative statement that the three authors want to make, namely that their purpose is "to inspire rather than direct." A light touch distinguishes the drawings as it did the recipes. The number of ingredients is deliberately minimalized; cheese, usually associated with so many traditional pasta and pizza recipes, is used judiciously. Martine Labro's evocative "Pasta Garden" with its tempting vegetables and herbs visually lures the reader to Alice's "Garden Notes" in the back of the book. Writing about garden favorites from chives to tomatoes, she supplies the kind of information that distinguished her *Cook's* magazine columns, including planting instructions, growing patterns, varieties, and harvesting tips. And the glossary of ingredients introduces many of the foodstuffs that Alice and her colleagues take for granted to a wider audience, who have to import fresh anchovies and red torpedo onions.

Sitting in her colorful garden in Vence, Martine Labro recalled sharing with Alice many of the recipes she had learned from her mother. During the actual writing of the book, she flew to Berkeley twice for concentrated working sessions and also exchanged ideas by phone and mail. In addition to contributing recipes, she did the illustrations. "Everything I painted is here," she said, pointing to the garden stretching in front of and along the side of her Provençal house, "like my cat and the raspberry trees. The only things not here were the duck and goose in the fall illustration."

Patricia Curtan, who for years had been associated with the restaurant, also contributed recipes and designed the book, overseeing the type and page layouts. Inspired as much by Provence as by Italy, the pasta and pizza recipes showcase the café's strong Mediterranean affinities. Alice's genius in bringing together as many different talents and tastes as possible was evident again.

If *The Chez Panisse Menu Cookbook* established Alice Waters as innovator extraordinaire, *Chez Panisse Pasta, Pizza & Calzone* earned her a reputation as "the culinary oracle of the eighties." Following her lead, cafés dotted the culinary map, "open kitchens" with wood-fired brick or stone ovens became de rigueur, and "designer pizzas" assumed theretofore unimaginable culinary importance, using "California" ingredients such as goat cheese, shiitake mushrooms, grilled artichokes, and shellfish. Even Wolfgang Puck, who had hired former Chez Panisse cook Mark Peel to man the kitchen at Spago, acknowledged his indebtedness to Alice for transforming original and delicious pizzas into restaurant fare.

In the relaxed atmosphere of the Chez Panisse café, the British food writer Jane Grigson ordered a pizza topped with "girolles in a general creaminess, spiked with a little Parmesan and onion." When it was served and she had tasted it, she said, "I saw what Alice Waters was about: the ordinary made extraordinary by the fine unusual ingredients . . . put together by a skillful and unusual taste." No doubt about it, pasta and pizza were "in," even in America's most respected establishments.

When *Chez Panisse Pasta, Pizza & Calzone* was published in June 1984, Alice and Fanny promoted the book from coast to coast. While Alice demonstrated pasta and pizza making at gourmet cookware shops and on the morning talk shows, Fanny dined on her latest food fancy—strawberries, bananas, and a bit of yogurt supplied by room service. Inevitably, the proprietor-chef of Chez Panisse was questioned about Fanny's eating preferences. Literally raised in the kitchen of Chez Panisse, Fanny had for her first solid meals little purees of pork and fruit—"all the classical things" Alice thought would entice her daughter to like the dishes that she liked herself. But Fanny proved fickle and at least for the moment preferred fruit and yogurt to grilled quail and peeled grapes. "I had to laugh about Alice and Fanny," Marion Cunningham said. "Even in the very beginning, when Fanny was barely big enough to be in her high chair, Alice would make her tiny little Chez Panisse meals." Educating Fanny's palate became a high priority for a mother who had only discovered how wonderful food could taste in her nineteenth year.

Before the birth of Fanny there seemed to have been no single defining moment in Alice's life. But since that momentous day in August 1983, and the wedding of Alice and Stephen Singer on September 23, 1985, Alice's personal and professional life became more focused and certainly more private. "I had never believed marriage made a difference one way or another," she replied when asked why she had not made the commitment sooner. "You were either committed or you weren't—a piece of paper wouldn't change that. But then I realized it meant a lot to him [Singer], and it became important to me because I knew I was going to stay with him forever and ever, amen."

After their honeymoon in Tuscany, Alice's wish for a more private life became a priority: "My ideal is still that Pagnol time. But I don't know how to make my life that way." There was only so much time in a day. Fanny needed much of it. Stephen, a self-employed artist, wanted some of it and eventually took on a second career as a wine merchant because it complemented Alice's work. So there was not much time left for the many friends with whom she had been intimate.

Old friends said that the delicate-looking lady who used to work herself blind in the restaurant's kitchen had learned to pace herself. Others said that she had become more professional, limiting her day-to-day involvement in the restaurant to participating in menu planning, tasting, and ombudsmanship. She also brought her own family into the Chez Panisse family. Her parents purchased a home in Berkeley, and her father continued his role on Pagnol et Cie.'s board of directors. A younger sister worked in the restaurant. Another sister and her husband became Alice's partners and the managers of Café Fanny, a smart, stand-up, European-styled eatery, which since its opening had attracted an enthusiastic Berkeley following with its big bowls of café au lait, buckwheat crepes, toasted country bread, imaginative sandwiches, and vintage Champagne sold by the glass.

A certain amount of distancing was also evident in the cookbooks that came to be known as "Chez Panisse" books, inspired by Alice although not written by her. When a dessert cookbook composed of Lindsey Shere's recipes was proposed by Alice's agent for "such and such an advance," Alice urged Lindsey to take on the project and promised to be "official taster" and facilitator.

Lindsey's talent for fine desserts had evolved as she progressed from *Gourmet* reader and "Julia Watcher" to innovative pastry chef when Chez Panisse opened in 1971. In those early days, she worked in the kitchen of a little cottage just steps behind the converted two-story house, bringing her cakes and pastries over to the restaurant before they were supposed to be served. Alone or with the assistance of one of the cooks on special occasions, Lindsey produced from three to five à la carte desserts (her famous almond tart and chocolate mousse were regularly on the menu) and the planned finales that were part of the special menus. Over the years, her pastry staff gradually grew to four full-time chefs, with the most substantial increase occurring after the opening of the upstairs café in 1980. At that time also the à la carte dessert menu became a feature of the café menu, and the weekly menus of the downstairs dining room featured a single dessert that harmonized with the other courses of the dinner menu. In dessert planning, Lindsey's guiding principle was seasonal availability and appropriateness with respect to the other courses. Alice described the success of Lindsey's efforts to prepare desserts "of the right flavor and texture to complete the meal, something to amuse and surprise the palate one more time—never overwhelming or dulling.''

A network of suppliers already in place assured fruits and berries of superior quality, but the quest for varieties not previously available led to opportunities to achieve the taste and texture most suitable for a particular tart, ice cream, or compote. Lindsey also experimented with flowers, herbs, spices, and wines in dessert making, using violets and rose petals as well as vanilla beans to flavor sugars; gathering plum, acacia, and mimosa blossoms to lend flavor and scent to ice creams; and growing basil, lavender, lemon thyme, and angelica to flavor custards and poaching syrups. The results, Alice said, ''were restrained—yet exotic, and wild. They leave you charmed, surprised, and satisfied.''

A cookbook that collected these one-of-a-kind desserts would have to be as unique in organization and visual imagery as it was in content. After an impressive introductory chapter, "The Basic Repertory," consisting of fundamental techniques needed to make the desserts in the book, Lindsey develops chapters with recipes grouped around dominant ingredients in a seasonal context. Chapters for winter—"Apples, Pears, and Quinces" and "Citrus Fruits"—begin the cycle, offering the staples of the winter table until the start of the especially long California spring. These are followed by "Tropical Fruits," "Flowers, Herbs, and Spices, "Berries," and "Cherries." "Figs, Melons, and Other Fall Fruits" complete the annual cycle. With additional chapters on "Nuts and Dried Fruits," "Chocolate," and "Wine and Spirits," the book contains over 300 recipes. In the spirit of nouvelle pâtisserie, Lindsey avoids classical buttercream–filled cakes, fondant frostings, desserts flambéed with liqueur, and elaborately decorated confections.

Just as fresh fruit, whether in gratins, mousses, sauces, or sherbets, have come to be the distinguishing feature of the new French cuisine, fresh fruit and berries are the dominant ingredients in Lindsey's desserts, with the added imperative that they be seasonal, picked at the peak of ripeness, and served immediately. Tarte Tatin warm from the oven, ice cream made in small quantities for the evening's service, Bing cherries so plentiful that quick sautéing with sugar, kirsch, and balsamic vinegar create a perfect compote—these grand finales are quintessentially Chez Panisse.

An organized person, well-known for carrying a notebook containing recipes, jottings, clippings, and "things to try" with her at all times, Lindsey completed the manuscript in ten months. Because she wanted her book to exhibit the same attention to visual detail that had made the two earlier Chez Panisse cookbooks so distinctive, Lindsey and her husband, an art and music critic, contacted Arizona-born artist Wayne Thiebaud. When he agreed to illustrate the book, designer Patricia Curtan gave one of his paintings a prominent place on the dust jacket. Tortes, ice creams, and fruits painted in broad strokes and primary colors introduce the unfussy and imaginative desserts presented in the book.

Published in 1985, *Chez Panisse Desserts* was hailed as "poetical and beautiful" by Elizabeth David, "lovely and unusual" by Richard Olney, and "innovative, refreshing, and irresistible" by Diana Kennedy. More to the point, three cookbooks emanating from Chez Panisse in four years kept the restaurant in the vanguard of California's culinary scene.

Although Alice had retired temporarily from the long hours of prep work in the kitchen, she continued to promote the concept of fresh and seasonal that had become synonymous with Chez Panisse, taking the idea far beyond nothing canned, nothing frozen, nothing pre-prepared, and nothing made with preservatives. Most of the restaurant's produce came from the growers' cooperative, the Chinos' farm, Bob Cannard's organic farm, and the Green Gulch Zen Center Farm. A regular source for eggs was New Life Farms, and enormous strides in finding good meat sources for the restaurant were being made. With a broader and more controlled network of suppliers providing the kitchen with a variety of foodstuffs that even Alice had not envisioned five years earlier, she urged Paul Bertolli to write a cookbook that would not only collect many of his innovative recipes and forays into organic gardening but also tell the story of Chez Panisse in the second decade of its existence.

Motherhood had reinforced Alice's convictions about quality food in spite of the fact that two-and-a-half-year-old Fanny's eating habits still mystified her mother. "One day she'll be interested in pasta and bread, and the next day she'll want to eat vegetables," she told an interviewer. "I thought she didn't like strong tastes, yet she likes olives and garlic. Every time I develop a theory about it, she breaks the rules." But whether it was pasta simply served with parsley, garlic, and olive oil or a bowl of steamed peas right from the garden, Alice insisted that her daughter's food be nutritious, and pleasing to both eye and palate. The idea of irradiation to kill off bacteria or preserve shelf life was as distasteful to her as sprouting supermarket potatoes and midwinter hothouse tomatoes. "Once you taste a tomato in the summer, you won't eat a tomato in the winter" was Alice's philosophy, whether at home or at the restaurant.

There wasn't a scheme or a plan to promote her philosophy of fresh and seasonal that she did not enthusiastically endorse. She wanted to revolutionize the food services of the Oakland Museum by introducing a food gallery that would include a bakery with an old-fashioned brick oven so people could see how breads and tortillas were originally made. She also proposed a restaurant that would serve traditional and contemporary California dishes along with a café that would offer light lunches that could be eaten in a garden where the salad greens and vegetables for the restaurant could be grown. At another time she joined forces with Berkeley's Mayor Eugene Newport to create new jobs for the city's unemployed by giving them opportunities to grow vegetables on vacant lots. And she had a long-range dream of a cooking school within the public vocational high school system. These schemes were only a prelude to the Oakland Market project, which she wanted to develop within the next two years.

Hers was a crazy mix of politics, food fanaticism, and friendship. But as Tom Luddy often said, "She'll never be able to rest completely and become complacent and rich or allow herself to be merchandised like some of her heroes who've done commercials for frozen food." Once bitten, twice shy, Alice had made a commercial with Wolfgang Puck for the Pacific Bell Telephone Company and later regretted it. "They caught me in a weak moment," she said. "I wanted the money to do my garden, but I'll never do a commercial again." Working with the writers and producers, she realized the extent to which anyone can be manipulated, and it was simply not worth it.

Although highly photogenic, she was also a bit prickly about glamour shots and the use of makeup. One of a group described by a friend as the Diane Keatons of the restaurant community, Alice had long distinguished herself by wearing faux-period clothing from a local shop called Bazaar Bazaar. Dressing down in the kitchen at Chez Panisse, she also chose to wear a black Oriental-style silk tunic over black drawstring trousers instead of traditional kitchen whites. And when she joined other chefs in the preparation of a benefit dinner, she followed the same practice. It all contributed to an image she assiduously cultivated.

During the second half of the 1980s, the cult of superstar chefs reached its apogee. In the spring of 1986, Alice, along with former Chez Panisse chefs Jonathan Waxman and Mark Miller, Boston chef Lydia Shire, and Campton Place's Bradley Ogden, were invited by Barcelona to cook a meal for its food establishment in exchange for a tour of the best restaurants of the city. "I went," Lydia Shire said, "because I wondered what it would be like to work with Alice Waters. To me she's an idol." Mark Miller and Jonathan Waxman already knew her talent for bringing out both the best and the worst in people. And Bradley Ogden had shared the spotlight with Alice at various San Francisco culinary functions. The events that ensued were frenetic, fun, and food-filled around the clock, but they also exemplified the camaraderie within the culinary community that would soon be enlisted to promote causes larger than financial and professional success.

In June 1987 Alice spearheaded a fund-raising effort to benefit the San Francisco charities serving victims of AIDS. Dinner for approximately 1,000 people was prepared by more than a dozen of the San Francisco area's leading chefs. Eiko Ishioka, Japan's foremost art director, supervised the decor at Fort Mason's Pier 2, and Tom Luddy helped produce the entertainment for the evening. Two months later Alice was en route to New York to participate in a James Beard Foundation fund-raiser.

At times she seemed to be juggling more than a dozen projects simultaneously, and she reluctantly admitted, "I find it almost impossible being successful at both mothering and entrepreneurship. It's as though I'm in perpetual motion." But she seldom departed from her regular schedule. A typical day often began with getting Fanny off to preschool, doing some routine household chores, and spending time with her secretary. By ten o'clock Alice was on her way to Café Fanny for café au lait and a bite of this or that, often tasting a dish (which might or might not pass muster for luncheon service). A stop at Café Fanny frequently also included an impromptu conference with Tom Luddy, Kermit Lynch, or another friend as well as an interview. From eleven o'clock until midafternoon, when she usually picked up Fanny at school, Alice spent most of her time at Chez Panisse, and she often returned in the evening to greet a special guest or join family or friends for a special occasion dinner. By the late 1980s the kitchen was staffed by a dedicated team of chefs that allowed Lindsey Shere, Paul Bertolli, and, especially, Alice to range a bit. But Alice never forgot that the final responsibility was hers.

In the late 1980s Paul Bertolli's cookbook also claimed a considerable amount of her attention. She began as its "provocateur" and eventually spent more time than she had planned in its completion. The first working title was "Tuscan Variations." And, indeed, in every projected chapter the staples of the Italian markets—capers, basil, fennel, onions, garlic, tomatoes, and bitter greens—appeared in the recipes. Using them showcased the restaurant's dedication to freshness and seasonality and Bertolli's conviction that "in the best cooking, the cooking itself does not show." And while some dishes like "Cotechino Sausage" seemed more appropriate for a professional audience, most of the recipes were accessible to everyone.

In many ways, despite Bertolli's focus on the dishes served at Chez Panisse, this was also a personal book. He shared his memories of the wonderful flavors of his grandmother's saffron risotto, his mother's potato gnocchi, and of an incomparable platter of grilled porcini mushrooms served in an unassuming *osteria* in the foothills of the Italian Alps. Moreover, his descriptive introductions to chapters and recipes conveyed a working chef's understanding of foodstuffs and grasp of culinary techniques as well as his personal passion for purity of taste.

The more he worked on the book, the more he wanted to make it all-inclusive. In the late 1980s, with the quality and safety of meats and poultry becoming an issue for groups like Americans for Safe Food, many farmers focused on humane practices for raising meat animals and more suppliers became known to the restaurant's forager as sources for quality products. Standards as well as definitions for organic foods were also increasingly available, and Bertolli's plan to include this kind of information in the cookbook shifted the focus from Tuscan variations to the second working title, "From the Earth to the Table at Chez Panisse."

Sometime during the years the manuscript was in progress, Bertolli and Alice also decided to return to the menu theme of the earlier *Chez Panisse Menu Cookbook,* and they devised a chapter that included the making of a menu, seasonal menus, menus for friends, celebration menus, and wine menus. Again the working title changed. The third title, "Nature of the Feast," included a play on the word *nature* and created a context for a group of seasonal menus, which featured some of the recipes in the book. Two more groups of menus repeated the format of the fanciful "Memorable Menus" of Alice's first book. "Menus for Friends" were acknowledgments of the mentors, friends, and patrons who were an integral part of the restaurant's history, and "Celebration Menus" reinforced the restaurant's commitment to bring friends and family together to commemorate holidays, anniversaries, birthdays, and special days with an appropriate feast. But again the title did not quite convey the multiple themes and variations in the book, and the search continued.

When *Chez Panisse Cooking* was published in 1988, it presented the most comprehensive statement to date of the kind of cooking that had made Chez Panisse a "cutting edge" restaurant for over fifteen years. Illustrated with Berkeley-based Gail Skoff's hand-colored photographs, the book has a handsome format, and, as always, Patricia Curtan designed the jacket and layout. Dishes that cajole diners into paying attention to their food and dishes that prove that a creative cook can use a week's supply of fava beans in yet another wonderful recipe appear in the text amid the simplicity of recipes like spinach soup and bitter apricot preserves. On the other hand, brilliantly devised double soups, pimiento soup with polenta sticks, grilled eggplant tart in a puff-pastry shell, and roast pigeon salad stylishly carry out Alice's basic conviction that recipes originating at Chez Panisse should "shock."

That *Chez Panisse Cooking* caught the attention of environmental magazines as well as periodicals devoted to food and wine was not surprising. Articles in *Organic Gardening* featured Alice and Paul Bertolli engaged in spit-roasting a family meal in the fireplace of Alice's kitchen. The two chefs were in sync; they both believed that "the best food is the simplest food. It's food that is so perfectly what it is that the cook can just let it be." And in the *New York Times*, food writer Florence Fabricant suggested that the chapter "Fresh and Pure Ingredients" about organically raised foodstuffs "deserves to be printed separately as a tract and given the widest distribution." Clearly, the cookbook had a substantial subtext. Between the recipes are miniessays on a diversity of topics—collecting wild mushrooms, bread making, quality ice cream, and menu planning—all embedded in the text. Alice commented that "with this book Paul has turned a page." And from that page, he and the staff at Chez Panisse would "move on to another place."

Although Random House did not use "From the Earth to the Table at Chez Panisse" as the title, the book emphasizes the amount of time and energy that Alice and her staff devote to the kitchen garden and to green markets, where the variety and generosity of the soil are everywhere in evidence. And within the constraints of an increasingly fragile ecology, the book is a clarion call to preserve the environment "amid the threatening pile-up of packages and cans." As a keeper of the flame, Alice also promoted the various uses of the fireplace by alerting Mill Valley's Rose and Gerard garden shop to the availability of a free-standing Tuscan grill perfectly suitable for grilling in an indoor fireplace, which they then listed in their catalog.

In the informal ambience of her own kitchen, she refused to be separated from her guests, preferring to gather them around the reconstructed fireplace that dominated the entire west wall. With family and friends joining in the preparation of a meal, she usually began a course with whatever she had pulled from the garden. She sprinkled tiny potatoes with herbs and olive oil, wrapped them in foil, and roasted them directly on the grill. Or she might place a caldron of savory beans and greens in the hot ashes to cook. She also frequently baked small pizzas in the bread oven for Fanny and her friends.

When she was not overseeing the smooth running of her restaurants, collaborating on the latest Chez Panisse cookbook, or speaking before agricultural, food, and wine groups, Alice and her family did manage to escape to Del Mar Beach, a favorite getaway that was adjacent to the Chinos' farm. And late in 1987 Alice decided to take a six-month sabbatical leave beginning in April 1988, before Fanny's school schedule would limit the family's trips.

With her husband and daughter, Alice returned to France, a year after she had been named the only American and the only woman in the prestigious *Cuisine et Vins de France* magazine's listing of "Les Meilleurs Chefs du Monde" in 1987. "The fact that they have to give me a certain credibility," she later said, "is in a perverse way pleasing to me." And the award really meant more to her than many of the other accolades she had received on both sides of the Atlantic. She was tenth on a list that included Fredy Girardet, Joël Robuchon, Michel Guérard, the Troisgros brothers, and Paul Bocuse. In such company, Alice felt that Gault-Millau's recommendation to cross the Atlantic to dine at Chez Panisse paled a bit, as did her inclusion in *U.S. News & World Report*'s "New American Establishment."

Ranking with world-class chefs also validated her basic belief that "the search for the perfect soufflé—or whatever technical knowledge—is not the important thing at all about food and eating. . . . At the restaurant people come to eat thinking they want some fancy and elaborate and formal 'dining experience.' But it seems to me that they're really hungry for interaction and a good time. So I try to make Chez Panisse unpredictable and informal, surprising and fun. And I want them to eat real food, in season—it doesn't matter a bit whether it's supposed to be fashionable or not. I don't want people to expect inappropriate, out of season, expensive food: no truffles in July or peaches in December. There's a lot of pretension and snobbery and one-upmanship when it comes to food. Just because it's exotic or French or costly doesn't necessarily mean that it's any good."

Hers was a curious blend of savvy public relations and a conviction that sitting around a table with good food, good friends, and good conversation was the only way to overcome the onslaught of culinary commercialism that had been alienating growers and consumers since the turn of the century. Certainly accolades in prestigious magazines and awards for best chef and best restaurant of the year were important. But what probably pleased Alice more was when her friend Martine Labro described dining at Chez Panisse as "ecstasy." From first course to dessert, there was a striving for excellence, a balance of flavors, and a perfectionism that made the Michelin-starred French restaurants in which she and her husband occasionally dined wanting by comparison. To be sure, there were brilliant flashes in these well-known establishments, first courses that were imaginative and beautifully executed, but there was the inevitable letdown when the entrée was served or when an overbearing waitstaff distracted from the service.

At Chez Panisse, whether the patron was Francis Ford Coppola with twenty guests, Janet Malcolm conducting an interview, Ansel Adams and Edward Albee dining on opposite sides of the dining room, Miloš Forman conversing with Mikhail Baryshnikov, Herbert Gold with Stephen Spender, Richard Baker (an abbot on leave from the Zen Center) accompanied by former governor Edmund G. Brown, Jr., Richard Avedon and actor-gourmet Danny Kaye, or the president of Chase Manhattan Bank, he or she could dine and be happy. For the famous and not so famous, Chez Panisse became a benchmark against which other restaurants would be measured. And that was satisfaction, indeed.

Chez Panisse was also a Berkeley institution. Local residents paid attention to and were vitally interested in what was happening there. The comings and goings of staff members, where Alice was on any given day, and even the weekly menus were important and collectible information. And Alice was in the vanguard of those restaurateurs who began offering diners a backstage view by reserving a small spot in the kitchen, or chef's table as it is popularly called, for friends and family.

One of Alice's guiding principles is that very few things do not need changing. It is certainly true in the commercial world of the marketplace but no less operative in the everyday world of Chez Panisse. And she has always been particularly concerned that neither she nor the staff at the restaurant rest on their laurels. For that reason, whenever she had the opportunity, she traveled, talked with chefs, and sampled the local products of a region.

Renting a house in France for three months during her 1988 sabbatical, Alice, Fanny, and Stephen followed their usual pattern of mixing business and pleasure. Restaurants, especially the ones in *la France profonde*, were a source of new ideas for Alice, and Stephen was interested in establishing contacts for his wine business, Singer and Foy Wines. Returning to the States in June, they spent the last three months of Alice's leave in Napa Valley.

During the six months of travel and leisure, Alice had spent more time with Fanny than their routine in Berkeley usually permitted, and she realized that her daughter's observations and eating habits might well contribute to another cookbook. Ever since Fanny was an infant, Alice had been asked for advice about what children liked to eat and recipes that a child could follow easily. So a child's cookbook became a natural choice. A collection of Fanny's recipes was also an opportunity to tell the story of Chez Panisse from a child's perspective.

Back in Berkeley in September, Fanny began first grade and the serious study of French at a bilingual private school. And Alice acquired a new editor at HarperCollins and assembled a team to create the Fanny cookbook. Like the four earlier Chez Panisse cookbooks, this was an "in-house" production, with one of Fanny's best friends, screenwriter Bob Carrau, telling the story of the restaurant from the little girl's point of view. Still-life painter and neighbor Ann Arnold was commissioned to enhance Fanny's story with illustrations. And Patricia Curtan brought the text and illustrations together on every page and designed the book jacket. But it was Alice who made the story happen.

While she didn't exactly put a whisk rather than a rattle in Fanny's hands in those toddler days, Alice applied all of her Montessori training, years of hands-on experience in Chez Panisse's kitchen, and passion for fresh, seasonal food in educating Fanny's palate and encouraging her to experience the joys of cooking and eating. In the beginning there was the big kitchen in the lavender-colored cottage where Fanny lived with her mother and father. It had a fireplace, a big yellow and green Oriole stove, a refrigerator, a worktable, and a large dining room table where family and friends gathered to shell peas, eat, and converse. Outside there was a garden with a section planted especially for Fanny, where she could pick peas, beans, parsley, lettuce, spinach, and strawberries, bring them into the kitchen, and enjoy them.

On the worktable, counters, and cabinet shelves visible through the glass doors were many of Alice's favorite things—a very large mortar and pestle, dishes with many patterns, bottles of olive oil and vinegar, jars of chestnut honey, anchovies, a basket of fresh fruit, and bottles of wine from Stephen Singer's shop. Alice's intention was clear: "Children have to learn about food with all their senses, to know what things look like, feel like, smell like, taste like, and sound like when they're being pounded." And Fanny was given the opportunity to do just that. Alice admitted, "We play around a lot in the kitchen. It's not really cooking in the sense of following recipes. She loves to make salads—go to the garden, collect the greens, then arrange them. She loves to cut and stir. And she loves to eat odd things."

There was, moreover, the brave new world of Chez Panisse, which Fanny describes in her book. For as long as she could re-member, "my mom used to stick me in the empty stockpots stand-ing on the counter. They were just like little playpens for me. I used to stand up in them and watch everything that was going on in the kitchen." Besides being privy to Fanny's acquired likes and dislikes in food, the reader of Fanny at Chez Panisse learns many things about the restaurant, its staff, and Alice's multifaceted role there. The tell-all naïveté of a child's voice brings to life her extended family of pizza chefs, maître d's, managers, pastry chefs, and cooks. Furthermore, themes that were introduced in the earlier books are repeated in the stories told by the little girl. Fanny picking over the raspberries, composting the "real garbage," separating the violet blossoms from the stems and leaves, and shaping a pizza in the form of an olive bottle makes the point about the restaurant's dedication to recycling, hand labor, and creativity in the kitchen with style.

In her fictional voice, Fanny talks knowledgeably about cooking, especially about following her "Mom's Special Rules." The forty-six recipes that accompany her stories were definitely learned at the elbow of a famous "mom" chef. Aioli, calzone, pooris, risotto, and tisane are only a few of Fanny's favorite things; she's also into making cornbread, blackberry ice creams, and 1-2-3-4 Cake. In the Chez Panisse tradition, she likes to put recipes together "to make up whole meals." So Fanny shares her menus for "My Birthday," "Class Pizza Party," "Spring," "Summer," "Fall," and "Winter" before she skips off to another adventure.

In a publishing climate where cookbooks proliferate in increasing numbers each year, what can be said of the five cookbooks in which Chez Panisse is showcased and of Alice Waters as author, collaborator, or provocative spirit behind them? At the very least, the cookbooks transcend many typical chef-author titles because they collectively document more than twenty years of an exciting and continually evolving restaurant. The books also communicate the philosophy of a determined woman who in August 1971 opened a restaurant in Berkeley "to capture the sunny good feelings of another world that contained so much that was incomplete or missing in our own." They are about a style of cooking, about "good food on the board and good wine in the pitcher," and about the age-old pleasures of the table. Fresh and seasonal ingredients are a refrain, as is the conviction that recipes are suggestions, not ironclad procedures to stifle the creativity of the cook—who ideally will start with the freshest available ingredients and then select a recipe, which is the real meaning of good cooking emanating from the garden.

Like her mentor Elizabeth David, Alice would undoubtedly say that a person cannot learn to cook entirely from books, "but if the cooks, celebrated or obscure, of the past had believed that written recipes were unnecessary, we should be in a sad plight indeed. The culinary skill of several centuries of practitioners, both professional and amateur, are distilled into the cookery books we now inherit." Reason enough, if one be needed, to add the Chez Panisse cookbooks to a culinary historian's "essential" list, because they document Berkeley's "second (and more enduring) revolution."

As the twenty-first century approaches, Alice Waters' private and professional goals are very much the same. Whether expressing concerns about agriculture by serving on the advisory board of the Land Institute in Salinas, Kansas, or speaking at conferences sponsored by the American Institute of Wine and Food, or lending her name to Chefs Helping to Enhance Food Safety, the Public Voice group, and Mothers and Others, she is a tireless advocate and a concerned mother. She has also convinced other restaurateurs to purchase produce grown by the participants in Cathrine Snead's criminal rehabilitation program in the Bay Area. Dedicated to raising funds for the victims of AIDS, she not only organized San Francisco's Aid and Comfort benefit in 1987 and took charge of the University of California's cosponsored AIDS benefit in 1990 but also solicited funds for the victims of AIDS by designing a dream kitchen for *Metropolitan Home*'s Show House 2, which opened to the public on March 7, 1991, in New York City.

Described as "rare and well-seasoned," the Show House 2 kitchen re-created the atmosphere of a European farmhouse with soapstone countertops, a copper sink, grained hickory cabinetry featuring open drying and storage racks, and a triple-duty oven that could heat the room, bake bread and pizza, and grill. It was modeled on the kitchen that she and architect James Monday had created in her Berkeley home, and it conveyed the lived-in, broth-scented, kettle-humming conviviality of her personal kitchen with the added details of darker, richer colors, more burnished copper, and a nineteenth-century wing chair from the Orkney Islands ideally suited to daydreaming by the fire. In her older-is-better philosophy, all those dents, scratches, and patches, along with drawers that did not quite shut tight, were the visible signs that told the story that every kitchen should tell to the generations that would pass through it. With Fanny cooking by her side, Alice continues to be mindful of generations.

When Alice and the staff celebrated Chez Panisse's twentieth birthday in August 1991 they were more than a little aware that the restaurant's initial search for the freshest and purest ingredients had grown into a larger mission, in which food was at the heart of some of the most urgent environmental and health issues of these troubled times. One full-time employee was designated an official "forager." At the moment, Alan Tangren "does nothing but scout for ingredients," going out on the road, meeting purveyors, and documenting products and the conditions under which they are grown. The network of quality producers has also expanded, and Sibella Kraus in cooperation with Chez Panisse sponsored the Taste of Summer Produce Festival on Shattuck Avenue to showcase regional growers of high-quality produce and to emphasize the farm-to-restaurant connection that has been crucial to the the restaurant's success.

There were also other changes at Chez Panisse. To everyone's sorrow some of the staff, including Royal Tom Guernsey III, have been lost to AIDS. Alice spends more time at the restaurant, cooking two days a week. And she wonders if the restaurant should be opened to the public even more in order to be warmer and more "house-like." Escalating costs have also changed the eclectic mix of the clientele. When the restaurant opened in 1971, the prix fixe dinner was $6.50. In 1993, the price of a five-course dinner on Fridays and Saturdays escalated to $65, but a special three-course dinner featuring hearty fare often served family style was offered for old friends on Monday evenings for $35. Luncheon and dinner in the café are still modestly priced.

Many other things, however, simply do not change. Despite its popularity, the restaurant is still not a financial success. Although there are usually 100 covers downstairs and 150 in the café each night that Chez Panisse is open, the cost of ingredients is high, and 100 employees (more than double the usual for an establishment of its size) make deep inroads into profits. Prosperity is an illusion, Alice says, "somehow we just can't net a fish." In the European tradition of preparing special meals to celebrate holidays, Bastille Day and the Garlic Festival continue to be joyous occasions (three such celebrations were captured in Les Blank's film *Garlic Is as Good as Ten Mothers*). As always, friends' birthdays are remembered in gracious, even dramatic ways.

In the spring of 1992, Alice masterminded a seventieth birthday party for Marion Cunningham and more than a hundred of her friends. Creating a menu of Marion's favorites—chicken potpies with wild mushrooms, red and yellow beets, iceberg lettuce [a particular favorite] with green goddess dressing—Alice and the Chez Panisse staff led the marathon preparations for the surprise lunch, held at the Robert Mondavi Winery in Napa Valley. With eighteen birthday cakes donated by Marion Cunningham's food famous friends and several decorative breads designed by Steve Sullivan, the party was a huge success and a testament to what former Chez Panisse pastry chef David Lebovitz called the Chez Panisse mafia: "You are there for life. You become a card member."

And that is perhaps the most unchangeable thing of all. Alice remains the fixed center of a family whose members range widely and frequently return, as Jean-Pierre Moullé did at Alice's request in 1992. Is it, as Fanny says, because "the restaurant is really a house?" Or because Alice's mission to nurture is so compelling? Or is it because Alice Waters saw in Berkeley the site of a revolution more far-reaching than the Free Speech Movement and Power to the People's Park? Entertaining President Bill Clinton for dinner on August 18, 1993, Alice improvised a special menu for a meal she had learned about only a short time before the arrival of the president's party and more than twenty Secret Service agents. It was exactly the kind of challenge she has always responded to with energy and style. She personally served the president pasta with crab and corn, a salad with wild mushrooms and green beans, a pizza, and blackberry ice cream, as well as a lemon custard with wild strawberries. And after his visit she followed up with a note, assuring him that "we can mobilize a small army of restaurateurs across the country who share a common belief that the choices we make about what we eat can transform our society. We are delighted that your health care reform efforts are acknowledging the connection between diet, nutrition and public health. Because of this we feel more strongly than ever that the White House can set a powerful example of where health and happiness begins. We hope that you will consider how wonderful it would be if the garden at the White House were to emulate Jeffersonian ideals of practicality, sustainability, and seasonality."

Celebrating her fiftieth birthday by once again visiting Paris in April 1994 marked an important chapter in Alice Waters' life and demonstrated the enduring strength of her conviction that eating well is the radical's best revenge.

CHAPTER EIGHT

Golden State

*The whole idea of California cooking is being heavily overdone,
over-written, overpublished.*

M. F. K. FISHER

*The more my food took on a Californian feeling, the more difficult it
became to write a menu in French.*

ALICE WATERS

*On Saturdays, my friends and I would . . . go to San Francisco and have
artichokes and cinnamon toast. We thought we were so elegant.*

JULIA CHILD

The seeds of the culinary ferment that distinguishes California today were sown during the years that spanned the founding of twenty-one missions from San Diego to Sonoma in the eighteenth century to the baptism of Robert Mondavi's dramatic Mission-style winery in 1966. The more than two-hundred-year chronology, with its waves of immigrants, saw European cuttings and seeds transported to a congenial soil where they produced a similar, yet distinguishable, wine and food. Spanish colonizers from Mexico, Russian fur traders from the north, native Americans and Yankees from the east in search of gold, immigrant Chinese laborers, and German, French, and Italian wine makers all brought with them a taste for the foods and wines of their former homes and an unquenchable desire to replicate them in this new land called California.

To the foods cultivated by the Indians—maize, beans, squashes, and peppers—were added a cornucopia of foods from the Spanish colonizers south of the border, such as avocados, figs, and dates, as well as the Spanish *barbacoa* (barbecue). Later on when the number of Chinese immigrants who had added their foodways to the area was eventually restricted, Italian craftsmen, stonemasons, and laborers joined the workforce and planted olive, lemon, and almond trees as well as artichokes, tomatoes, rice, and other staples of the Italian garden. Early California propagandists stressed the climate, potential agricultural wealth, abundant game, and coastal waters filled with seafood. In the rush of the gold mining era, the promise of a quail under every bush and an abundant supply of oysters in every saloon lured ranchers and gold-seeking adventurers into a variety of newly opened boarding houses, taverns, and restaurants.

Since the late nineteenth century San Francisco, like New York, has had its tradition of French restaurants, such as Poulet d'Or and Maison Riche, where patrons came to expect haute cuisine on the plate and hauteur at the door. But there were also Japanese, Chinese, Italian, and other ethnic restaurants catering to the diversity of the city's population, plus early and still thriving maverick establishments like Jack's (1864), Sam's (1867), and the Tadich Grill (1849), which offered a host of signature dishes such as Hangtown fry, deviled crab, and cioppino. And a word must be said about the "barngrills," a word coined by *San Francisco Chronicle* columnist Herb Caen when he defended the Washington Bar & Grill against the negative remarks of a restaurant critic: "[The critic] seemed not to understand that the regulars go there for something besides the food. Friendship, warmth, noise, fairly decent shouted conversation, a great staff." The bar and grill experience combined the best features of a French bistro, an Italian trattoria, and a gold miner's dream of an "oyster saloon." According to food writer James McNair, this uniquely San Franciscan institution was practically as old as the city itself.

With wine and food there is always a question of influence, whether of time and place, soil and climate, or the vagaries of human endeavor. And whether the crossings are of grape cuttings from Mexico and Europe to California in the eighteenth century or from California's root stocks to those European countries whose vines were decimated by phylloxera in the late nineteenth century, cuttings have gone back and forth and will continue to do so. The same can be said of food trends. Whether it be an emphasis on lighter fare or a cultivation of regional dishes, crossways have prevailed.

While the dynamics of the professional wine and food world encouraged these crossways, there was ultimately something agreeable in the sun and sea and soil that made the crossing so successful, along with the individuals who had the will to do so. At the turn of the century, names like Rossi, Sebastiani, and Gallo as well as

Schram, Frug, Wente, Korbel, and Beaulieu became well known in California's wine tradition. And in the 1970s, a highly publicized "winery revolution" took place throughout California, virtually doubling wine production in less than eight years. When the wine makers' emphasis on the pairing of wine and food and the fresh and seasonal ingredients offered in California attracted nationwide attention, the land and its cuisine became more than a journalist's paradigm. And the ragtag term *melting pot* invited deconstruction.

By accident and not by design, the three women who have substantially changed the way many Americans think about food have had a special relationship with California. And they have established their own personal crossways between France and California and created their own private geographies of both places. While not a native Californian, M. F. K. Fisher lived in and was identified with both the southern and northern parts of her adopted state. The French Chef, Julia Child, was born and raised in Pasadena and plans to retire eventually to her home in Montecito Shores. And while Alice Waters perhaps has the shortest residency in the Golden State, she enjoys a continuing visible presence in the place known on both sides of the Atlantic simply as Berkeley. But residency is only a partial explanation for the special affinity that these three women have to this prelapsarian state. For M. F. K. Fisher and Julia Child, there was an early identification of California as a kind of Eden where, Mary Frances believed, "smog, pollution, effluence, ecology itself were still part of an unsuspected semantics"; for Alice Waters, California had to be reinvented.

As America's most prolific gastronomical writer, Mary Frances ranged comfortably between France and California, drawing inspiration and subject matter from her beloved Provence and her various homes in the Golden State. By writing about her childhood in Whittier, she dramatized the often contradictory influences of the parade of cooks employed by the Kennedy family and the dietary rules of Dr. Kellogg advocated by Grandmother Holbrook. Mary Frances also introduced compelling aspects of French cuisine to a coterie of devoted readers in the late 1930s, when *The Fannie Farmer Cookbook* and *The Settlement Cookbook* had widespread authority. And when most of her fellow Americans were more familiar with brands of baking powder and nutritionally balanced meals, her books referred to Brillat-Savarin and *Larousse Gastronomique*, recounted the pleasure of a *pâté de foie gras en brioche*, and praised the ripe bouquet of a Chambertin 1919 in a great crystal globe. As a traveler, aspiring viticulturist, and writer, she irrevocably linked France and California in America's culinary consciousness by simply spinning out stories, telling gastronomical tales, and reminding everyone that eating is not only a necessity but an art.

It is of no little significance that M. F. K. Fisher's first published article appeared in the California publication *Westways* and was about Olas, a fictitious name for Laguna Beach, her family's summer retreat. The artists' colony was, she wrote, "much more my spiritual home, from my fourth to perhaps my thirty-second year, than ever was Whittier, or Vevey, or probably Dijon, or Hemet." Living there was easy and uncomplicated, with most meals gathered from the sea and the local farmstand, prepared simply, and savored out of doors.

Stronger than the great stretch of Laguna's shore, however, was Mary Frances's gravitation toward vineyards and the company of vintners. After her father's death, she moved north to St. Helena and then later to Glen Ellen to live in wine country. At a time when memories became her mainstay, the cycle of pruning, budding, tending, and harvesting helped her to relive vicariously her brief vineyard haven with Dillwyn Parrish in Vevey, and her childhood forays from San Gabriel to San Diego with her father to restock the ranch's supply of wine. And in her last years the rhythm of the seasons went beyond remembrance to vitalize the present.

In that sunny, fragrant land just a few hours north of the Golden Gate Bridge, she, like the grape growers whose vineyards bordered the Bouverie Ranch, embraced a satisfying way of life. A loaf of Sonoma sourdough bread, a jug of local wine, and a wedge of Teleme Jack cheese were the staples of her kitchen, along with fresh fruit and vegetables either supplied by her neighbors or available at the market. They were the bounty of California's soil, a celebration of fresh and seasonal foodstuffs that she had known since childhood and had frequently written about. Captured in her prose is the immediacy, the sensual experience of dining well in company or alone, in one place or another. In her various Provençal and

California kitchens, fresh fruits and vegetables were rushed to the table dressed simply with a vinaigrette. By evening they were cooked to stave off their quick progression from ripeness to decay. It is no accident that Mary Frances's prose is infused with thoughts about "fine preserving," with capturing the magic of the moment or saving the remnants of a basket of cherries, zucchini, or tomatoes.

Although she spent some years away from California, Mary Frances made her home in cities and small towns from Baja to the Russian River. And it became increasingly impossible to think of her without assigning "a local habitation and a name" to the places in the stories she told. In Whittier the large brown house on Painter Avenue and the ranch on the rural extension of that same street were backdrops for what she later called her "ghetto" years in the Quaker enclave. Despite the fact that by the late 1950s Whittier's population had grown to over 100,000, and "the soft hills [had] been cut into recklessly, to make holes and cliffs for houses, and native plants like poppies and lupine and sage [had] been shaved away forever," the Whittier of an earlier time lives in *Among Friends*. The same can be said for the sparsely settled, undeveloped, raw beauty of Mary Frances's Laguna Beach.

Her accounts of dining in Los Angeles contrasted sharply with the asceticism of the dining room where Grandmother Holbrook's food preferences prevailed. Mary Frances enjoyed her first restaurant meal in Los Angeles's Victor Hugo dining room, where chicken à la king foreshadowed many future elegant meals—entrées served under glass, buffets of salads, and flambéed desserts. After a day of shopping there were also memorable visits to an ice cream parlor called the Pig 'n' Whistle, where Mrs. Kennedy and her two daughters sat in a highly polished booth and ate ice cream scooped into long silver boats before boarding the Red Car at the Pacific Electric Depot for their return to Whittier.

Farther away from Whittier, the City by the Bay was "an escape hatch." Initially Mary Frances's parents went to San Francisco to visit the Pacific Panama Exposition in 1915. Souvenirs from the city made it magical and desirable to Mary Frances and her sister Anne. In 1924, when they attended the Bishop's School in Palo Alto, they had the opportunity to venture into San Francisco on

Saturday afternoons and walk around Union Square or meet their mother, who frequently spent the weekend with her daughters, treating them to tea at the Garden Court and taking them on excursions into Chinatown. Years later, when Mary Frances's own daughters were in schools either in or near San Francisco, the city took on additional importance. And in Mary Frances's last years, the city became the point beyond which it was almost impossible to travel. Throughout her life, she wrote, "San Francisco stayed firmly in our credo as the cure, the salve and balm, the escape hatch."

Mary Frances also wrote about living in places as dissimilar as an untillable and previously haunted ranch called Bareacres near Hemet and a one-room apartment only a short distance from Paramount Studio in Hollywood. She spent many happy years also in a hundred-year-old house in St. Helena. But surely Mary Frances's most quintessentially California residence was in the Valley of the Moon. The-two-and-a-half-room adobe-style *palazzino* was designed and built for her on the Bouverie Ranch a few miles north of Sonoma. Situated on more than 500 acres of land, the ranch offered privacy, security, and a sampling of every terrain that can be found in California except a sea line. A subtropical canyon, 150-foot waterfall, pasturage, vineyards, birds, wildflowers, and groves of madrona, eucalyptus, and bay trees afforded Last House an ever-changing pattern of fragrances, sounds, and views.

As culturally and climatically important as California was to Mary Frances's lifestyle, however, she etched her own private geography of the Golden State into her writings. California was the promise of adventure, beachcombing, and lush orange groves that had made her father decide to push westward from Albion, Michigan, with his wife and two young daughters. Although for him the adventure dimmed, there were opportunities and space enough to escape to the seashore and eventually to the ranch he bought on the outskirts of Whittier. As soon as it was possible, Mary Frances, in turn, escaped to France, only to return. Like her father, she made California her permanent residence and settled into a journalistic career, still hoping for more.

There is no doubt that those early days in California exposed Mary Frances to some of the best and worst traditions of American cooking. Homemade peach pie bathed in fresh cream, the pervasive smells of jellies and preserves cooking in the kitchen, rare grilled steak served on a bed of fresh watercress were the pluses. White sauce over carrots and dried beef, overcooked root vegetables, and tomatoes stewed with soggy bread were the preferences of a strong-willed grandmother. The latter made a strong case for the former. The cooking of France was a feast for her eyes and palate that totally changed her attitude toward food and affected the composition of every meal she would ever serve when she returned to California.

At Last House a typical lunch consisted of a bottle of local wine, a gratin of eggplant, peppers, celery, or endive served at room temperature, sourdough bread, salad greens, and fresh berries with crème fraîche. Mary Frances usually wrote very early in the morning. Depending on the hour, she then prepared various dishes for the day's meals and enjoyed a light lunch and good conversation well into the afternoon. At about four o'clock she attended to correspondence and more writing until early evening, when she either entertained or dined alone. Beginning with a glass of sherry or her favorite Campari, vermouth, and gin aperitif, she preferred a simple meal consisting of vegetables *à la grecque* or tomatoes with a hint of pesto, followed by soup or a simple gratin, baby lettuces, and fresh fruit or ice cream for dessert.

When asked about the phenomenon called California cuisine, she often stated that she was "fed to the teeth with the word *California* in connection with any cuisine at all." But she did feel that the trend away from heavy sauces, too much butter and cream in cooking, and the excesses of haute cuisine, especially in restaurant service, was a welcome one. And she readily admitted that the food associated with California had always been interesting to her "because it combines so many elements—New England, Oriental, southern France, and Italy." As a final caveat she emphasized that California cuisine was not new and that eclectic regional influences had been in place for years. In 1946 she had read with pleasure Genevieve Callahan's *California Cook Book*. In the 1950s Helen Evans Brown had published a series of books; one of them was called *Patio Cook Book* and much of it was devoted to charcoal cooking. Although mesquite replaced charcoal, the principle was the same. It was a well-known fact, furthermore, that grills with open fire pits were commonplace in the tent-and-shack San Francisco of 1849 and, years earlier, in the missions.

Under the barrage of articles on nouvelle cuisine in the 1970s, some of which were good and some misinformed, Mary Frances viewed the latest culinary preoccupation from afar and talked the matter over with Julia Child. Whatever the "style" of the food or its presentation, she concluded that nouvelle cuisine's most important, and perhaps only, contribution was in providing young, talented chefs a chance to show their inventiveness. By the same token, she was pleased when its excesses quickly gave way to capitalizing on regional differences and tastes. Independent, innovative, and certain in her likes and dislikes, Mary Frances paid little or no attention to food fads and defined gastronomy as the art of eating and drinking with intelligence and grace. That she chose to practice that art in California made a statement: "This is the way my past, my education, my environment all taught me to live now. I could never say that I like all of my pattern, and I recognize that I am perhaps too cozily removed from the rapacious activities of other parts of my planet Earth. But I am here. The wine is almost perfect."

Not only was California a refuge, escape hatch, and a bountiful place for Mary Frances to live as a career woman, single parent, and "national treasure," but the "laid back," nonjudgmental ambience of the West Coast was conducive to creating the unusual blend of sophistication and high jinks that have made her books so memorable. While in her eyes her work might have been simply "sit down at the desk kind of journalism," or "upper-class comment on the pleasures of the table," M. F. K. Fisher's first five books broke with a pattern of food writing that concentrated on nutritional information, balanced meals, and entertaining tips. A keen observer of French foodways, and a successful translator of them into a contemporary idiom, she attracted a coterie of readers and imitators.

Scores of magazine writers have appropriated the "I, myself" syntax, food stylists deliberately remember the aromatic kettle of chowder on Grandmother's stove while using their high-tech cooktops, and culinary arrivistes romanticize the bread boxes of their growing-up years. Unfortunately, most of them lack the authentic-

ity of the "gastronomical she," and their work does not resonate
with the depth of continuous reminiscence. Too often M. F. K.
Fisher's imitators write about food instead of hunger, culinary
history instead of the universal rites of cooking. They develop
recipes to be followed at the worktable instead of recipes begging
to be read and enjoyed because they are essentially literary and
belong not to the literature of knowledge but to the literature of
power. Still, imitation lends its own kind of favor, and it is certainly an acknowledgment that M. F. K. Fisher in addition to
creating a genre of gastronomical writing heretofore nonexistent in
American prose also improved the quality of culinary writing in
this country. That she chose to do it "nowhere but here," suggests
that California was as congenial to her muse as it was to her.

Julia Child's relationship with her birth state has always had a
different comfort level. California is a part of her inheritance, a link
with her pioneering ancestors. Pasadena was the place of her birth
and growing up, the scene of many family gatherings at the home
she loved. During the years that she and Paul lived abroad, the
sunny communities ringing Los Angeles were places to revisit to
see family and friends. Later on when her sister and brother-in-law
moved north of the Golden Gate Bridge and her longtime friend
and assistant Rosemary Manell located in Belvedere nearby, San
Francisco drew Julia and Paul to the West Coast as often as their
schedule permitted. And in the 1980s, when travel to the south of
France became increasingly difficult, Julia decided that she not only
could but would go home again.

Julia's college years in New England and brief career in New
York City did not really convince her that the East Coast was a
better place to live than California. Paul Child did. In the man
she met in Ceylon, she discovered a cosmopolitanism that family,
friends, the Junior League, and would-be suitors in California had
never offered. She readily "turned her back on all that," as she
put it, to be his wife. Listening to him converse about the many
regional varieties of Chinese food, meeting his artistic twin
brother and talented family in Pennsylvania, and realizing the extent to which they were conversant with music, art, literature,
and politics motivated her to change what could only be called a

self-deprecating self-image: "I was a real hayseed, having never been outside of the USA except for China," she said. Paul Child, on the other hand, was an intellectual, an artist and photographer, who had traveled extensively and had been involved in sensitive operations with the OSS in the Far East. Julia happily shared his travels, changed her political allegiances, and learned as many foreign languages as she could.

Through the accidents of time and place, Julia began her career when Paul's was beginning to wane. But in regard to living arrangements, his priorities prevailed. When he retired, they chose the intellectual milieu of Cambridge, Massachusetts as their permanent home and built their small retreat in Plascassier for social and professional reasons. In the early 1980s, however, they purchased an apartment in Montecito Shores for convenience, climate, and a certain cachet. Julia wrote enthusiastically about the new condominium, which was simple and functional inside with an enclosed balcony for Paul to use as a studio. She created a makeshift writing area for herself by blocking off the dining room from the living room. The views from the large windows opened to the Pacific shoreline, where she sighted fishing boats offshore, people strolling the beach, and "trees of every California description."

Crossing the country on tours promoting her books and various TV series, Julia was continually reappraising certain things in "Le Far West." California, north and south, had catapulted into culinary prominence, and Julia's 1984 TV series, *Dinner at Julia's*, which was filmed in Santa Barbara, annotated some of the authentic and some of the superficial features of what had become known as California cuisine. Unfortunately, the Rolls-Royce crowd who gathered in "Julia's Santa Barbara Showplace" suggested that the cuisine of the moment belonged only to those who could afford to dine in designer clothes and party with the rich and famous. And her selection of guest chefs, both American and French, focused attention on the current cultivation of megastar celebrity chefs. All together, it was a little more Tinseltown than a demonstration of what Jeremiah Tower called "that American straightforwardness of personality that really helps in cooking."

The "gathering" segments of the show featured Julia touring Zacky Farms Chicken Ranch, shrimping in the Santa Barbara

Channel, foraging for wild chanterelles in the hills above Santa Barbara, and picking artichokes at Borchard & Sons Ranch as well as other collecting, picking, and fishing scenes. Fortunately, even the "designer duck" and "soufflé crepes" could not distract from the quality of foodstuffs available in California and in the Pacific Northwest that flashed across the colored TV screen. The entrées of leg of lamb roasted with only the addition of herbs and mustard, Alaska salmon steamed in white wine, and grilled jumbo shrimp that were prepared during the course of the thirteen shows made a strong statement about ingredients that were fresh, light, and prepared in uncomplicated ways to preserve their natural flavors. And those preparations were closer to what was really going on in California's private and professional kitchens than were the remnants of haute cuisine.

Perhaps the most helpful feature of Dinner at Julia's was the involvement of California's wine growers in the pairing of appropriate wines with the various courses presented at the dinners. To an audience only too familiar with the "jug" wines produced en masse from grapes grown in the San Joaquin Valley, the information that "boutique" wines were being made and were frequently not available beyond the borders of the state was a coup de foudre. Seeing Richard Graff suggest a Pinot Noir 1974 as an appropriate wine for the cheese course, Richard Sanford pair a Pinot Noir Vin Gris 1981 with stuffed mushrooms duxelles, and Robert Mondavi offer a Botrytis Sauvignon Blanc 1978 with the apple tart dessert course introduced the age-old marriage of food and wine to middle America via television. And it gave that audience a positive image of the hardworking people behind the wine labels.

When an ever greater emphasis was placed on the totality of the wine and food experience in the 1980s, Julia was enlisted to participate in Robert Mondavi's "Great Chefs of France and America" cooking programs, which were held at his state-of-the-art winery in the Napa Valley. Not only was the food prepared to complement some of the "newer" styles of wine he was promoting, such as Chenin Blanc and Fumé Blanc, but Mondavi also took on the role of "actually sculpturing the wine to enhance the food." Whether served in the dining room, where the windowed walls provided views of the Mayacamas mountains to the west, or served outdoors on the patios, terraces, and gardens that were an extension of the winery, these Lucullan dining experiences epitomized California entertaining. Although Julia participated, she still remained very much "the French Chef," and not a practicing innovator defining more precisely the new California cuisine.

Neither Julia's participation in these typically California-style food events nor Santa Barbara's epicurean reputation, which has grown substantially since Julia selected Montecito Shores as a winter retreat, has really influenced the articles she continues to write. Named with Marcella Hazan and Jacques Pépin as one of a trio of contributing editors of *Food & Wine* in October 1992, Julia began her first article with a recipe for beef stew which she prepared while saying farewell to her little house in Plascassier. It was made with braising beef from the *supermarché*, which now has replaced the small village's butcher, baker, and vegetable shops. The stew was also marinated in Provençal olive oil, local onions, tomatoes, garlic, and half a bottle of hearty neighborhood red wine and finished in her blue enamel-lined iron casserole. In that article, as in so many of her recent pieces, she draws on her years in France and offers recipes she loves, like Classic Fish en Croûte, and Steam-Roasted Duck, the recipes she feels a need to share.

Julia has no appetite for "trendy souped-up fantasies." She has little tolerance for "kiddy food," which she describes as "Grilled. Half of it is burned, and half of it is raw." She abhors food that is prepared without a knowledge of sound French principles. But Julia refuses to be typecast. While she has undoubtedly done more to encourage basic cooking techniques and share the "pleasures of the table" than any other TV cooking teacher, she never stops in her efforts to improve professional cooking standards in this country and to bridge the gap between "master chefs" and home cooks. It is a mission she has dedicated herself to. She readily admits that there are passionate chefs like Alice Waters who "just sprang forth with no formal training—she's a genius, very influential, and just revolutionary," but she also maintains—as she wrote in *Cooking with Master Chefs*—that the desire and willingness of serious cooks and chefs to learn new things "turns home cooking and the pleasures of the table into a wonderful adventure."

Diplomatically, both Julia and Alice respect generational differences. And for Alice it is simply obvious that "Julia made it happen." She made Americans from coast to coast aware of the
difference between brioche and croissant, piqued their curiosity
about French restaurants, and got them into the kitchen to make
dishes with a distinctly French accent. Alice also acknowledges that
Julia paved the way for the success of a restaurant like Chez Panisse.
But what Julia took away from France was a vastly different experience from Alice's and it took the *Cooking with Master Chefs* series
in 1993 to find common ground between the two.

Opening a restaurant to give her friends a place where they
could discuss politics and enjoy food similar to the meals she
prepared in her own dining room, Alice Waters unwittingly
broke with the tradition of a typical "restaurant," yet she captured the dynamics of many of the Bay Area establishments of
the earlier days that were famous for their fresh but simply prepared foods. And certainly what some have called California's
"laid-back style," openness, broad-mindedness, and receptivity to
new kinds of experience, played no little part in her willingness to
do her own thing and offer the same prerogative to the other
cooks in her kitchen, becoming thereby the mentor for dozens of
successful chefs.

Culinary history records very few instances of these lineages, but
Alice and her restaurant belong to their number. At least thirty
years earlier, Fernand Point established one among his apprentices
at La Pyramide in Vienne, and Paul Bocuse, Alain Chapel, the
Troisgros brothers, Louis Outhier, and François Bise became *chefs-
patron* of restaurants dedicated to a simpler, lighter style of French
cuisine. A similar, although not quite comparable, phenomenon
occurred in New York City when Henri Soulé owned Le Pavillon
and the chefs who were trained by him went out to establish
restaurants of the caliber of La Grenouille, La Côte Basque, La
Potinière, Le Veau d'Or, and La Caravelle in Manhattan. Even
more recently Charles Palmer, the paterfamilias of the River Cafe,
listed nine protégés who have left his kitchen to supervise other
restaurants, and Alfred Portale at the Gotham Bar and Grill has
sent out at least five chefs to take charge of trendy local eateries. But
even they acknowledge that New York is too competitive to foster

many restaurant lines of descent. Boston also boasts a lineage of sorts, beginning with Jasper White and continuing with Lydia Shire, Gordon Hamersley, and Jody Adams. The West Coast, however, is better known for its expansiveness, and Alice Waters is without equal in promoting the careers of the succession of talented cooks who have entered the back door at Chez Panisse. It is simply a different kind of restaurant.

Beginning with the chain of command, which is minimal at best, there was no resemblance between the old-style French kitchens, which were authoritarian, and the freewheeling creative spirit that has always distinguished Alice's kitchen. In its early days, Lindsey Shere confessed that they really didn't know what they were doing, but Alice's spirit kept them together. Jeremiah Tower, probably Chez Panisse's most enterprising graduate, describes his apprenticeship at the restaurant more dramatically: "It was so chaotic that I didn't have a chance to think for two years." Together with Willy Bishop, an out-of-work beatnik, he learned to cook by doing it all, including most of the prep work, and "when necessary, the dishwashers became cooks." But when he left in 1977, he knew exactly what he wanted to do to make his mark on the Bay Area culinary scene.

After Tower's departure, Alice, joined by Jean-Pierre Moullé and Mark Miller, worked the kitchen, where each prepared one of the courses of the dinner menu. Miller credits Alice with teaching him "to understand a lot about my own abilities. She always pushes you to the edge to be really adventurous." A different course every day gave him a basic repertoire of more than 500 dishes in the three years that he was at Chez Panisse before leaving to develop his own southwestern-style cuisine at the Coyote Cafe in Santa Fe and later at Red Sage in Washington, D.C.

In the creative turmoil of the kitchen at Chez Panisse, it was not unusual for a cook to stay for less than a year, as Jonathan Waxman did. When he moved on to a position as chef at Michael's in Santa Monica, he created signature vegetable and fruit composed salads that distinguished the kitchen of one of Southern California's innovative restaurants. And he ultimately introduced the freshness and lightness of California-style cuisine to New York when he opened Jams.

Nor was it unusual for kitchen associates, paid or unpaid, to remain at Chez Panisse indefinitely or for long periods of time. Paul Bertolli replaced Jean-Pierre Moullé in 1982 and was executive chef of the dining room until 1992, when he left to pursue a degree in medieval philosophy. To complete the circle, Jean-Pierre Moullé returned to share the kitchen with Alice and reintroduce a French flavor into the menu.

While many of Alice's protégés did not open their own restaurants, they became respected and famous in the food world in other capacities. Assistant pastry chef Mark Peel joined Wolfgang Puck at Spago, Steve Sullivan opened the Acme Bread Company when kitchen space at Chez Panisse became too limited, and Paul Johnson propelled Monterey Fish into a successful business.

Alice also broke new ground by opening her kitchen to women in an unprecedented way. Since the opening of Chez Panisse, women have risen to the top in more than a score of restaurants in San Francisco. No other city in the States can match that number. And while there are financial as well as social reasons for this, many women in the cooking profession cite Alice Waters as an inspiration. The chef and co-owner of Zola's simply says, "Alice was definitely a role model and very encouraging for everyone."

Beginning with Chez Panisse's first chef, Victoria Wise, and the restaurant's continuing pastry chef, Lindsey Shere, the list of celebrated women who have worked with Alice is long. "She was responsible for giving me my break," said Joyce Goldstein, who in ten years has gone from cooking teacher to assistant baker and Café Chez Panisse manager to chef-proprietor of her own restaurant, Square One. Charlene Rollins also opened a restaurant, called the New Boonville Hotel, in Boonville, California, where she and her husband literally lived Alice's dream of raising everything served in the restaurant. Deborah Madison went from Chez Panisse to the vegetarian restaurant Greens in San Francisco and on to a successful career as a teacher and cookbook author; Judy Rogers did a stint as chef at Union Hotel in Benicia and then became co-owner of Zuni Cafe in San Francisco. Carolyn Dille became a caterer in Rockville, Maryland. And after working for three years in the kitchen at Chez Panisse, Sibella Kraus was instrumental in developing a liaison between food producers and restaurants in the Bay

Area and in creating a permanent public market in San Francisco.

While Alice has always said that she is not "a feminist per se," she has been very supportive of women and hired them as cooks in the kitchen. "I'm attracted to the kind of energy women have," she says and cites Cecilia Chiang, who opened the Mandarin restaurant in San Francisco in 1961, as one of her own inspirations. She quickly adds, however, that even though it is less formal and more open-ended on the West Coast, women chefs have to work twice as hard and twice as long to achieve success as do their male counterparts. Asked if women cook and run restaurants differently from the way men do, Alice responds affirmatively. "Women have an instinctive desire to feed. As far as I'm concerned, food that tastes good is what a restaurant is all about. Women are more concerned with whether people like their food and want to eat it than with making a statement." Maybe that's why she keeps a sharp eye on the refuse bin, and why her disciples, both men and women, discovered she was an exceptional teacher and credit her obsessive pursuit of perfection for the improvement of raw ingredients not only in California but all over the country.

The Chez Panisse dining room and café were not only "California restaurants" but also Berkeley restaurants. And their success was consistent with the particular blend of revolution, thought, cosmopolitanism, and "flashbulbs flashing" that made Berkeley a unique epicenter for what was happening in the seventies beyond the carry-outs, fast food, frozen food, and mass feedings that made America the culinary schizophrenic "sea to shining sea" country that it was.

The previous decade, in spite of "the French Chef's" high visibility, had been accented by only a scattering of commercial enterprises with special commitments to food. Stores dedicated to cheeses, fine coffees and teas, spices and fine herbs, as well as stores offering specialty cookware were rare. Only Asians cooked with woks; crepe pans and Croque Monsieur grills were, for the most part, only available through mail order. Describing the rapidly developing culinary scene in California less than ten years later, Ruth Reichl wrote in *New West*, "Suddenly you can't walk down the street without bumping into cheese stores that stock eight kinds of blue cheese and ten varieties of chèvre. Coffee, freshly roasted, of course, is tenderly brewed in all kinds of contraptions, and the home espresso machine is quite commonplace. Pâté is purchased at the corner store. Not so long ago few of us were fond of fish; we now eat it raw. Our tastes have changed."

Berkeley was in the vanguard. The culinary spotlight which focused on Alice Waters' Chez Panisse in the late 1970s also drew attention to a cluster of shops—bakeries, charcuteries, fish and vegetable markets—that residents exhibited to visitors more proudly than Sather Gate. Some believe that the community's "culinary education" began in the 1960s. The Co-op was the major market, and since it was owned by its customers, board elections were bitterly fought in a faction-ridden political climate. Revisionists were not convinced that butter was better than margarine. People who had been raised on supermarket products like frozen vegetables were surprised when they tasted vine-ripened produce that was pesticide-free. Protesters who could not destroy the political system could wage war on mass-produced food dependent on preservatives. Even the most skeptical of the new breed of food enthusiasts were reminded that "Ho Chi Minh had been a pastry chef for Escoffier." Experimentation was rampant, and, according to *San Francisco Chronicle* food critic Patty Unterman, there was a general sense that "we weren't coming out of any tradition. We were creating one." Former students and even faculty members opened either cooperative specialty food shops or fairly priced fresh food markets. As one student said, "Anyone who cuts corners to make money is a sellout." Conversely, anyone who offers quality, whether in a shop or in a restaurant, is a hero of the revolution.

Expressed in nonpolitical terms, what Alice and her fellow chefs initiated was labeled California cuisine. But that concept was quickly rejected by the initiators. "It's a trendy catchword," Alice said. "We used what we could find. We were looking for fresh stuff. It just became California because of that." Jeremiah Tower (who composed the menu that started the myth) dismissed the label as "absolute rubbish"; Joyce Goldstein thought it "a nasty pigeonhole." Without exception the restaurateurs and chefs who were its practitioners agreed that California cuisine was created by and for the media. The practice of grilling meat was older than the state.

Wine and fresh produce characterized the area from the beginning. Without even an American cuisine in place, confusing a cuisine with a cooking style obscured the fact that, as Tower said, "American food peaked in the nineteenth century and then fell by the wayside. In the 1940s and '50s, a number was done on the American housewife to convince her that food was better if packaged. It was cleaner and politically more acceptable to prepare food out of packets. . . . American food is Russian, African, German, Scandinavian, French, Mexican, Italian, South American. One of the strengths and inspirations of what's going on over here now is the ethnicism."

In 1982 *Newsweek* described Alice Waters and other young, innovative cooks as "pioneers." "The land they are clearing is what remains between the highway stops where food is dispensed like gas and the 'gourmet' temples where food is fed to the expense account. Their homesteads are restaurants that run the gamut of American taste—from international to patriotic to regional to 'home style.' Whatever the fare, these restaurants remind us of the enormous variety of natural produce that Americans can grow and cook fresh." Ten years later, the pioneers have become a coalition with enough clout to write to President-elect Bill Clinton, "We, chefs from across the country, believe that good food, pure and wholesome, should not just be a privilege for the few, but a right for everyone." Revolutionary still, Alice says "It's the first time I feel we have a little access," although she warns, "It's a long time before we develop an 'American cuisine,' but at least we're beginning to look at what's *really* here."

Three weeks later, Julia Child, as spokesperson for the American Institute of Wine and Food, sent another "Dear Bill" letter, and, while praising the LBJ period for the quality of White House dinners, she denounced another administration for honoring a high French official with "airline food served without grace in a smoke-filled room. An embarrassment to this country." She continued with the hope that as the 1990s progress, official White House food will be given serious consideration, saying, "We are raising wonderful fresh produce, we are training accomplished chefs, we are turning out world-class wines. It is time we took pride in displaying our accomplishments."

If M. F. K. Fisher were still in residence in the Valley of the Moon, she might say she detected a bit of "Yankee Pank" in the discussion and then answer the question about the existence of an "American cuisine" in the negative: "There are some regional things, but we're just too young and too enormous. I think the same thing is true about wine. A great many wine people are Anglo-Saxon, but most of the wine people are basically French or Italian or German." And to the end of her life she admitted without reluctance that there was from "40 per cent to 60 per cent" more "me" in France than here. "I'm more alive there, although I don't know about now."

And "now" is the point. Even the most dedicated francophile has detected less insistence on quality and perfection in France's favorite preoccupation. There has also been a decline in the prominence of formal French restaurants. Ten or fifteen years ago, when a new generation of French chefs worked out new techniques for sauces, borrowed from the Japanese and other cuisines, and popularized nouvelle cuisine, it was difficult to know who affected whom and to what degree. Crossways between France and California and California and France had enormous vitality, and new ideas were rampant, especially in the direction of fresh, seasonal, and less fussy. In France, all this played out in the renewed attention toward bistros and "regional" cuisine. In California, it meant a return to and an updating of what James Beard wrote about in *Delights and Prejudices* and in *American Cookery* and what Alice Waters heralded in 1971 as cooking from the garden. By the late 1970s, California's chefs had counterparts all over the country. The "New American Chefs," from Larry Forgione and Barry Wine in New York, Lydia Shire and Jasper White in Boston, Jackie Shen and Richard Perry in the Midwest, and Anne Greer and Mark Miller in the Southwest to a host of "California" chefs from San Diego to San Francisco, were creating their own personal cuisine and adding status to the concept of chef. And today they are joined by another generation of "master" chefs who, indeed, believe that the culinary arts are a respected profession.

In the beginning there was M. F. K. Fisher, dining elegantly and simply, writing about food sensually, and dignifying hunger. Then there was Julia Child, transforming the kitchen into one of the most important rooms in the nuclear family's house and teaching the joy of French cooking to an audience who listened with amazement and watched in unabashed amusement. And ten years after *Mastering the Art of French Cooking*, Alice Waters opened a restaurant with a French name and a Berkeley modus operandi and, quite unintentionally, became the mentor for dozens of successful chefs, who, like Alice, have gone forth from California and tried to change "the nationalizing and homogenizing of American food tastes and habits."

Reading between the recipes of M. F. K. Fisher, Julia Child, and Alice Waters, food enthusiasts will find La Belle France of open markets, family dinners, and the pleasures of the table. They will also find the "pure California" that Sylvia Thompson says the Chumash Indians never saw: "groves of orange, avocado, fig, walnut, and pomegranate trees; thickets of kiwis, grapes, and olives; and amid these splendors vast horse ranches, cozy cottages, and a sparkling reservoir." Aspiring cooks will find more. They will discover three women who learned to live in another landscape, women who "from the kitchen, oven, and stove *ruled*."

S O U R C E S

M.F.K. FISHER

UNPUBLISHED MANUSCRIPTS AND LETTERS

The Arthur and Elizabeth Schlesinger Library, Radcliffe College. Cambridge, Mass. Mary Frances Kennedy Fisher Papers, 1929–1985. Unprocessed Collection 71-58-87-M68.

BOOKS [FIRST EDITIONS]

Serve It Forth. New York, London: Harper and Brothers, 1937.
Consider the Oyster. New York: Duell, Sloan and Pearce, 1941.
How to Cook a Wolf. New York: Duell, Sloan and Pearce, 1942.
The Gastronomical Me. New York: Duell, Sloan and Pearce, 1943.
Here Let Us Feast: A Book of Banquets. New York: Viking, 1946.
Not Now But Now. New York: Viking, 1947.
The Physiology of Taste, Or Meditations on Transcendental Gastronomy by Jean Anthelme Brillat-Savarin: A New Translation by M. F. K. Fisher with Preface Annotations by the Translator and Illustrations by Sylvain Sauvage. New York: Limited Editions Club [George Macy Co.], 1949.
An Alphabet for Gourmets. New York: Viking, 1949.
The Art of Eating. New York: Macmillan, 1954.
A Cordiall Water: A Garland of Odd & Old Receipts to Assuage the Ills of Man & Beast. Boston: Little, Brown, 1961.
The Story of Wine in California. Berkeley: University of California Press, 1962.
Map of Another Town: A Memoir of Provence. Boston: Little, Brown, 1964.
The Cooking of Provincial France. New York: Time-Life Books, 1968.

With Bold Knife and Fork. New York: G. P. Putnam's Sons [Perigree Book], 1969.

Among Friends. New York: Alfred A. Knopf, 1970.

A Considerable Town. New York: Alfred A. Knopf, 1978.

As They Were. New York: Alfred A. Knopf, 1982.

Sister Age. New York: Alfred A. Knopf, 1983.

Two Towns in Provence. New York: Vintage Books, 1983.

The Standing and the Waiting. Fallbrook, Calif.: Weather Bird Press, 1985.

Spirits of the Valley. New York: Targ Editions, 1985.

Fine Preserving: M. F. K. Fisher's Annotated Edition of Catherine Plagemann's Cookbook. Berkeley: Aris Books, 1986.

Dubious Honors. San Francisco: North Point Press, 1988.

Answer in the Affirmative & The Oldest Living Man. Vineburg, Calif.: Engdahl Typography, Canto Bello Series, no. 3, 1989.

The Boss Dog: A Story of Provence. Covelo, Calif.: Yolla Bolly Press, 1990.

Long Ago in France: The Years in Dijon. New York: Prentice Hall, 1991.

To Begin Again: Stories and Memoirs, 1908–1929. New York: Pantheon, 1992.

Stay Me, Oh Comfort Me: Journals and Stories, 1933–1941. New York: Pantheon, 1993.

JULIA CHILD

UNPUBLISHED PAPERS AND LETTERS

The Arthur and Elizabeth Schlesinger Library, Radcliffe College. Cambridge, Mass. Julia McWilliams Child Papers, 1953–1980, Unprocessed Collection—1964–1983.

BOOKS

Mastering the Art of French Cooking, Volume I [with Simone Beck and Louisette Bertholle]. New York: Alfred A. Knopf, 1961.

The French Chef Cookbook. New York: Alfred A. Knopf, 1968.

Mastering the Art of French Cooking, Volume II [with Simone Beck]. New York: Alfred A. Knopf, 1970.

From Julia Child's Kitchen. New York: Alfred A. Knopf, 1975.

Julia Child & Company [in collaboration with E. S. Yntema]. New York: Alfred A. Knopf, 1978.

Julia Child & More Company [in collaboration with E. S. Yntema]. New York: Alfred A. Knopf, 1979.

The Way to Cook. New York: Alfred A. Knopf, 1989.

Cooking with Master Chefs. New York: Alfred A. Knopf, 1993.

ALICE WATERS (CHEZ PANISSE)

CORRESPONDENCE AND PAPERS
Private collection.

BOOKS

The Chez Panisse Menu Cookbook. New York: Random House, 1982.

Chez Panisse Pasta, Pizza & Calzone (with Patricia Curtan and Martine Labro). New York: Random House, 1984.

Chez Panisse Desserts by Lindsey Remolif Shere (preface by Alice Waters). New York: Random House, 1985.

Chez Panisse Cooking by Paul Bertolli with Alice Waters. New York: Random House, 1988.

Fanny at Chez Panisse: A Child's Restaurant Adventures with 46 Recipes (with Bob Carrau and Patricia Curtan). New York: HarperCollins, 1992.

Araldo, Josephine, and Robert Reynolds. *From a Breton Garden*. Berkeley: Aris Books, 1990.

Ascher, Carol, Louise DeSalvo, and Sara Ruddick, eds. *Between Women: Biographers, Novelists, Critics, Teachers and Artists Write About Their Work on Women*. Boston: Beacon Press, 1984.

Balzer, Robert Lawrence. *The Los Angeles Times Book of California Wines*. New York: Harry N. Abrams, 1984.

Beard, James. *American Cookery*. New York: Little, Brown, 1972.

———. *Delights and Prejudices*. New York: Atheneum, 1964.

———. *Hors D'Oeuvre and Canapes*. New York: M. Barrows, 1940.

Beck, Simone [Simca]. *Simca's Cuisine*. New York: Alfred A. Knopf, 1972.

———. *Food and Friends*. New York: Viking, 1991.

Belden, Louise C. *The Festive Tradition: Table Decoration and Desserts in America, 1650–1900*. New York: W. W. Norton, 1983.

Bernstein, Richard. *Fragile Glory: A Portrait of France and the French*. New York: Alfred A. Knopf, 1990.

Blake, Anthony, and Quentin Crewe. *Great Chefs of France*. New York: Harry N. Abrams, 1978.

Brown, Ellen. *Cooking with the New American Chefs*. New York: Harper & Row, 1985.

Brown, Helen Evans, and James A. Beard. *The Complete Book of Outdoor Cookery*. New York: Doubleday, 1955.

Burns, Jim, and Betty Ann Brown. *Women Chefs: A Collection of Portraits and Recipes from California's Culinary Pioneers*. Berkeley: Aris Books, 1987.

Clark, Robert. "Carneros," *Journal of Gastronomy*, vol. 5, no. 3 (Winter 1989–1990).

David, Elizabeth. *French Country Cooking*. London: Penguin Books, 1959.

———. *French Provincial Cooking*. London: Penguin Books, 1960.

———. *An Omelette and a Glass of Wine*. London: Penguin Books, 1986.

Degler, Carl N. *At Odds: Women and the Family in America from the Revolution to the Present*. New York: Oxford University Press, 1980.

Diat, Louis. *French Country Cooking for Americans*. New York: Dover, 1978.

Dosti, Rose, ed. *The New California Cuisine*. New York: Harry N. Abrams, 1987.

Douglas, Ann. *The Feminization of American Culture*. New York: Alfred A. Knopf, 1977.

Eichenbaum, Luise, and Susie Orbach. *Between Women: Love, Envy, and Competition in Women's Friendships*. New York: Viking, 1988.

Ellwanger, George H. *The Pleasures of the Table: An Account of Gastronomy from Ancient Days to Present Times*. New York: Doubleday Page, 1902.

Erenberg, Lewis A. *Steppin' Out: New York Nightlife and the Transformation of American Culture, 1890–1930*. Westport, Conn.: Greenwood Press, 1981.

Fischler, Claude. "The Michelin Galaxy: Nouvelle Cuisine, Three-Star Restaurants, and the Culinary Revolution," *Journal of Gastronomy*, vol. 6, no. 4 (Autumn 1990).

Friedan, Betty. *The Feminine Mystique*. New York: W. W. Norton, 1963.

———. *It Changed My Life: Writings on the Women's Movement*. New York: Random House, 1976.

Fussell, Betty. *Masters of American Cookery*. New York: Times Books, 1983.

Gay, Peter. *The Bourgeois Experience: Victoria to Freud*, vols. 1 and 2. New York: Oxford University Press, 1984.

Gilbert, Sandra, and Susan Gubar. *No Man's Land: The Place of the Woman Writer in the Twentieth Century*, vol. 1. New Haven: Yale University Press, 1988.

Girardet, Fredy. *The Cuisine of Fredy Girardet.* New York: William Morrow, 1984.

Goines, David Lance. *The Free Speech Movement: Coming of Age in the 1960s.* Berkeley: Ten Speed Press, 1993.

Grover, Kathryn, ed. *Dining in America: 1850–1900.* Amherst: University of Massachusetts Press, 1987.

Guérard, Michel. *Michel Guérard's Cuisine Minceur.* New York: William Morrow, 1976.

Hartman, Mary S., and Lois Banner, eds. *Clio's Consciousness Raised: New Perspectives on the History of Women.* New York: Harper & Row, 1974.

Hartman, Susan M. *The Homefront and Beyond: American Women in the 1940s.* Boston: Twayne, 1982.

Hayden, Dolores. *The Grand Domestic Revolution: A History of Feminist Designs for American Homes, Neighborhoods, and Cities.* Cambridge, Mass.: MIT Press, 1981.

Heilbrun, Carolyn G. *Writing a Woman's Life.* New York: W. W. Norton, 1988.

Hooker, Richard J. *Food and Drink in America: A History.* New York: Bobbs-Merrill, 1981.

Jones, Evan. *American Food: The Gastronomic Story.* New York: Random House, 1981.

Kamman, Madeleine. *When French Women Cook: A Gastronomic Memoir.* New York: Atheneum, 1976.

———. "Nouvelle Cuisine or Cuisine Personnelle?" in *In Madeleine's Kitchen.* New York: Atheneum, 1984.

Kelley, Mary. *Private Woman, Public Stage: Literary Domesticity in Nineteenth Century America.* New York: Oxford University Press, 1984.

Lee, Hilde Gabriel. *Vintner's Choice.* Berkeley: Ten Speed Press, 1986.

Levenstein, Harvey A. "The New England Kitchen . . . ," *American Quarterly,* vol. 32, no. 4 (Fall 1980).

———. *Revolution at the Table: The Transformation of the American Diet.* New York: Oxford University Press, 1988.

———. *Paradox of Plenty: A Social History of Eating in Modern America.* New York: Oxford University Press, 1993.

Lucie-Smith, Edward. *The Story of Craft: The Craftsman's Role in Society.* Ithaca, N.Y.: Cornell University Press, 1981.

Lynch, Kermit. *Adventures on the Wine Route: A Wine Buyer's Tour of France.* New York: Farrar Straus Giroux, 1988.

McNair, James. *Bar & Grill Book: Exciting New Recipes from San Francisco's Bar & Grill Restaurants.* San Francisco: Chronicle Books, 1986.

MacNeil, Karen. "Eleven Good Cooks: A Roundtable Discussion," *Journal of Gastronomy*, vol. 3, no. 4 (Winter 1987–88).

Matthews, Glenna. *"Just a Housewife": The Rise and Fall of Domesticity in America.* New York: Oxford University Press, 1987.

Olney, Richard. *Simple French Food.* New York: Atheneum, 1974.

———. *The French Menu Cookbook.* New York: Simon & Schuster, 1970.

Pappas, Lou Seibert. *Winemakers' Cookbook: Culinary Adventures with America's Premier Vintners.* San Francisco: Chronicle Books, 1991.

Pellegrini, Angelo. *The Unprejudiced Palate.* New York: Macmillan, 1948.

Rector, George. *Dine at Home with Rector.* New York: E. P. Dutton, 1937.

Roberge, Earl. *Napa Wine Country.* Portland: Graphic Arts Center, 1985.

Root, Waverley. *The Food of France.* New York: Alfred A. Knopf, 1958.

Root, Waverley, and Richard de Rochemont. *Eating in America: A History.* New York: William Morrow, 1976.

Rorabaugh, W. J. *Berkeley at War, the 1960s.* New York: Oxford University Press, 1989.

Senderens, Alain. *The Three-Star Recipes of Alain Senderens.* New York: William Morrow, 1982.

Singer, Mark. "The Chinos' Artful Harvest," *The New Yorker* 68, November 30, 1992.

Smallzried, Kathleen Ann. *The Everlasting Pleasure: Influences on America's Kitchens, Cooks, and Cookery, from 1565 to the Year 2000.* New York: Appleton-Century-Crofts, 1956.

Sokolov, Raymond. "When Dinosaurs Ruled Restaurant Row: A Food Critic's Memoir," *Journal of Gastronomy*, vol. 3, no. 1 (Spring 1987).

Thompson, Bob, and Hugh Johnson. *The California Wine Book.* New York: William Morrow, 1976.

Verdon, René. *The Enlightened Cuisine: A Master Chef's Step-by-Step Guide to Contemporary French Cooking.* New York: Macmillan, 1985.

Vergé, Roger. *Roger Vergé's Cuisine of the South of France.* New York: William Morrow, 1980.

Villas, James. *American Taste: A Celebration of Gastronomy Coast-to-Coast*. New York: Arbor House, 1982.

Waters, Alice. "The Farm–Restaurant Connection," *Journal of Gastronomy*, vol. 5, no. 2 (Summer–Autumn 1989).

Wheaton, Barbara Ketcham. "Petits Riens and Pommes Barigoule: Food in France After the Revolution," *Journal of Gastronomy*, vol. 5, no. 3 (Winter 1989–90).

Williams, Susan. *Savory Suppers and Fashionable Feasts: Dining in Victorian America*. New York: Pantheon, 1985.